CIDER

50 BC onwards

Author credits

I would like to thank the Top Tips team (see end of the book) for sharing their invaluable advice and experience. Rob Bradshaw, Matthew Veasey, Simon Thomas for their unpaid proofreading.

Also, my wife Lisa for her loving patience and understanding.

First published in May 2014

A catalogue record for this book is available from the British Library

ISBN 978 0 85733 283 7

Library of Congress control no. 2013955824

Published by Haynes Publishing,
Sparkford, Yeovil,
Somerset BA22 7JJ, UK.
Tel: 01963 442030 Fax: 01963 440001
Int. tel: +44 1963 442030 Int. fax: +44 1963 440001
E-mail: sales@haynes.co.uk
Website: www.haynes.co.uk

Haynes North America Inc.,
861 Lawrence Drive, Newbury Park,
California 91320, USA.

Printed in the USA by Odcombe Press LP,
1299 Bridgestone Parkway, La Vergne, TN 37086.

CIDER

50BC onwards

Enthusiasts' Manual

A practical guide to growing apples and cidermaking

Bill Bradshaw

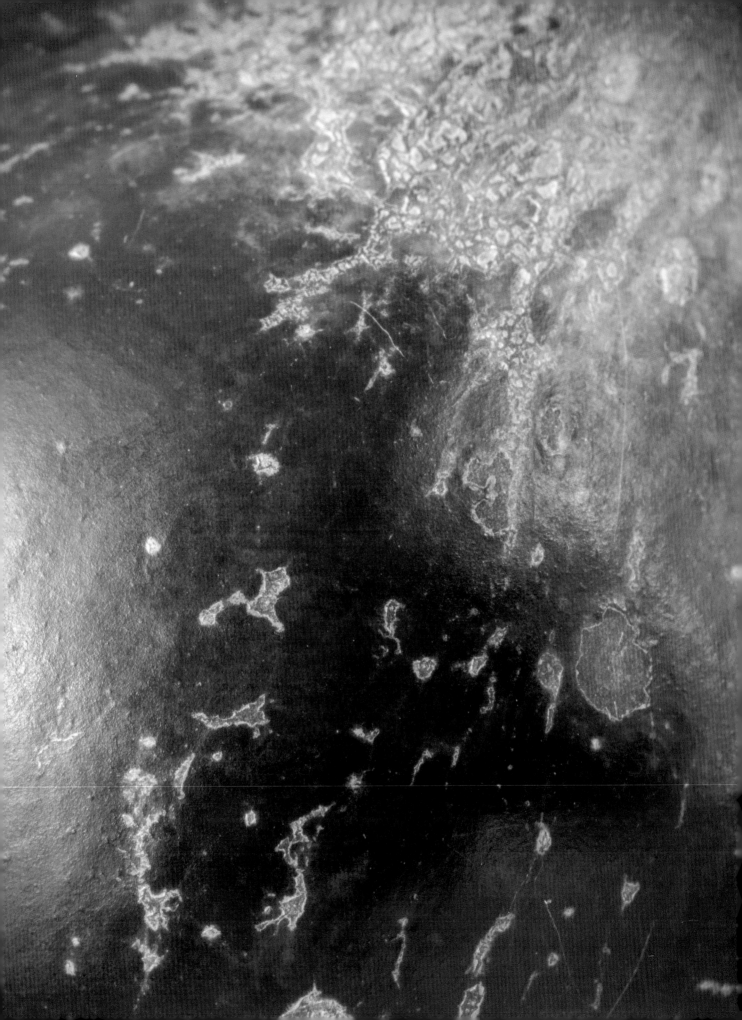

CONTENTS

INTRODUCTION

For many, enjoying cider is a lifelong passion. The cider world is made up of folk who are often as eclectic, colourful and diverse as the fruit that makes the juice itself. Cider has a cult following, sometimes referred to as a 'broad church', full of zeal, opinion and devotion. My first attempt at making cider led me to realise that it's not quite as straightforward as I had been led to believe and that I needed help to steer my way through the seasons. The delight I felt upon opening my first flagon was quickly replaced with disappointment, as I realised it was infected and undrinkable. Failure at the final stage is one of the bitterest lessons to learn in life, but is also the most effective because hopefully you only do it once. Since then I have gone on to discover how cider is made all over the world and the one thing I know now, more than ever before, is that everyone does it slightly differently. This is part of cider's inherent appeal.

Like many things, such as photography or music, cider making is a peculiar mix of practical technique and creative freedom. Practical technique is something we can all be taught and is fundamental to a successful outcome. We can use the science involved to reduce the chances of failure and steer towards a particular style or flavour. Creative feel, however, is a more elusive quality and can be a difficult concept to grasp. The desire to make great cider means committing to learn the science involved, while allowing yourself the confidence and freedom to remain true to the fruit. You need a good understanding of the fruit at your disposal and an idea of the final product you wish to create.

Cider was born from farming and has been produced where I live – Somerset, UK – for a very long time. Cider has also been made in many other places, each with their own apples, techniques, customs and traditions. Some countries have a more recent relationship with it, seeing a significant surge of interest within the last 10–15 years, whereas much of Europe has been experimenting with making and enjoying it long before it arrived on Britain's shores.

These days both apples and cider are commodities that are appreciated all over the world and the industry that surrounds them is worth billions. Like all the cultures that celebrate it, cider itself has a long, colourful history, the origins of which can only be speculated over. Cider found its way here from Europe shortly after the crucifixion of Christ, and spread further afield, travelling over oceans, birthing new cider cultures and apple varieties. This in turn gave rise to the variety available to us today as far wide as USA and Australia.

No one book can tell you everything you need to know about cider making and this is an introductory guide to the maker's world. It's aimed at taking anyone interested in small- to medium-scale cider production through the first few seasons of cider making, and providing a thorough basis on which to start. I urge anyone starting to make cider to build on their own personal experiences through travel and experimentation. Increasing your knowledge by visiting or working with cider makers: being around a cider farm and among the orchards will give you invaluable first-hand experience. It will also hone your instincts and increase your respect for nature and the artisan approach.

The *Cider Manual* introduces the maker to all aspects of cider from the history and culture, the apples and orchards, to the cider-making process itself. Throughout you will notice some hints, tips and suggestions from top cider makers and apple growers. Each one is a hand-picked, personal bit of advice from some of the greatest orchardists and cider makers around. It also might mean the difference between a five-minute wonder that you give up because it frustrates you, or a lifetime of enjoyable and successful cider making.

Bill Bradshaw

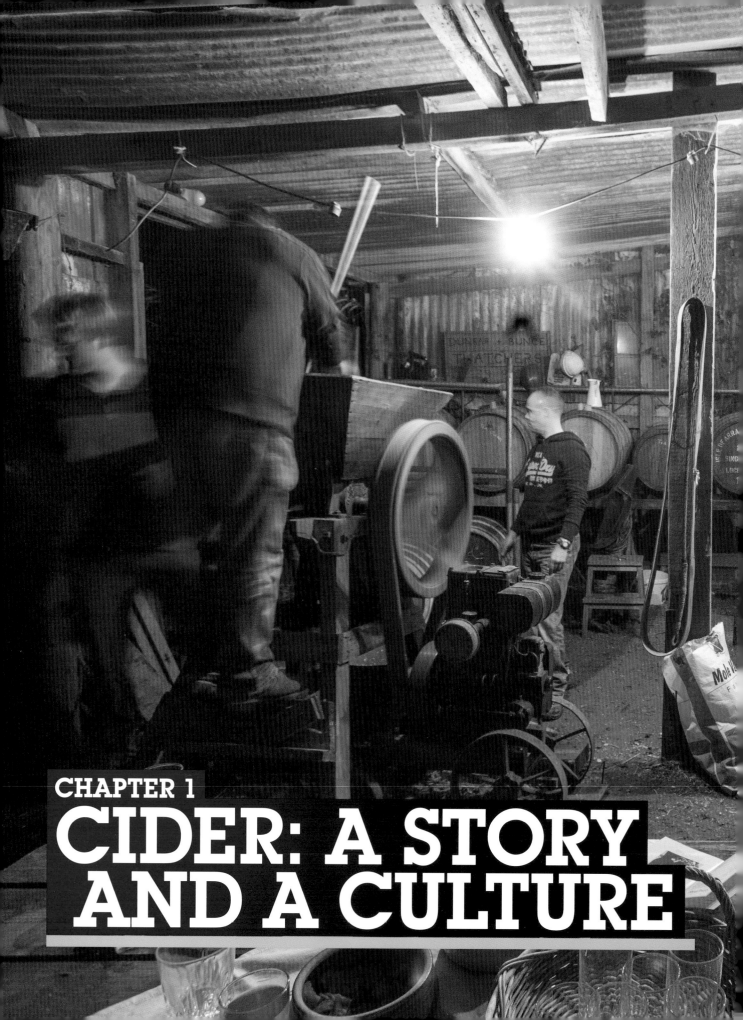

CHAPTER 1
CIDER: A STORY AND A CULTURE

What exactly is cider? In different places the word has come to mean slightly different things, so to clarify, cider is the fermented juice from apples. At least is it in the UK. In the USA, cider refers to unpasteurised, freshly-pressed apple juice and the alcoholic version is often referred to as *hard cider*, but these days it often means both, so it's always worth checking. In Wales its *seidir*, France it's *cidre*, in Spain *sidra*, in Germany *apfelwein*, in Austria *möst* and so on.

In the context of this book cider is fermented apple juice. It can vary in strength depending on various factors from around 3% ABV to 8.5% ABV or more, but the natural amount of fermentable sugars in a normal season's apples will typically produce a cider of 6–8% ABV. The process of cider making will also have a bearing on how strong it can be.

It's enormously popular in the UK and we drink more of it that any other country in the world, but other countries such as Spain and France also have strong cider cultures. Beyond Europe, cider's popularity is growing at a speedy rate. These days cider is made in all corners of the world from Chile to Indonesia, to Russia and Canada, and many places in between. Each place will bring its own unique influence into it whether cultural or physical.

Despite cider simply being fermented apple juice, the end product varies enormously and that's part of the fascination for enthusiasts. Much like grapes are to wine and winemakers, apples and the process of producing cider is governed by the variables of the fruit (and the *terroir* of the orchards) as well as the skills of the cider maker. These days a skilled cider maker can pretty much fix any problems and make their cider taste how they want it to. As such there is more of a movement than ever to return to traditional methods, pure juice, wild yeasts and respecting the fruit.

Technically cider can be made from any apples, but traditionally the majority of what are considered to be the best ciders are made using specialist cider apples. These are quite different from the eating and cooking varieties that we're used to seeing day to day. As well as the usual sharpness and sweetness you expect from an eating apple, the skin of a cider apple contains tannin, a bitter compound similar to those found in the skin of wine grapes, which imparts an extra level of complexity and dynamism to the final drink. Tannins can contribute to dryness, texture (mouth-feel) and bitterness. The use of traditional cider apple varieties will add tannins and a newer level of complexity introducing a level of bitterness (like wines). True cider apple varieties are grown specifically for these unique flavours and each region has its own apple varieties that are most suited to local growing conditions and are held in high regard. Most contain the particular proportions of acids, sugars and tannins useful for fermentation, yet they're often distasteful to eat. Bite into one and see for yourself. However certain regions (East/South East UK, Germany, USA, Australia, *etc*) have traditions of making cider using dessert fruit. Many of these ciders are also of high quality but differ in style due to the apparent absence of tannins.

As strong cider-producing regions with an established culture tend to use their own cider fruit specific to that place, many places such as Normandy, Brittany and Asturias can only use certain listed varieties and legally call it cider. Many of these areas are protected by status such as PGI (protected geographical indication) and PDO/DO (protected designation of origin) an EU-wide mark/label that forms part of a legal framework intended to protect the names and quality of traditional foodstuffs from certain areas. Ironically in the UK, while much of Herefordshire's cider has a PGI status, many producers in Somerset don't want one. They want to preserve the variety of processes, fruit and techniques employed through out the region, which makes it virtually impossible to agree a definition.

Consequently, cider comes in many styles. The look can vary from the clearest, elderflower-pale perry, through to a dark, hazy, ale-like brown of an aged farmhouse scrumpy. Also the taste can vary from very sweet, fresh fruit juice to mouth-numbingly dry and horse-leathery bitter. Some ciders are quite sharp and some are mellow and buttery, some are delicate while others are bold. Traditional farmhouse ciders can be completely flat, and crafted bottle-fermented ciders are as feisty uncorked as the finest Champagnes. Some have a thick 'body' to them while others are much thinner. Accordingly, cider is served in a variety of ways, some by the pint and others in a flute or wine glass.

Types of cider

FARMHOUSE OR SCRUMPY

Typically, UK farmhouse cider made traditionally is flat, hazy and golden in colour. Often sold 'loose' from a vat or barrel at a cider farm, it is the oldest and the most traditional style cider in the UK. Farmhouse ciders have become more popular in recent years and some of the best ciders are found down quiet country lanes.

Typically, they are 100% apple juice and made from a blend of traditional cider apples. A strict traditional approach also calls for the use of wild yeasts that are already present on and in the apple, rather than resorting to a laboratory-grown, single yeast strain. The use of wild yeast isn't for everyone, as they are often fermented to dryness, may have a 'farmyard' taste, they can be quite tannic and sharp, but more ideally a balanced combination of these. They are often cloudy, rich in colour, full-bodied, juicy and sometimes benefit from low levels of vinegary sharpness. The most popular examples are usually medium dry with some residual sweetness, an obvious tannic presence and a full-bodied, fruity mouthful. It is cider in its rawest form and relies heavily on the apples used and the skill of the cider maker. Some makers still press it through straw, although this is less common these days. Of all the cider styles you could approach, this is arguably the simplest and the most difficult to master, with great potential for mishap. This style is often referred to by cider fundamentalists as 'real cider' as it's raw, unfiltered, unpastuerised and unabated.

CLEANED AND BOTTLED

These ciders are popular and, generally speaking, of good quality. Many bottled ciders available these days are taken a stage further from the farmhouse ciders. They usually have a reasonably high level of cider apples and some are still pure juice.

It's a modern, retail-friendly way of ensuring cider is approachable to new cider drinkers. It's easy on both the eye and the palate. These ciders are often made using an approach that is sympathetic to traditional methods but employs the use of some modern equipment and techniques to help with production and consistency. Some will be sweetened with sugar, sweetener or even fresh juice to reduce fermented dryness. They are often pressed using a belt press, fermented with cultured yeasts, micro-filtered for clarity, pasteurised for shelf life and carbonated. Some believe this destroys the finer nuances of a raw product, but it does have the advantage of appealing to a much wider audience and makes storage and sales somewhat easier.

BOTTLE CONDITIONED

Bottle conditioning is another traditional technique that sees a second fermentation occurring in the bottle, allowing for a natural sparkle. It's the technique used to make sparkling wines like Champagne, Prosecco and Cava, and also fine beers. Initially, in a process the French refer to as the *methode ancienne* the cider is allowed to ferment to a certain stage, by which time most of the sugar has converted into alcohol. It is then bottled into a strengthened bottle and corked. Any residual sugar and yeast in suspension will then slowly complete the fermentation inside the bottle. This has the advantage of self-carbonating as the carbon dioxide released during the process is sent back into solution under pressure and not released until the cork is popped (hence the fizz.) It will always leave a natural sediment in the bottle too. Ciders fermented and aged this way have a tendency to have more complex aromas and flavours.

Although pioneered first by the British cider and perry makers in 1662, what's now referred to as the *'methode champenoise'* was perfected by the French who evolved the process slightly further still by removing any sediment and adding a small amount of sugar back before final bottling. After an initial fermentation, and ageing on the lees in the bottle, the cider is allowed to continue fermenting in a special rack (*pupitre*) that stores the bottles upside down. It is turned a quarter turn on a regular basis so the yeast and lees work their way down towards the cork and settle in the neck of the bottle at the underside of the cork. When ready, the cidermaker removes the yeasty lees by temporarily freezing the neck of the bottle, removing the cork and the plug of sediment slides out effortlessly under pressure from the dissolved CO2 inside. Before replacing the cork, a small *dosage* of fresh juice (or sugar) is added to allow for final conditioning. The bottle is re-sealed and left to age until ready.

This process adds a natural sparkle to the cider, but ageing it on the lees will add another level of dynamism to the aroma and final complexity of flavour. Due to the extra time and handling required by these processes, bottle-conditioned products are generally regarding as premium and fetch a higher price.

KEEVED

Keeving is an old production technique, now more established in France than anywhere else where's it's know as *'le chapeau brun'* (the brown hat). During fermentation, the cider splits into three parts: a brown hat (yeast layer); the cider in the middle; and the lees on the bottom (dead yeast and protein). The addition of calcium by the cider maker can force the separation, and the cider maker racks off the middle layer of cider to another vessel where fermentation continues much more slowly. The result is a much fruitier style of cider that is naturally sweeter and lower in alcohol and typically accompanies food. The process allows the cider maker much greater control over the fermentation, but it can be quite difficult to achieve and it is also quite wasteful.

INDUSTRIAL

Science and production are the two forces that dominate this style. It may be a long way from its farmhouse roots but the principles are basically the same. The apples are washed and pressed as per usual but the juice is then condensed into a concentrate that will be stored. To order, the concentrate is then fermented, water is added and it's sweetened and packaged, all within a few weeks. The ciders are nearly always clear, carbonated, lower in alcohol than their more traditional counterparts and much simpler in taste and aroma. To make large quantities of anything, to keep it consistent and affordable you need some high-tech equipment and to be super-safe in terms of hygiene that might affect flavour and consistency. Many of the better modern industrial British cider makers make their own concentrate from cider fruit that they grow or buy, but historically concentrate is shipped in from anywhere in the world.

The use of apple concentrate is a contentious subject for many people and causes passionate debate! UK law states that you can use no less than 35% apple juice if you want to sell a product as cider. Personally, 35% is too little for my taste buds, and I'd struggle to consider anything a cider at only 36% juice. Indeed, some makers may also add artificial aromas and various other adjuncts to create an impression of apples or other fruit flavours and aromas in what they are selling. However, they are very popular with millions of people.

Mass-produced ciders taste the way they do because they are popular and people like them. Some like to market themselves based on the mystique of an old and traditional artisan heritage, yet in reality, making and selling traditional cider in the same quantities is impossible. There is always going to

be a compromise, albeit one that benefits many smaller artisan producers who don't have to compromise to the same degree but do have to charge more for a premium product.

Some of the better mass-produced ciders actually help move people on from industrial fizz to artisan finery. These 'gateway ciders' are made to look and taste more like traditional farmhouse cider but are still made in huge volumes. They are available nationally and bring cider to the attention of drinkers who may usually drink wine or beer. Many enthusiasts will deride this type of cider, but there are benefits of having some big businesses sharing the sector with small producers. The UK has a interesting and often overlooked symbiotic relationship between commercially produced ciders and artisan ciders.

WHITE CIDER

The most shameful abomination to ever have been born from of the cider world has to be white cider! It can still be spotted on the bottom shelves of supermarkets as pale, fizzy, sweet liquid in large two-litre bottles at a very cheap price. It was conceived as a low-cost product that is the result of processing together enough of the cheapest bare essentials to get away with calling it cider. In flavour it's always been much more like a soft drink but with the added punch of 6%–7% ABV of an alcopop. As such, it appeals to young drinkers, which recently brought about a tightening of UK law to increase the amount of apple juice in any cider (although it is still too low) and called for an increase in tax on these kind of products. White ciders have given cider in general a bad reputation – they are as far as you can get from real cider and are more of a ghoulish, tumorous growth associated with it.

PERRY

Perry (or pear cider) is the name given to the fermented drink made from pears, so for all intents and purposes, it's exactly the same as cider with the exception of its chief ingredient. It's simply assimilated into the term 'cider' when people write or talk about it, but in reality, perry has its own identity and unique history.

True perry pears are similar to cider apples in that they are virtually inedible. They often contain high levels of tannins and so are only suitable for perry making as they add a pleasing complexity to the flavour of the juice. They are strange looking fruit and often much smaller and rounder than a normal dessert pear. The trees themselves live for a much longer time than apple trees, often still producing useable volumes of fruit after 300 years! One famous tree still existing today is the Holme Lacey Perry Pear tree and is the largest known recorded pear tree. It once covered 0.75 of an acre (approx. 3035 square metres) and offered a crop of over six tonnes annually. The remnants of the tree still survive today, although the trunk has disappeared, but the branches that remain have grown and matured into individual trees by their root system.

The Romans enjoyed eating pears and developed orchards so it's understood that they introduced the domesticated varieties of dessert pears to UK, as they did with apples. The most common theory is that these varieties hybridised with wild pears producing the early variety perry pears. Early saints who travelled widely preaching their beliefs were said to have a strong association with perry, one or two even claiming to live on it alone! There are numerous accounts of Christianity's association with wine and viniculture as missionaries carried vines with them to the new world, so it's likely the same is true of pears and perry. Welsh Saint Teilo apparently took perry pears to France. Saint Carantoc travelled extensively throughout what are now strong cider regions (Wales, South West UK, Brittany, Ireland) and with him would have travelled the knowledge and culture of perry and cider making. Perry making seems to have got a foothold in mainland middle Europe after the Romans had left, and wasn't really established in the UK until after the Norman Conquest. Perry production within the UK is now at its strongest in Worcester, Gloucester and Herefordshire and also over into Wales, in Monmouthshire as people realised they could grow perry pears in places where cider apples might struggle. Bottled conditioned perries are popular for celebrations, and can be seen as a more sustainable alternative to champagne.

Babycham was the first commercially produced pear cider and it was very popular in the 1960s and 1970s. It was the first alcoholic drink to be advertised on UK television.

◀ **Sparkling Perry is one of the most delightful drinks ever produced.**

Outside the UK, France produces a sweeter version known as *poiré* in the Domfrontais region and it is also found in Austria where there are perry pears in abundance, and it is known as *möst* (pronounced mosht).

Perry is trickier to produce and requires a greater deal of skill and patience than cider. The general approach and practices are very similar – but with a few crucial factors that every perry maker must learn. Pear trees are very slow growing but will live for hundreds of years, so planting some for production is an investment (most likely for the next generation). As such, perry production is more of a specialism, because perry pears are so hard to come by and there just aren't enough to meet demand. They are also more difficult to deal with. The fruit rots from the inside out, is more vulnerable to pests and disease, the tall trees are difficult to reach up to, higher levels of citric acid in the pears mean it is more vulnerable to aecetification… the list goes on. Having said that, perries are really popular, so enthusiasts make as much as they can!

In recent times, perry made from dessert pears has come to be known as 'pear cider' consequently the quality of the juice isn't as high (as it has very few tannins in it) and so makes a much less complex beverage. One advantage the perry pear has over a cider apple is that while they may contain more sugar than apples, perry pears also contain a small amount of unfermentable sugar and so will offer the producer some residual sweetness. Because of this and its delicate flavour, it's probably best appreciated when fermented to dryness, or near dryness.

Any cider maker considering perry production will benefit, quite literally, from having the patience of a saint! Several seasons of cider-making experience, some first-hand advice and nerves of steel also help.

FRUIT CIDER

Putting 'fruit' into cider has had a hugely polarising effect in recent years. The 'real cider' community despise what they see as 'alcopops' being labelled and sold as 'fruit cider' as business jumps on the cider bandwagon. Industrial producers can take advantage of the minimum 35% apple requirement to make a white cider whilst using fruit concentrate to colour and flavour it according to the latest market whims. Millions of these drinks sell daily, they are hugely popular and generate massive revenue. Whilst they may still be classified as cider, they are surely a long way from their full-juice cousin.

Ironically, the practice of adding fruit (and spices) is quite an old one and has been documented as far back as the 17th century, Cider's heyday, where things like raspberries were used to add to a small cider (or ciderkyn) as an alternative for women to drink, so its no new idea. In Normandy, some producers still press blackberries and apple to ferment in small batches to make a traditional Kir Normande.

Origins: A is for Apple

"Although it took some 6000 years for the apple to be brought from the Tian Shan to western Europe, it took only 300 years for it to reach the other temperate parts of the world – at the hand of the colonising European powers."

Barrie E. Juniper, 2006, *The Story of the Apple*

This will give you some idea of the time frame we're dealing with and in which millennia *Malus sieversii* (or *pumila*), the wild apple and ancestor of domesticated apples, became available in Europe. The apple's arrival here, via existing wine producing regions, its unbelievable genetic diversity and its ability to reproduce easily meant that for the first time factors were right for the notion of 'cider' to first be possible. As primates, we were eating fruit long before we were human, so when you consider the journey of the apple as we know it today and what it has come to mean as an everyday part of our lives as the world's most important temperate fruit crop, the appropriate place to start is the moment those two worlds collided.

That relationship started about 5000–7000 years ago and came about from our need for nutrients. Our inability to produce our own vitamin C is an inadequacy rare in mammals, but is the reason we started searching for it in fruit. Wild crab apples contain large amounts of it and considering the health benefits to us from a regular intake, coupled with the fact that apples literally grow on trees – you can easily argue that man was destined to form a strong and binding relationship with them. There is evidence that we've been eating dried apples for at least 4000–5000 years, but the geographic distribution of apples was much more limited then, so analysing its spread will give us a clearer idea of where man's affinity with the apple started and developed.

The apple trees were huge in comparison to the modern versions we now grow and existed in vast forested areas. It's likely they were eaten and distributed further afield by bears, and as humans started to eat them, we too played our part. The transient lifestyle of nomadic peoples and traders meant apples were dried or consumed and their cores discarded along their journeys. Seedlings that germinated from direct human contact would have done so in or along centres of human activity, further reinforcing our bond.

Malus sieversii (or pumila) are believed to have originated from the lower mountain slopes of the Tien Shan mountains of central Asia, a mountainous area in Kazakstan. Brought west in the stomachs of horses and the packbags of the people who owned them, it brought the sweetness and size (volume) to what we generally refer to as today's domestic apple.

Central western Europe has its own native, tiny, bitter crab apple *Malus sylvestris*, quite different from *Malus sieversii*. During Neolithic times, wild crab apples were eaten here in the UK – the fossilised pips have been found and analysed. We also have evidence from around 3000BC that wine was being made in Egypt and that Mesolithic peoples here in Europe were halving and quartering wild crab apples (*Malus sylvestris*), which they dried and stored for later use. This combination also makes cider making likely or even inevitable at some stage.

After arriving via trade routes, like the Silk Route, into or around Turkey at the eastern edge of the Mediterranean the effects of newer *Malus sieversii (or pumila)* on the existing native crab apple spread north towards Bulgaria and Georgia. Its influence also spread across the Mediterranean following sea-based trade routes throughout the area, coming into contact with what was Celtic Europe about 2400 years ago. These long-established shipping routes took the apple past Gibraltar and north, up the west coast of modern-day Spain, France and the UK.

Inevitably, when the new *Malus sieversii* species eventually arrived in the area of modern Europe, genes were exchanged and a multitude of newer hybrids were born.

In 2010 the genome of the Granny Smith apple was analysed. It was discovered that the apple had a greater variety of genes than a human being, which illustrates the incredibly diverse potential in each apple and partly why we have so many today. If you plant an apple seed, the plant that grows from it will produce different fruit from the one it came from. It may, by chance, be nicer to eat but more likely it would be more suited to cider production, as pippins (apples grown from seed) tend to revert to a more wild state when grown from a pip.

As populations began to exploit their properties, apples were eaten, reproduced, carried further west and north. This ongoing process of cross-pollination (of the sweeter, larger eating apples of *Malus domestica* and the native crab apples already present in northern Europe *Malus sylvestrii*) is believed to have been responsible for the birth of the particular cider apples we use today. The *domestica* contributing to an increased size and level of sweetness and the *sylvestrii* adding tannins and acidity – all vital for modern day cider fruit.

The Gulf Stream is a factor that has certainly aided the

success and sculpted the geography of apple-growing and cider-making regions in Europe. Its benefits include mild weather and increased rainfall, two important influences in the colder climes of northern Europe, and for thriving on free-draining soils.

We may have had the climate, and the desire for more from an apple, but crushing one is much more difficult than a grape for wine, so the tools to crush this hard, dense fruit, let alone the knowledge and skills to ferment and condition the juice, had to wait until technology caught up.

CIDER: A BRIEF HISTORY

We've been ingesting fermenting fruit and grains for their alcoholic properties far longer than we've been recording it. It's impossible to say who first understood that collecting fruit, harnessing its natural ability to ferment and ingesting it for pleasure would be of an advantage. What is well known is that as a species, we hanker for the intoxicating effects of it. Historians still debate and argue over who first started

harvesting apples to crush into juice because someone wanted to make cider.

The etymology of the word 'cider' is still hotly contested. It may come from *shekar*, a Hebrew word for 'strong drink' and there is certainly a similarity both in sound and effect. In northern Europe, the ancient Britons and Celts already used wild crab apples as a part of their diet and it's important to note that the idea of cider was possibly introduced to Britain earlier than is generally accepted by travellers. The Druids of the UK and Ireland worshipped apple trees and used their wood to make their wands – maybe they started it?

The area of northern Spain is made up of Asturias, Galicia and the Basque country and this region certainly has strong claims for having the oldest cider-making culture. Eduardo Coto, a fellow cider enthusiast, believes that their story starts about 60 BC. Strabo was a Greek philsopher and historian and is credited with a book *Geographpikon* in which he writes about people from the North Atlantic coast of Spain saying "*zytho etiam utuntur, vini parum habent*" ('they also drink Zythos, they have little wine"). Although, *zythos* means 'beer' in Greek, barley was grown in really small amounts, so most archeologists and historians think that something similar to cider would be more

▼ *Malus Sylvestris*, a wild apple, in full bloom

likely. Coto's speculation grows still more when we read about the Cantabrian wars – Asturias and Cantabria being the last areas in Spain to be conquered by Romans.

It required 7 Legions, the Roman fleet and 10 years to complete! (The same amount of time it took Caesar to conquer the whole of Gaul.) When it was finally conquered, around 19 BC, Asturians were subsequently enlisted into the Roman army who then went on to conquer ancient Briton. If each of the 500 strong newly formed regiments carried a thirst for cider with them, then it stands to reason they probably carried some idea of how to make it too. It may be the case that this was indeed the birthplace of cider.

In reality it's more likely that cider making happened simultaneously in several places using differing techniques that were predominantly determined by local culture and climate.

Although apple cultivation is documented as early as 1178 BC in Homer's *Odyssey*, cider making itself enters written history much later thanks to Pliny the Elder (AD 23 – August 25, AD 79) who records in *De Rerum Naturum*, of the use of apples and pears for fermenting in the first century.

The Romans, influenced by the Ancient Greeks and Persians (who probably picked it up via the Phoenicians), are widely acknowledged with introducing 'domestic' apples into Britain – sweeter eating apples that had been grafted to preserve genetic pureness. They certainly introduced cider making on a small scale too. Although we were already growing wild apples in Britain at this time, the Romans brought about a much more organised approach to their cultivation. As an encouragement for army veterans to remain, they were given land on which to grow fruit, a practice probably undertaken all over the Roman empire. As it grew, so did its influence and they certainly played their part in creating cider, cider apples and perry pears as we know them.

When the Romans abandoned the UK in the year 410, Britain became vulnerable once more and was subjected to waves of invasions from the European mainland by Saxons and Angles. As life became harder for people and the country fragmented, orchards were neglected and suffered, so cider making fell to the Church for its survival. Monasteries had orchards, vines and presses (and bees) as well as the knowledge of cider making, so it became the preserve of monks and saints.

Meanwhile throughout Europe, the Frankish Empire was slowly expanding. By the time Emperor Charlemagne, came to power it covered much of modern Europe. The *Capitulare de Vallis*, an 8th century document (created by Charlemagne or his son Louis the Pious) clearly outlines an idealised decree of how royal estates should be run. It requests:

That every steward shall have in his district good workmen – that is, blacksmiths, gold- and silver-smiths, shoemakers, turners, carpenters, shield-makers, fishermen, falconers, soap-makers, brewers (that is, people who know how to make beer, cider,

▲ The granite base for a long-gone traditional cider press.

▼ Charles the Great (Emperor Charlemagne) decreed apples and pears be planted for cider production.

perry or any other suitable beverage)... [and also goes on to list plant types that should be planted, to include] various kinds of apple, pear... The names of apples are: gozmaringa, geroldinga, crevedella, spirauca; there are sweet ones, bitter ones, those that keep well, those that are to be eaten straightaway, and early ones. Of pears they are to have three or four kinds, those that keep well, sweet ones, cooking pears and the late-ripening ones.

The reach of his empire was huge – it spanned from what we understand today as northern Spain, across France, northern Italy, up through Slovenia, Austria, Germany to Denmark, Holland and back down through Belgium! Given that any of the surrounding territories were also dependent on it too, the size and influence of the Frankish empire at the time, was absolute. Countless estates governed using these guidelines and stretching over these distances would really have strengthened any Roman influence with regards to cider making and the growing of apples and pears.

▼ A first edition of *Vinetum Brittanicum* published in 1676.

CIDER IN BRITAIN

The Norman conquest of 1066 also brought their culture, technology and knowledge to Britain. Coming from a place where growing apples and making cider was already a strong tradition, they are credited with popularising cider making in the UK as we know it today. To everyday folk throughout the country, the ability to grow their own apples and make their own cider became more widespread. Not only did they introduce new types of apple to these shores but they also brought the technology in terms of mills and presses. The legacy of Charlemagne had reached Britain and cider making blossomed as tax records of the time attest.

Both the middle ages and tudor periods saw apple growing and cider making continue to expand throughout both Britain and mainland Europe. Water was still unclean and unsafe to drink. In the 14th century there is even evidence of monks baptising children in cider.

By the mid 16th century European apple varieties started appearing throughout the UK. French varieties were imported and distributed by the King's fruiterer and by the beginning of the 17th century all the major cider regions of the UK today were well established and cider's heyday had arrived. Both the quality of the fruit and the resultant cider were important

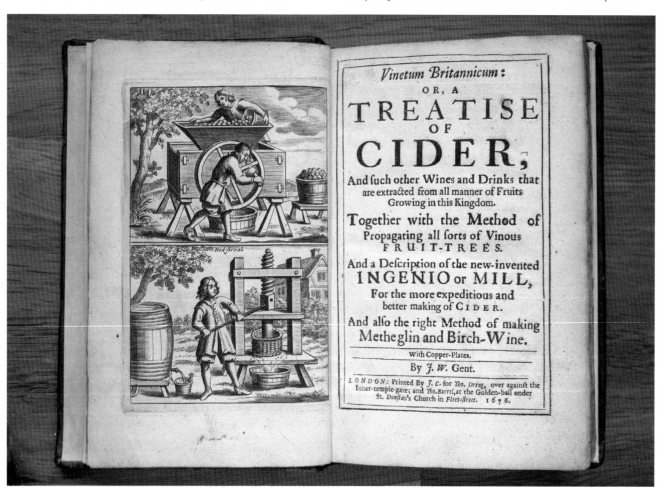

Vinetum Britannicum:
OR, A
TREATISE
OF
CIDER,
And such other Wines and Drinks that are extracted from all manner of Fruits Growing in this Kingdom.

Together with the Method of Propagating all sorts of Vinous FRUIT-TREES.

And a Description of the new-invented INGENIO or MILL, For the more expeditious and better making of CIDER.

And also the right Method of making Metheglin and Birch-Wine.

With Copper-Plates.
By J. W. Gent.

LONDON: Printed By J. C. for Tho. Dring, over against the Inner-temple-gate; and Tho. Burrel, at the Golden-ball under St. Dunstan's Church in Fleet-street. 1676.

enough to merit books and papers being published on the subject. In 1662, a paper by the Royal Society in London was published in which the addition of sugar to wine to give it sparkle was documented. This was the Champagne method years before Dom Periginon had even started and it was pioneered by Lord Scudamore of Holme Lacey, in Herefordshire. He had the advantage of using stronger English glass that could hold the intense pressure of bottle-conditioning. By now cider was being enjoyed in various forms and was drunk by every sector of society, be it a pint of scrumpy for lowly agricultural laborers or a crystal flute of best perry known as 'English wine'. It was shipped all around the country from ports like Bristol and Plymouth. In 1676 John Worlidge wrote *Vinetum Britannicum: A Treatise on Cider'*. It was the first book of its kind to show understanding and discuss the importance of farming apples as an industry. Worlidge identified the value British cider had over imported wines – growing apples better suited our climate so the profits of the industry would remain British, not foreign. It's recognised as one of the most important pieces of literature in the cider world.

In 1763 the British government proposed the Cider Bill, and led by Lord Bute they tried to levy a tax of four shillings on every hogshead (a 52 gallon barrel) of cider produced. The effect this had was widespread and immediate: riots broke out in the streets and the law was eventually repealed.

With regards to cider making in the 20th century, commercialisation, fashionable tradition and innovation are the main influences. Many of the oldest existing cider-making businesses that are still in production today such as Aspalls may have their roots in the 17th and 18th centuries, but their real size came about from the industrialisation of the process during the 20th century. For example, inspired by a firm of champagne producers in Epernay, HP Bulmer & Co undertook to produce a bottle-conditioned sparkling cider in the UK on a large scale. In 1906, it was released and although rebranded several times it survived until the 1980s. By then they were, and still are, the largest cider maker in the world.

Post-war Britain welcomed industrially processed foods and pioneered many of the modern techniques that improved shelf life, production speed and consistency. Apple juice can be heated and reduced to a thick, sugary concentrate that allows factories to make cider in variable volumes any time of

▼ **Cases of Bulmer's Pomagne (marketed as 'Champagne Cider' until the 1970s) are loaded onto a train at Hereford.** (Bulmers)

▲ Bulmer's bottles, often reused and recycled by customers, pass along the production line at Hereford, ready to be filled. (Bulmers)

▼ Traditional cider producing regions in the UK. (Charlie King)

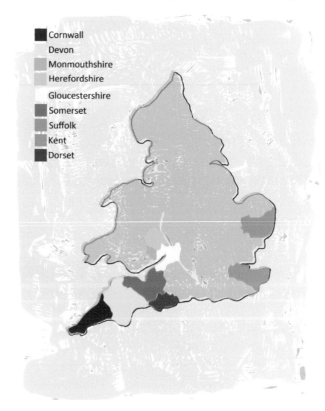

Cornwall
Devon
Monmouthshire
Herefordshire
Gloucestershire
Somerset
Suffolk
Kent
Dorset

year. Modern yeasts in controlled conditions ferment the liquor speedily and then it it watered back to the desired alcoholic volume before being packaged and distributed. This factor suits a more generic business model rather than a traditional agricultural one, regardless of flavour and tradition. With such speedy and efficient production methods, cider could be ordered, made, packaged and distributed all within a few weeks. Artisan and farmhouse producers suffered as a result, and the 1980s and 1990s saw orchards being grubbed out and replaced with alternatives, as farmers and landowners needed the land for more lucrative crops. When Magners was launched in the UK in 2003, it revolutionised the industry. It reminded millions of people that drinking cider was still a good option and brought new drinkers to the market from wine and beer. Promoting it as a great drink served with ice might have offended many traditional cider drinkers, but it worked and it totally reinvigorated the sector. The renaissance of cider has happened all over the world and it's more popular than it has ever been before.

A SUSTAINABLE DRINK

Since 2004 the global cider market has grown each year and this is continuing, but no boom lasts forever. To modern ideals cider does have some great features that *should* at least help it continue with creditability and longevity. It is (and certainly has the potential to continue to be) a very environmentally green product. In Somerset, typically cider is sold on the same farm on which the apples are grown (often within a mile or two), pressed and fermented. It is stored carefully and sold 'loose' straight from the barrel. Customers, often bring their own vessel (sometimes on a bicycle) to decant into, pay their dues and be on their merry way. Traditionally, there is very little processing and packaging involved, so the carbon footprint of traditional cider is very small and if made simply, fundamentally and ecologically, it's arguably carbon negative. When compared to beer, it is very green indeed. In a comparison to wine, there is less of a need for importing so its not only greener in that respect, (wine is never available loose in UK) but it can also be considered a healthier alternative (by volume) being only half the alcoholic strength, or less.

Orcharding and cider making themselves take us back to the land and brings seasonality back into our lives, an increasingly rare experience these days, so in those terms they offer modern lives something precious and of value. Orchards are wonderful places.

CIDER AROUND THE WORLD

Which country has the oldest cider-making tradition is not known, although it is still passionately contested. What's more important is enjoying and celebrating the wonderful diversity of the many unique and long-held traditions around the world. After the many obvious similarities, each culture is unique and as diverse as the country it spawns from.

Spain (sidra)

Arguably, Spain is one of the oldest cider-making nations and boasts some of the oldest records regarding its production. There are two regions for cider production, both in the north against the Atlantic coast, and both with strong Celtic roots.

Their *sidra* is characterised by its unique flavour, and really tastes like no other cider on earth. To a cider drinker from the rest of Europe or the USA, it is often perceived as an inferior drink due to the high levels of volatile acidity it contains, giving it a vinegary element. However, by pouring it properly, from a good height into the right kind of glass held at the correct angle, you temporarily infuse the cider with a short-lived but very pleasant sherbety effervescence. It's tart, delicious and refreshing and the style has evolved to go particularly well when accompanying local cuisine of meats, spices, cheeses and seafood. The first time you see it done well is quite a sight to see: a bottle of *sidra* is held aloft in the pouring hand as high as the arm will go, the other hand is extended fully downwards and holding a glass at an angle (approx 45°). Looking forward, the *escanciador* starts to pour the sidra (this is known as 'throwing the cider') bouncing it off the side of the glass and allowing it to splash furiously and effervesce. This temporary aeration gasses the drink and the glass is filled to about an inch from the base. It is then handed out and consumed in one before being returned so the process can be repeated. The glasses are always shared. Drinking sidra with the locals in Spain can often mean eating (and singing) a lot too. Both regions have strong and passionate zeal for their *sidra* and so festivals are popular. To protect their traditions they use a

legal framework (DOP). New ciders are now appearing on the market and are know as *nueva exression* (new expression), and while not as traditional as the *sidra natural*, offers the drinker a slightly more mellow alternative that is more wine-like in style.

The two regions where cider is made are Asturias and Basque country. It is claimed that the Asturians drink more cider per person than anyone else in the world. Their cider, although still sharp in comparison to other ciders, is rounder and has a slightly longer-lasting flavour than that of their Basque brethren where it is called *sagardo*. Made and presented with just as much passion as their western neighbours and very similar in style, the Basque cider is slightly more intense and robust. Cider has been popular here for centuries and it is commonplace to visit a *sagardotegia* (cider house) sometime between March and May when the new cider is ready.

▼ Teaching youngsters the importance of throwing *sidra* in Asturias.

▲ Typical architecture of a Normandy cider farm.

France (cidre)

Anyone who has tasted French *cidre* will realise it tastes fruiter and is fizzer than most of the cider in the UK. The French still use a traditional technique called keeving or *chapeau brun* in French, which is used to maintain a higher level of fruity sweetness in the final juice than other styles. There is also a tradition of bottle fermenting the cider to give it a pleasant carbonation or *mousse*. No cider is flat in France. It's a popular style globally of cider going with food very well, and as such more producers around the world are experimenting at re-creating it. The French also have a strong tradition of distilling their cider into cider brandy, *Calvados* in Normandy or *Lambig* in Brittany. Rather cleverly, someone thought to try blending some of the cider brandy with some apple juice (probably to preserve it.) As it aged it for a few years in oak barrels it gave rise to another French idea – *Pommeau*.

Like the Spanish, the idea of protecting the regions and local techniques of cider making is very important and they too use a PGO legal system in place throughout Europe. The two regions where cider is made, although not exclusively limited to, are Brittany (known as *chistr*) and Normandy. Within France, cider drinkers argue that Brittany has a better cider culture, as Brittany's cultural identity is still quite independent. They still have their own language, their own flag, and are more resistant to influence from the outside. Their *terroir* is also unique and as such has a unique effect on the apples that grow there.

Normandy *cidre* both benefits and suffers from its proximity to Paris. Many wine-drinking Parisians take weekend trips and holidays to Normandy, and the influence they have on the Norman cider culture is thought to be limiting, as they tend to think of it as an inferior product to wine. To the benefit of Normandy's cider makers, some of their ciders have found great success outside France and can now be found in some of the best restaurants in the world (ask to see the cider list next time you are in one).

Strict rules govern precisely what pieces of land specific apple varieties can be grown on; these are known as 'parcels' and are basically small pockets of land where the geology meets certain criteria. French cider is acidic, sweet and tannic, and as such it is full-bodied and often has a very strong sense of *terroir*. Wild yeasts are used to ferment their apples and so the *cidres* are also complex and tend to be more floral.

Germany

Germany has a thriving *apfelwein* culture and it is the official drink in the state of Hessen, with Frankfurt as its stronghold, although it is also made in other regions too. Frankfurt's Sachsenhausen district contains many of the traditional a*pfelweinhäuser* (cider houses) where they serve it from a blue and white jug called a *Bembel* into a particular style of glass with lozenge cuts in it. The Germans often drink it alongside cold meats and cheese. A typical glass of their of cider is flat, slightly hazy and a mildly tannic. Traditionally, the amount

▲ *Apfelwein* being served in Frankfurt.

▼ A typical line of perry pear trees in Austria.

of tannin can be increased by adding Spierling fruit (*Sorbus domestica*) but these days many producers are reducing the amount of tannin in their cider to suit more modern tastes. They are also experimenting with bottle-conditioned champagne-style ciders with some residual sweetness in an effort to woo wine drinkers.

Austria (möst)

Unbeknown to many outside the country Austria has a very strong and old cider and perry culture. Apple and pear trees are grown all over the country in an open system, rather than existing in orchards only. In one region of Lower Austria the success of cider in the region brought so much to the area it became known as the *Mostviertal* (literally 'cider quarter'). Here the tradition of growing pears and making perry is stronger than cider and so the landscape is typically characterised by lines of pear trees alongside roads and pathways as far as the eye can see. There are very few fences and walls and so the trees are planted out in lines and new ones are added regularly, so much so that it is now the largest pear-producing area in Europe.

The most successful of these cider makers are known as The *Mostbarons* and they live along a tourist route now known as the *Moststraße*.

Within the last 20 years, it has seen a revolution in production methods to 'improve' the quality with massive influences having been taken from the wine industry. A large

proportion of the perries available now are single variety. Many modern techniques have been employed, the availability of additives is more widespread so the *möst* (pronounced mosht) is now cleaner than ever. However, these improvements are somewhat subjective as the traditional drinks are now left to individual farmers who keep the more traditional approach alive. They still blend all their fruit and use wild, native yeasts to ferment with, which means their ciders have more character than their modern counterparts.

Wider Europe

Various types of cider and perry are made in small amounts throughout mainland Europe including Italy, Switzerland, Belgium, Holland, Denmark, Poland, Scandinavia and beyond.

England and Wales (cider & seidir)

The UK has a really established cider tradition and is well known throughout the cider-drinking world, which is illustrated by the huge volume we consume as a nation. To give you some idea of the scale, the market value of the UK cider industry in 2013 was valued at £3 billion and in 2012, we drank 1,500,000,000,000 (1.5 billion) imperial pints. The UK is one of the few countries in the world were cider is drunk more like beer (in 20oz/568ml pints), rather than like wine in smaller 125ml/250ml measures.

Historically, its roots were as a drink made for the working class in southern and central agricultural areas where the climate and soils are perfect for growing apples. It's well known that cider made up an important part of an agricultural labourer's pay, with him collecting a daily allowance that increased in the summer and harvest periods until it was abolished by an addition in the Truck Act of 1887. It was a healthier alternative to the available water in many areas. So families and children consumed weaker, watered-down cider as a matter of course.

As an island nation, our strong maritime history also boosted the cider-making economy. In the south west where much of our naval and maritime industry was based, cider was sent to sea with merchants and sailors after the admiralty realised it helped prevent scurvy on the long sea voyages. These days the West Country is synonymous with cider and it is a bastion of traditional cider making. The Three Counties (Gloucestershire, Herefordshire and Worcestershire) have a historically rich heritage for cider and perry making and some of best (and the biggest) cider makers in the world are based there. Nearby Wales, where it is called *seidir*, has seen a resurgence in cider making in the last decade from a point of virtual extinction. Societies like the Welsh Perry & Cider Society have done much to promote and develop it there.

Today's UK cider scene is varied and rich with cider makers producing ciders of every type: traditional, dry, hazy, tannic farmhouse ciders to golden, clear, wine-like ciders to sophisticated bottle-conditioned perries that are comparable to the finest champagnes. Our heritage is alive and well and younger drinkers are drinking more of it than they have in decades. Orchards are being planted again and innovation is rife.

▼ Frank Naish, renowned as the UK's oldest traditional farmhouse cider-maker.

▼ Welsh Perry & Cider Society festival glass.

WASSAIL!

'*Waes Hail*' is an old English phrase meaning 'be in good health' and in that spirit, it has given name to the best kind of cider party you could ever hope to attend! The pagan celebration, Wassail, is held annually around Twelfth Night (17 January) where people gather in the orchard to celebrate a good harvest and inspire another one. The basic idea of a wassail is to give thanks for the last season's bounty, thanking the orchard for the apples and its guardians (robins, *Erithacus rubecula*) for protecting them. Although each wassail is unique, there are some core elements. Cider is mulled with spices, sometimes using a red-hot poker, and there is generally a bonfire and a procession into the orchard to the base of the oldest and largest tree. Toast is dunked into the cider before being placed into the branches to encourage the robins to stay, and cider is offered back to the orchard itself by being poured around the base of the tree. Singing and making lots of loud noise is important at some stage to ward off any evil spirits and also to awaken the trees. Some people use pots and pans to bang together, but in Somerset we often use a volley of shotguns just to make sure.

Wassails vary from fun, family events to learn about the local cider, to wild, raucous parties where a lot of cider is consumed. It's not uncommon to experience middle-aged men dancing around in badger suits to Bluegrass, and the best wassails tend to be a mixture of the two. The British countryside in the middle of January is about the bleakest, coldest, wettest and darkest place you could ever hold an outdoor event, so dedication is required by all attendees, and waterproof trousers are a must!

Old apple tree, we'll wassail thee,
And hoping thou wilt bear.
The Lord does know where we shall be
To be merry another year.
To blow well and to bear well
And so merry let us be;
Let every man drink up his cup
And health to the old apple tree.
Spoken:
Hatfuls, capfuls, three-bushel bagfuls, and a little heap under the stairs.
(Traditional wassail song)

USA (hard cider)

The USA was once home to about 15,000 apple varieties and in the late 1700s, hard cider was North America's most popular beverage, but it virtually lost all its original cider-making culture by the early 1900s. Today its popularity is growing exponentially and both artisan and industrial producers are struggling to find fruit. What a typical American cider tastes like is difficult to say, because it's made in many ways, in all corners of the continent and is consequently subject to a huge degree of variation and influence. Louisa Spencer from Farnham Hill Cider in Lebanon, New Hampshire, passionately rejects attempts to define the long-awaited arrival of an 'American style' and looks to the notion of *terroir,* that could take decades to understand in itself. '*Terroir* is really the only sound basis for regional style, and US ciders need more time,' she advocates.

One of the issues currently facing the cider industry in the USA is a lack of true cider apples. Since their apple-growing culture is so strong, there are thousands of acres of apples grown in the north east, north west and Great Lakes regions. However, the fruit has always been for eating and fresh juice rather than cider making, so their apples are often low in tannins and high in sugar. Most of the apples grown are modern eating varieties but a recent trend has been more towards heritage varieties unique to each region. As many

US units/measurements

There are differences in every country. Some will be legal whilst others are cultural. The USA has some particularly complex differences that readers should be aware of when researching or learning more about apples and cider production. Examples include two sets of laws regarding the production and sale of alcohol; federal laws are governed nationally (see www.ecfr.gov/), whilst state laws vary all over US. They also have a very complicated alcohol distribution set-up, which requires a separate licence for each state. Until very recently, nearly all of the apples grown in the US were grown for eating and so the way fruit is processed (picked, packed, stored etc) has a focus on preservation of perfect hand-picked fruit rather than cider making. Regulation and best practice are therefore significantly different and warrant further local research. In a fermentation scenario the use of Brix (°Bx) is a popular and widespread difference. Degrees Brix are used to measure the amount of sugar dissolved in a liquid: 1 degree Brix being the same as 1gram of sugar dissolved in a solution as a percentage by weight (%w/w.) Most US home-brew information will be calculated using Brix, unlike the UK.

▲ A New England cider orchard. (Farnhum Hill Cider, NH)

▶ A drier Pacific northwest orchard. (Tieton Cider, WA)

Top tips

There is no typical 'American cider,' as one might refer to a 'Normandy cider' or 'West Country cider.' Our growing conditions vary so widely from region to region of this vast continent that different varieties are relied upon more or less in each of them. Of course, this also depends on the preferences and idiosyncrasies of the apple growers. Ben Watson

producers use the apples that are available to them, much of the cider has less tannin in than in Europe. There is also virtually no tradition of using wild yeasts to ferment cider either although this is starting to change. The resurgence of craft cider making has meant true cider fruit is now at a premium, and many growers are top-working their orchards (grafting traditional cider varieties from

Europe or heirloom fruit from the US onto existing non-cider fruit trees) in the hope of boosting numbers. They are willing and skilled experimenters and will try virtually anything with regards to production in a logical, calculated manner until it either fails or succeeds. Either way – something will be learned and adapted or utilised for the future. This mindset has led to some new ideas in the cider market there and in that respect the USA is a really exciting place to be. Those credentials guarantee a healthy future in one of the largest markets on earth.

New England was the earliest part of the country settled by cider-drinking Europeans. During 1767, the average citizen of Massachusetts drank more than 35 gallons of cider and has become a stronghold for apple growing and cider production today.

The Pacific north-west area (or Cascadia as it's known locally) is more commonly associated with hops and beer thanks to the part it played in the US beer revolution. However, the area grows a huge amount of apples and has done for a long time, supplying about 55-65% of the apples eaten in the USA. This, combined with the region's strong winemaking culture and beer heritage has led to an interest in the production of hard cider. It's now a stronghold for some of the best ciders in USA.

South America

Since the 15th century, emigrants from Spain have populated South America, their cultural habits and similarities existing since then. Trade links between the two regions have been strong historically too. Around Christmas time, public holidays and other special occasions, the Argentinians turn to local carbonated ciders to celebrate, while Chileans have been making cider since colonial times.

Australia and New Zealand

Australia has a burgeoning cider scene and the number of producers is increasing continuously. Its southernmost island Tasmania is known as the Apple Isle for its long history of growing apples, and they were one of the first crops to be introduced by European colonisers. The climate there, as with many other of the cooler regions, is perfect for growing them with their rich soil and long warm days. Apples and pears remained a traditional crop until the 1970s when the acreage started to decline. Since then, and without realising it, Australia's strong wine culture has trailblazed for its infant cider market. The techniques used and the infrastructure

la bebida alegre del verano...

SIDRA-CHAMPAN

El Gaitero

available to winemakers has lead to producers transferring knowledge, techniques and skill to cider making.

Their cider market is so young still, it's impossible to offer a typical representation of style. Many producers are experimenting continuously and the ciders they are producing are evolving constantly. Currently, anything produced will reference another cider somewhere else in the world, but they are an enthusiastic bunch and it's a country to expect more from in the future.

Asia

Ironically, as the original apple area of the world, Asia has no long-established tradition of cider making, although there are now pockets of it all over. Japan, an area in northern India, and China, all have cider making of one description or another going on these days. They are all different from one another, all having examples of both 'traditional' approaches and modern alternatives.

Country/region	Sweet %	Bitter-Sweet %	Bitter-Sharp %	Sharp %	Original Gravity	Final Gravity	Total Acidity gr./L	Total Tannin gr./L	Description and Notes
Principality of Austria	10%	20%	30%	40%	1.045-1.055	1.000	3.5	1.5	Fresh and tart apple, tannic, quite vinegary but refreshing
Basque Country	20%	15%	15%	50%	1.045-1.055	1.002	3-6	1.2-1.8	Sharp with medium light volatile acidity, some vinegar flavours
Normandy	20%	50%	20%	10%	1.055-1.065	1.010	3	1.4	Fizzy, mild sharpness, juicy fruit balanced with tannin
Normandy 2	15%	80%		5%	1.060-1.070	1.012	2	1.5	Sweet apple, citrus fruits, fresh hay, rustic, complex, farmy and lingering
Brittany	30%	30%	30%	10%					Drier, more tannic and minerally than Norman style but similar otherwise
Germany	25%		50%	25%			3-6	0.35-0.7	Smooth, flat
UK Eastern	40%-85%				1.040-1.052	0.999-1.001		<0.75	Mild
UK Hereford and 3 Counties	5%	75%	50%	5%	1.045-1.055	0.999-1.001	3-3.5	1.2-1.3	Full-tasting bittersweet, appley nose, good body and acidity for balance. Spicy, leathery characteristics, rich colour.
UK West Country	10%	70%	10%	10%	1.040-1.060	0.998-1.001	3.5-4.5	1.5-1.8	Robust
UK Commercial	Unknown				1.045	1.010	3-4	1-1.2	Fizzy, clear, inoffensive balance of sweetness, sharpness and tannin
NE USA	45%	20%		35%			3.4	0.75-1	

'TYPICAL' REGIONAL CIDER PROFILES BASED ON APPLE TYPE, SUGAR, ACIDITY & TANNIN LEVELS. (AN APPROXIMATION – FOR USE AS A COMPARISON ONLY)

This table is intended to show the variation in approach to making and flavours in cider regionally throughout the world. It is very generalised and doesn't take into account specific terroir, seasonal differences, modern intervention techniques, MLF or even personal preference. It's intended as an indicator of just how much cider can vary from country to country. It is worth noting that these are approximations sourced from cider-makers in each area. 'Typical' is a generalisation based on both historical and current data.

CHAPTER 2
APPLES AND ORCHARDING

Apples

The best cider comes from the best cider apples, which is a simple fact I would encourage anyone interested in making cider to embrace and understand. Cider apples contain a particular mixture of acids, sugars and tannins – all of which have an influence on the final flavour. Cider can certainly be made with any kind of apples, but it may not have the classic bitter-sharp cider taste you are accustomed to. Bittersharp apples live up to their name, providing both bitterness and sharpness and are specially selected to give you that particular cider taste. For the purposes of demonstration, if an experienced cider maker were to make three batches of cider in *exactly* the same way, but using three different apple types they'll taste drastically different. So the final flavour of the drink starts with the fruit you use.

To my mind (and to cider makers all over the world) the inclusion of bittersweet apples is essential for a classic cider taste, and I could never imagine making cider without them. However, it's quite common for a professional cider maker also to include some culinary and dessert fruit alongside cider apples to boost acidity and sugars levels. Many first-timers collect unwanted fruit of this sort from wherever they can scrounge it and there is certainly no shortage of sources

across the UK. Tonnes of apples lie unused every autumn, both wild and cultivated, on private and public land. Many people are happy collecting these, putting surplus fruit to good use as cider.

Community orchard schemes are popular and more spring up on disused land for local residents to tend and use. Many of these are cooking and eating varieties, but in some cases they are cider varieties so the community can make cider annually. Proceeds raised tend to go towards funding further community projects in turn.

At best, owning land and growing fruit can be seen as a luxury, and aside from their bounty, orchards are wonderful places to be in recreationally. For many though, the idea of planting up an orchard on land that you own represents an added responsibility and requires both financial investment and extra time to maintain it. Commercial apple growers commit their land to 50 years or more when they plant an orchard, and can't expect to break even on their initial outlay for at least seven years. For a professional cider maker who wants complete control over their fruit, growing apples may be a desirable step to take. It allows for total control, starting with their favoured varieties used in cider production that offer the best taste, growing schedules and maintenance that suit their business ethos as well as more accurate timing and co-ordination between harvesting and pressing. They get to know exactly how their apples taste, how the trees react under certain conditions, which ones grow best on their land, where they ripen first, the likely yield of each orchard annually and so on. They also remove third parties from the equation so, while the initial outlay may be more, cider makers can become more self-reliant in the long term as their fruit supply is less influenced by market forces.

Consequently, never growing your own fruit will probably mean you will be slightly further removed from the deepest level of understanding about your main ingredient – the apples themselves.

Another consideration is location and space – urban cider makers will understand this problem more than most, and also welcome the chance to escape the town/city on the hunt for fruit. However, it must be stressed that not growing your own fruit or having space to do so doesn't rule you out of making great cider. Phill Palmer, an enthusiastic Welsh cider maker makes cider annually in a shed in his back garden in Cardiff, and was the winner of the 'Farmhouse Dry' category at the Royal Bath & West Show in 2012 (the largest and oldest cider competition in the world to date). I think it can best be summarised as being 'more ideal' to own your own fruit trees because it will always take you a step closer to the fruit itself.

For those who wish to take their cider-making a step further, growing your own apples is a giant leap forward. Like a chef, if you are really serious about creating a great flavour, you need to be serious about your ingredients, where they come from, what influences them and how to get the best out of them. The best way to get to know them is to grow them. I heartily recommend everyone go to the effort of growing their own apples and reap the many benefits of doing so. You will be introduced to new experiences and it'll give you an increased level of understanding of the juice that makes up your cider.

Being in an orchard regularly allows you to tune in to an 'awareness of season', it will increase your understanding

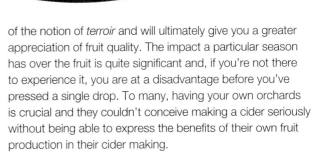

of the notion of *terroir* and will ultimately give you a greater appreciation of fruit quality. The impact a particular season has over the fruit is quite significant and, if you're not there to experience it, you are at a disadvantage before you've pressed a single drop. To many, having your own orchards is crucial and they couldn't conceive making a cider seriously without being able to express the benefits of their own fruit production in their cider making.

If you put your heart and soul into your apples, they will put theirs into your cider.

Top tip

"THE ONLY APPLE YOU CAN'T USE IS A BLACK ONE. IF IT'S GONE BLACK, IT'S GOT NOTHING LEFT TO GIVE"

ROGER WILKINS, cider maker

Growing apples

When planting an orchard, some important considerations need to be taken into account such as land, size, varieties and orchard type. A little bit of background research about what apple varieties go into the cider you already enjoy is a fairly easy and is a good starting point in terms of flavour (although process plays an important part too). Cider makers will be able to tell you what varieties they grow and prefer, and why, but as a general rule of thumb, the classic cider varieties will offer you the best flavour.

Specialist cider apple growers and nurseries, although not widespread are generally helpful and are happy discuss your interests. The site you choose to plant an orchard will have its own set of factors that will dictate how best to proceed, so careful planning is key. The fundamentals of what needs doing when planning a new cider orchard can, for the most part, be done yourself. But in a professional scenario some key help is advisable and there are specialists available to help you decide precisely what's best for you, on your site and in your location.

Books are written about growing apples (listed later), and cider apples specifically, and these will contain far more detail regarding best practice with regards to planning, planting and maintaining a successful cider orchard. For the most part, the good news is that cider apples have the same or very similar growing requirements as eating apples and as they tend to suffer slightly less from pest and disease, and are quite well suited for organic production. Following is an outline of the most important things.

CONSIDERATIONS

What particular cultivars you decide to grow will dictate what kind of cider you will end up with. It's not the only factor to consider, but it is the first one and an important one. From an international point of view, there are hundreds of varieties to choose from, but regionally certain cultivars prevail and usually offer the best results, so speak with local cider makers about what grows well.

To complicate things further, certain varieties are more susceptible to certain problems (like scab or mildew) that can inhibit growth and fruit quality more than others. The flowering season (and pollination) is another factor that needs considering as not all apples will blossom at the same time and so varieties that flower simultaneously should be grown in close proximity to each other in order to aid pollination. New orchards should be organised by flowering season, grouped together so the blossoming, insects and thus the pollination move down through the orchard. Group early varieties at one end and the latest at the other.

The type of orchard you have will determine the size of the trees you need and what rootstock you need those varieties grafted onto. Soil quality also plays a role in rootstock choice.

Site

Where you choose to grow your fruit will affect how it grows, how easily it is harvested and also the final flavour of your cider, so choosing the right site is important. Avoid places that have frost pockets as it will damage blossom and reduce your final yield – in the UK frost is one of the most damaging factors in fruit production. One of the major advantages of planting on a slope (as so many vineyards are) is that you not only get a great exposure to the sun but also it allows colder air to slide further down the slope, leaving the trees and their precious blossom slightly better off. A sunny, warm, south-facing gentle slope is perfect. However, slopes can cause problems during a wet harvest, so think carefully.

Sometimes a windbreak may be necessary to protect the trees from prevailing winds. Pollinating insects dislike strong wind so if you do need a windbreak, it needs to be planted before the apple trees and allowed to establish. It also needs to be maintained appropriately to protect your orchard, so build that into your maintenance plan. Avoid areas with yellow grass patches, too much moss or anywhere with big cracks in the soil as they are either too wet or too dry.

Understand that you should put your trees where *they* will do best, not where suits you.

Drainage

Look at the site over winter and try to find any wet patches. These will need avoiding or draining to sort out any water that is sitting on or just under the surface. Some of the most beautiful orchards I have visited have natural low dips towards one end that the landowners have allowed to remain boggy or even as ponds. These encourage wildlife and biodiversity that will benefit the orchard overall. Alternatively, you need to drain excess water off-site by digging a channel, filling it with gravel and a drain tube and running it elsewhere.

Soil

Apples don't particularly like shallow soil, but they can be grown successfully on a wide range of soil types. Avoiding heavy clay soils will help establish strong roots at an early age and help prevent further complications later in the tree's life. As a rule, heavier soils are prone to water retention and compacting (making heavy machinery like tractors and trailers more difficult to use) and lighter soils are more susceptible to drought and the leaching of nutrients. A thorough site inspection and a soil test are very important. Knowing the history of a plot may also throw some light onto how it is likely to behave.

Any nutritional imbalances should be rectified before planting commences. Work in nutrients by adding the necessary additives and fertilisers onto the soil and then ploughing them in. The most important soil requirement is that there is a combination of adequate drainage and moisture retention – that balance is crucial.

Layout

Unless you are a planting a modern bush orchard, avoid planting in a grid – follow a quincunx pattern (see diagram overleaf) that allows for the maximum numbers of trees per acre. There is a temptation when planting small maiden trees to put them closer together, so you have to try and imagine them as large, mature trees that need space and light around them.

If you do plant too closely, then following a quincunx pattern will mean that any future tree removal (to improve space) will be more effective and easier. When possible, rows should be aligned north to south. This helps ensure the trees are getting the maximum amount of light throughout the season.

Quincunx pattern:

x	x	x	x	x
x	x	x	x	
x	x	x	x	x
x	x	x	x	
x	x	x	x	x
x	x	x	x	
x	x	x	x	x
x	x	x	x	
x	x	x	x	x

The distance between each tree needs to vary depending on the variety, its vigour and any maintenance machinery used. As a rule of thumb, vigorous varieties should be planted about 3m (10ft) apart, moderate varieties 2–2.5m (6–8ft) apart, and smaller/weaker cultivars about 2m (6ft) apart.

Standard trees should be 9m (30ft) apart each, which may feel excessive upon planting but in time they will grow into the space, and still benefit from space around each tree.

VERGES

As a cider maker, orchards are the source of your most important ingredient and they may also be viewed as a conservation resource. When making plans for a new orchard, rough grass margins should be incorporated around the outside. Verges should be at least 4.5m (15ft) wide to help with air, light, access and biodiversity. It's critical not to underestimate the future size of your trees and the space they'll need, so larger verges encourage a more open side, allowing air to move and light to penetrate as the trees matures. You may need access for a tractor and trailer (maintenance and harvest time) and verges are of benefit here too.

The ideal perimiter of a typical orchard might be a mixed hedgerow of native species (that is pruned every other year), followed by a rough, un-mown grass strip between it and the apple trees. This long grass provides valuable habitat (summer and winter) for natural predators that will help keep your trees healthy. If livestock is in the orchard, these will need protecting too.

YIELD

No two apple trees are the same in terms of yield – their variety, age, size and general health all have a bearing on the quantity of fruit they produce. Some trees are more biennial than others (they crop more heavily every other year), and this is one of the most difficult things to anticipate as a cider-apple grower. When mature, it is reasonable to assume a standard orchard will give you five tonnes of fruit per acre. Apples, especially when grown as traditional standards, are biennial so there are always good years followed by bad years in terms of fruit volume, and this figure can vary widely.

A general rule of thumb using standard trees is that 40 trees per acre should yield about 5 tonnes of fruit. Bush orchards, planted at 250 trees per acre will yield about 15 tonnes of fruit. A tonne of fruit should yield 50–70% weight-to-volume, *ie* between 500 and 700 litres of juice. Some volume is lost during fermentation but not much.

HOW MANY TREES?

If you want to grow cider apples, deciding how many trees to plant needs careful thought. Ideally, you'll want to plant enough to give you slightly more fruit than you need. Consider how much cider you would like to make (or drink!) and work backwards. If you assume an average volume over a given period of time, you can start to get an idea.

As an example, consider the following as a homemade cider set-up. If you assume consumption in your house might average a pint a day (and two on Saturday!) over the course of a year you'll be consuming a gallon per week, or 52 gallons a year. This is easy enough to get through, especially if you include an annual party. About half a tonne (500kg) of fruit should be sufficient to produce enough juice for what you need. Depending on your press efficiency, and losing some naturally throughout the process of racking *etc*, for half a tonne of fruit, you will need about 5–6 mature standard trees. This will give you slightly more juice than you need to make approximately 1 hogshead or 52 gallons of cider.

LIVESTOCK

Secondary orchard usage is also worth considering early on – do you want to use the space for anything else too? If you want to share the space by grazing cows, sheep or pigs, the orchard type is important because the trees will need to be higher and will need protecting for longer.

If you do plan to use it for livestock, animals are normally removed seven or eight weeks before fruit is likely to be collected, to ensure lower levels of bacteria at harvest time. Traditionally, animals were always grazed on the same land, but removed prior to harvest. Occasionally the impact on flavour that comes from grazing livestock under fruit is seen as too strong, so some cider makers decide not to do it. But it offers an alternative to maintenance that more usually involves mowing or spraying to reduce the grass that competes for moisture with the trees.

Needless to say, if you are planning to house livestock in the orchard, it limits the type of orchard you can grow. A low-growing bush orchard, isn't a viable option in this scenario. Another factor is machinery – will you be using a tractor? In a bush orchard scenario, you will need a tractor-mounted grass mower and probably a spraying set-up too.

TREE TYPES

The number of trees you can grow is determined by the size of the area available and type of orchard you want to plant. So, after choosing what exact varieties you want, the next consideration is the type of orchard you want and the size of trees you want to grow in it. There are two main types of orchard these days – standard orchards (the traditional ones dotted about the countryside with large trees in) and intensive bush orchards (low-growing, high-density, modern versions usually set up by professional cider-apple growers or larger-scale cider makers.) Both are quite different and have their benefits. There are other tree sizes available such as semi-standards, which may be better for hand-picking fruit, as they are smaller trees, but they don't tend to be planted much these days as they make maintenance difficult without the benefits of yield. The yield of trees will increase with age but you can't expect much fruit for the first few years.

Standard trees

The long-term and most beautiful solution is a traditional standard orchard. It's a slower start and a lower yield but the trees will be useable for longer – even up to a century – and produce top quality fruit. The individual trees themselves grow up to 8m high. They are planted with a wide space (varying from 15-35ft!) between the trees and will start to bear fruit from five to ten years of age.

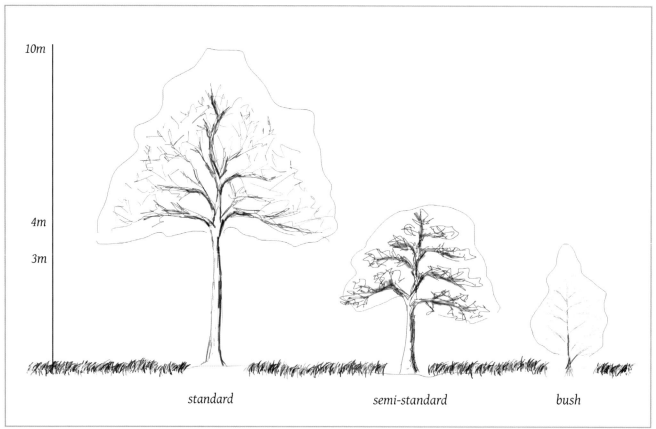

10m

4m

3m

standard   *semi-standard*   *bush*

ORCHARD TYPE FACTS

Tree size/ type	fruiting height		row spacing		tree spacing		trees per acre approx	yield per acre		advantages	disadvantages
	m	ft	m	ft	m	ft		kg	ton		
Standard	1.6–10m	5–33ft	9.1–10.6m	30–35ft	9.1–10.6m	30–35ft	40	5,080	5	double use land, long lived, beautiful	more biannual harvest, lower yields
Semi standard	1–4m	3–13ft	3.6–4.3m	12–14ft	3.6–4.3m	12–14ft	200	10,160–12,192	10–12	easy to maintain and pick	no tall livestock (cows, horses etc).
Bush	ground–3m	ground–10ft	5.5m	18ft	2.1–2.4m	7–8ft	310	15,240–20,320	15-20	massive yield, easier to access plants	heavily mechanised system, labour intensive, shorter lived, less attractive

Semi-standard trees

Similar in style to standards, but a little shorter growing, 4.5–6m.

Semi dwarf

Semi-dwarf trees are more common in garden situations and make trees easier to pick by hand. They are more vulnerable to cattle, however, so the land can only be doubled-up with sheep or pigs. The trees typically grow to 3.5–4.5m.

Bush orchard

The modern alternative is an intensive bush orchard. The trees are lower to the ground (and literally gown as a bush), but they

▼ An intensive orchard in mid-harvest, Somerset, UK

have the advantage of bearing fruit quicker and offering much higher yields. The disadvantage is that they don't tend to live as long (although with care they can live for quite a while), they don't look as nice and the orchard space can't be used for anything else. The trees themselves grow to about 3m.

ROOTSTOCKS

When cultivating apple trees it is necessary to grow them on a different set of apple roots, controlling the growth and size of the tree. Cider varieties are grafted onto 'rootstocks' and left to develop as a single tree before they are sold. If you look at the base, mid-section or top of the trunk carefully, you can often see the bulbous scar where the two join. Rootstock types are dictated by the combination of site and your needs with regard to the size of your trees (standard orchard, bush orchard *etc*). They exert the most influence on the final size of your tree; eg, a dwarf tree will grow to 2–3m, a semi-dwarf 3–4m a half standard 5–6m and a standard 6–8m. Seek specialist advice wherever you buy your trees, but it's worth considering the following:

M106 is the most commonly used rootstock and is semi-dwarfing because it imparts a moderate vigour and size (4–6m) to the tree. It's useful for growing vigorous varieties like Dabinett, Ashton Bitter and Harry Master Jersey, but is susceptible to rot and doesn't like wet sites or periods of prolonged damp.

M111 is a vigorous stock, producing larger trees than MM106 that are generally tougher. It's more tolerant of drought, wet, wind and limited soil depth. It's also useful for weaker cultivars like Dabinetts or Ashton Bitters that may need a bit of a boost.

M25 produces the largest and most robust trees, so is ideal for anyone who wants to grow standard trees. Because of its vigorour, it produces trees that are more disease resistant. If you have poor, hard ground or shallow soil, the inherent vigorour of M26 will really help your trees. However, particular varieties are more vigorous than others, such as Major & Ellis Bitter, in which case a more dwarfing rootstock is a better choice.

Laying out an orchard

As much as possible, run the rows north to south. When measuring out your orchard, use a piece of string to mark out where your first row will be (allowing for a verge of 4.5m or 15ft) and peg it down. This becomes your baseline for marking out the rest of the orchard. At one end will be your first tree so put a marker in. Using this position, mark out the position for the second tree in the row 9m (30ft) away for a standard orchard and mark it. This is repeated until you have reached the end of the row.

Then measure 11m (35ft) from the first row and use the string to peg down a second row that runs parallel to the first. Measure the halfway point between the first two markers on the first row. Use another length of string placed at a 90° angle from this point, and where it crosses the second row, this is the point where the first tree will be planted on the second row. Place a marker. Following this method and repeating it throughout the orchard should give you ample space and a quincunx layout pattern.

Bush orchards can be approached in the same way, but the distances are much shorter and the density of trees is greater at 250–300 trees per acre. It's a modern concept designed to maximise crop production and they're much more short lived (maybe 15–20 years) but do have the bonus of a significant increase in yield. Rows should be planted 5.5m (18ft) apart and trees 2.4–3m (8–10ft) apart.

When ordering trees from specialists, it's worth noting that most are grown to order and so can take a few seasons to get hold of. Unless you are replacing a few trees in an existing orchard, you will probably have a wait.

GUARDS AND STAKES

When planting a tree, you need to protect it against the wind while it settles and puts significant root growth down. It will also require protection from animals like rabbits, who like to chew the soft bark at the base of the tree, which can kill it. The cost of a tree guard and also a stake and tie must be added to the overall cost of planting an orchard. One apple grower I know says: 'All apple trees want to do for the first seven years in an orchard is try and lie down.' So you'll need to help them.

For a standard tree, you'll need a 2.4m post that is driven 75cm into the soil, a rubber tree tie and a rabbit guard. You can lose a tree overnight if you don't stake it properly – for example, a sheep could rub on the guard and knock it over, and a rabbit could chew bark round the base. A standard tree can take up to ten years to come right, so don't ruin your chances by skimping on the set-up. Stakes should be used on the windward site and should be substantial enough to support themselves and a young tree in the most inclement weather of the year.

PLANTING A TREE

Planting a tree properly means it only needs to be done once and should reduce the likelihood of problems later in the tree's life. Protect your investment by planting your trees correctly. It's best done in a team of two or more.

Plant while trees are dormant – the general rule of thumb for a dormant season is early December to late February. The middle of March in an 'average' year is about as late as you'd want to go, but it's safer to plant before the end of February.

Encouraging strong root growth is key to them getting a good start and 'bedded in' so the addition of bonemeal around the roots of anything you are planting will increase the capacity for root growth within the first season or two. If you want to use some manure, don't put it underneath the roots but at the top, or thinly on the surface. If you put it at the base beneath the tree and plant it on top, it can hold too much moisture around the roots, and as the manure rots, it will create a gap beneath the tree that destabilises it. If it's on the top or near the surface, the worms will bring it down as they want to.

If you are using bare-root trees, it's quite important to keep the roots themselves covered during the process, right up until you actually put them into the ground. Strong wind can suck the moisture out and kill a tree quickly so keep them adequately moist and covered right from the moment of delivery until you plant them. Careful planning and preparation should mean you are ready to do this at the time they arrive to minimise the potential for damage.

When you have determined the exact spot for your tree, the area of ground around the mark needs preparing properly. Firstly, you need to remove the grass for at least 1m (3.5ft) from the trunk in all directions. Then dig

down to a level that is both deep and wide enough to encompass the root system, removing any large rocks or stones that will get in the way. One of the commonest mistakes people make is to plant a tree deeper than it was planted initially. The level of the soil around the base of the trunk after planting needs to be the same as it was before planting (when it was at the nursery), not lower or the tree will suffer. It should, if anything, be planted slightly higher as you should allow for some sinking over the years as it matures. If you inspect the base of the trunk above the roots, you will probably see a darker soil line indicating the level at which it was growing in the nursery previously. Maintaining this level will help the tree establish quickly. Making a hole slightly too deep is better as it allows you to add some loose soil back in (along with some bonemeal) until you get to the correct height. Each tree will be slightly different.

The next thing to do is drive a stake into the hole. This is done on the windward side but off-centre in the hole (so the tree itself can be placed centrally) about 10cm from where the trunk will lie. Trees that aren't staked properly tend to flop about in the wind, weakening the base of the trunk and making it more prone to fungal attack in the worst possible place. When the stake is placed on the windward side, the tree will be blown away from the stake and therefore not damaged by it.

Place the turf from the top upside down at the bottom of the hole and chop up well with a spade. It contains nutrients and leaf matter that will help the new roots establish. This is also a good time to throw in some bonemeal.

When ready, place the trunk about 10cm from the stake and place some loose soil over the roots. As the soil is put back into the hole, gently shake the tree to encourage the soil around the roots, so as to not leave any pockets. When filled approximately 7.5cm from the top, the soil over the roots needs firming down but not packing too tightly. It needs to be pressed and firm, not compacted and squashed. Using your heel, push the soil around the trunk so it's firm and steady. Then add the remaining soil and press down lightly with the sole of your foot.

The addition of well-rotted manure as a mulch on the surface of the soil around the base of the tree will encourage moisture retention and soil aeration (via worms), both also helping establish healthy growth. Be careful not to let too much of the mulch come into contact with the trunk as it may hold damp and cause rot, a small gap around it will suffice.

Always place the tie at the top of the stake to help prevent damage to the trunk when it's blown about in the wind. A staple in the stake at that height will prevent the tie slipping down as the tree moves. Lastly, fit a rabbit guard around the base of the tree to protect it – make sure it's well fitted all the way down to the soil level.

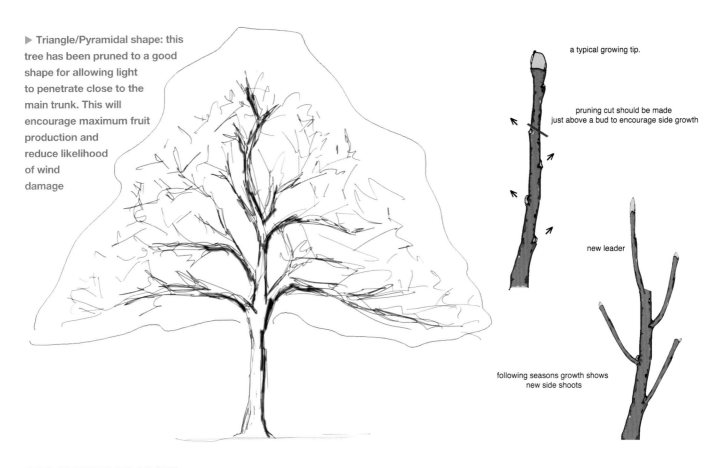

▶ Triangle/Pyramidal shape: this tree has been pruned to a good shape for allowing light to penetrate close to the main trunk. This will encourage maximum fruit production and reduce likelihood of wind damage

a typical growing tip.

pruning cut should be made just above a bud to encourage side growth

new leader

following seasons growth shows new side shoots

MAINTENANCE

Orchards do need regular maintenance to get the best out of them. Although they may crop every year and look healthy enough, without some routine care and attention, they won't thrive and your yield will be much lower than its potential. Other than pruning (see below), general maintenance duties throughout the year include replacing broken and rotten stakes, checking guards, loosening ties, checking boundary fences, sucker removal and checking for tree rock after gales.

The nutritional requirements of apple trees needs to be taken care of, so an annual addition of trace elements and minerals will improve the health of the trees and ensure bigger, better-quality fruit.

PRUNING

Pruning is an essential annual task for any apple grower, to remove dead or diseased wood and to allow light into the crown of the tree, so it's really important to get it right. Every tree is different, but it's generally accepted that cider-apple fruit benefits from growing a central leader trunk and allowing feathers (side branches) to shoot off from it. This is called apical dominance, and controlling or removing the central leader has the effect of regulating the tree's growth. When it's removed, the rest of the tree benefits by triggering more upward growth rather than flowering and fruiting. Allowing

a single trunk to grow upwards and encouraging feathered branches to spread out beneath it will allow the central leader to supply energy to the rest of the tree while fruiting as well. Without one, the tree will try for more growth instead and fruit production will suffer as a consequence. Different varieties will do this at different stages and some depend on a central leader more than others. Still, the most important aspect of pruning is to maximise light into the tree. Pruning apple trees is like farming light: good light means good leaf and good fruit. The more horizontal the branches are, the weaker their growth is and the more fruit they will produce, so encouraging the correct shape and development of a young tree is important. You can even try hanging small weights on individual young branches to encourage them sideways and help shape your tree.

In July, a young tree may have its top four or five buds removed from the central leader (but not the tip bud!) in order to encourage some of the lower buds to grow sideways. If you do it any earlier, the new growth tends to be too strong and more upright. Removing these will encourage side shoots that are more likely to flower the following year. Vigorous varieties can be pruned later in the year to check their growth, whereas weaker varieties (or trees on weaker soils/slower rootstocks) can be pruned early to help invigorate them. You want good leaves in August because that's when the trees set fruit buds for the following year, and that means fruit!

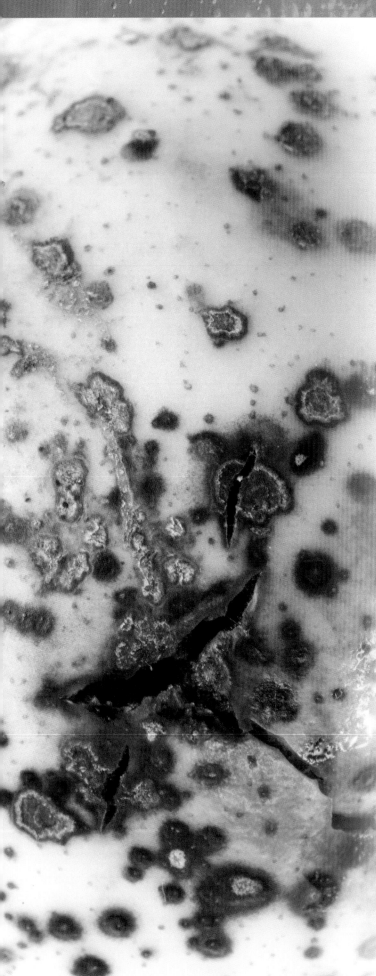

Pests and Disease

Among all the ailments that can cause problems for cider-apple growers, the most common are caused by fungi. Luckily, because they are common, good orchard management, biodiversity and vigilance mean they can be kept to a minimum.

SCAB

Apple scab is acumulative problem encouraged by moisture and humidity. It's a fungus, *Venturia inaequalis*, that overwinters on the leaves of the orchard floor and in wet weather, particularly in spring, spores infect new growth on the tree and affect young fruit as it develops. The most important impact it has is to reduce fruit size, so it does have an economic bearing on your harvest to some extent. But it doesn't harm the cider, leaving it perfectly safe to drink. Many apples suffer with scab, but the extent of the damage changes dramatically between varieties. Particularly vulnerable are Coates Chisel Jersey, Yarlington Mill, Harry Masters Jersey, Majors and Kingston Black. It is identified as brown or black scab-like blotches that appear on the skin of the apple from mid-spring until leaf fall in the autumn. When severe, it can lead to the splitting of the fruit.

Prevent it by spraying a copper-based solution in March, sometime before bud burst. Many organic farmers use this once a year before the buds break, and it offers a good start to the season. Alternatively, you can spray with sulphur as a programme throughout the summer every two or three weeks. Many apple growers don't worry about scab at all as in many cases the effects are negligible.

MILDEW

This is another common fungus that can affect cider apples, although it is generally less of a problem. Again some varieties suffer more than others – Somerset Redstreak, Dabinett and Ashton Bitter are susceptible. The spores overwinter in both leaf and flowers buds and then emerge in the spring when they go on to infect more of the tree. It also reduces the yield and quality of the fruit.

PESTS

Although apples are very popular with various invertebrates, most of them don't actually affect the size of your crop

◄ Intense scab damage.

▲ Sawfly.

▲ Rosy apple aphid.

too much. Encouraging biodiversity with recommended practices such as large verges and not using insecticides will mean that, in most cases, natural predators will control pests very well. Any infestation in large numbers will obviously need dealing with. Three notable pests to watch for are apple sawfly (*Hoplocampa testudinea*), rosy apple aphid (*Dysaphis plantaginea*) and codling moth (*Cydia pomonella),* all of which can affect your yield quite seriously. If you don't want to spray, you have to rely on birds to keep the insect populations down by promoting bird life as much as possible. Bird boxes for blue tits and great tits will help, as will some dead wood areas among the verges. These days you can even buy lacewing and ladybird houses to encourage them into your orchard – they are two voracious predators (as larvae and adults) that should be supported. In a domestic orchard –chickens are good for standard and semi-standard trees because they will seek out and eat overwintering pests such as blossom weevils, but they are no good if you are spraying!

Adult apple sawflies are active in late April–May and can

be seen visiting the open blossom. They are 4–5mm long with blackish brown heads and thorax and brown abdomens. They lay their eggs in the flowers, and the larvae tunnel into the developing fruit while it is still small. They can be treated by spraying with deltamethrin or lamdacyhalothrin-based chemicals, or you can remove infected fruits by hand.

Rosy apple aphid is a small pink-grey insect that infests apple blossom and damages the developing fruit quite seriously. They can be treated by a multitude of pesticides if you are happy to spray, or small, localised infestations can be pruned out from a tree.

For codling moth hang a trap in the tree in late May/early June when the males are flying to find mates. Check every day, and when a large number are caught then spray with whatever is recommended. Codling moth traps can be found in most larger garden centres. Larger animals such as badgers and deer can also damage orchards but tend not to affect them too much.

▼ Codling moth.

A *Hessle* Pear scion (top half) is joined to a *Pyrodwarf* rootstock (bottom half) using a tongue and groove technique.

The graft is then bound to protect it and stop it drying out whilst the join heals. (Matt Veasey, Nooks Yard Cider)

Grafting

When you have a cultivar that is favoured for its exact flavour characteristics, its important to be able to preserve it exactly how it is. If left alone, nature will ensure that the natural offspring of any apple will make it different from its parents. However, we want to preserve the original because they make great cider, so we take a piece of it and grow it on another tree, and this is called grafting. The Chinese started the idea a long time ago, but its widespread use in Europe came about thanks to the Romans, who loved apples and pears.

Two separate (living) parts of apple trees are joined together – the top part (which will grow and become the fruiting tree) is called the scion, and the bottom part, which is essentially the roots, is called the rootstock. The scion and rootstock are cut in a particular manner so that the living tissues (the green cambium layer under the bark) can join when held together and then wrapped in grafting tape, such as polythene strips or raffia.

Grafting requires some degree of skill, although with practice and patience many people can do it themselves. It's usually done in late winter/early spring before the sap starts to rise.

Pollination

Pollination is a crucial aspect of successful fruit growing and there are two major factors that affect pollination rates.

Apple trees can be divided into pollination types. While some cultivars are self-fertile (meaning they will always produce fruit without the help of other trees), others are not and always require pollen from other trees for fertilisation. Typically, a traditional cider orchard containing a good mix for flavour will also offer a sufficient mix of tree types to ensure every tree has what it needs to pollinate well. The greater variety of trees there are, the easier it becomes to pollinate them. In cases where large numbers of non-self-fertile trees are grown together and there is an insufficient amount of pollen available, many growers will use crab apples as pollinators to boost pollen levels amongst in the orchard.

Insects are the engine of pollination and so are an important consideration too. Honey bees (*Apis Melifera*) in the orchard will undoubtedly aid with pollination, as the bees and orchard owners will benefit from hives among the trees. Beekeepers and cider makers have long been partners, as both receive what they need from each. Wild insects such as hoverflies (*Diptera*), solitary bees (*Hymenoptera*) and bumblebees (*Bombus*) are also successful as pollinators and make up a large percentage of the insects responsible for pollination. They will thrive in large verges left on each side of an orchard, so encouraging biodiversity by keeping spraying to a minimum has meaningful benefits. A verge of 15ft around each edge of the orchard itself where the grass is unsprayed and uncut for much of the year will act as a safe habitat for such creatures to thrive in and their presence alone will in turn increase the natural predation of pests. This will have the knock-on effect of reducing the need for chemical intervention, also reducing costs and time whilst increasing yield.

As well as considering the balance of self-fertile trees to pollinating trees and the mechanics of insect pollinators, some consideration should be given to the organisation of the planting so that trees of a similar flowering season work side by side. As mentioned earlier, if you plant varieties that flower at the same time alongside one another throughout the flowering season it improves pollination and yield. In Normandy, cider orchards are often planted by the particular flowering season groups that they fall into. At one end of the orchard, the early-flowering varieties are planted together, which mix into the early middle varieties. The early middles are also all planted together and eventually they mix into the late middles and then into the lates and so on. By planting in such a way, the orchardist can ensure both the blossom and insects are concentrated together as the flowers open, and pollination moves down through the trees from one end of the orchard to the other.

Top tip

"When planing a new tree, keep the grass well away (1m/3ft) from the trunk for four years – it really competes for soil moisture with the tree in the early-establishment period."

Ed Landen, commercial cider apple grower

Harvesting apples

If you are sourcing free apples from a tree or an orchard where the exact cultivar is unknown, hold it in your hand and bite it. The flavour of the juice will tell you everything you need to know and, most importantly, if it's ripe!

If it's bitter and/or makes your mouth feel furry, it's either a cider apple or one that could be used for making cider because you can taste and feel the tannins in it. If it's sweet and juicy, it'll tell you the apple has little or no tannins in, but sweet, ripe and ready to press. If it's really sharp, it'll be good for the acidity levels you want in your juice. If you are collecting apples from someone's land (with their permission!), it's always a good idea to leave some for them or at least give them some cider in return to thank them.

Collecting apples can be back-breaking work, but the joys of being in an orchard on a crisp autumnal day do wonders for raising the spirit. It's an opportunity to bond with your favourite apple trees, socialise with your cider colleagues and appreciate the quality fruit you'll be using to make your cider. Handpicking is slow but is the first line of defence against unwanted detritus ending up in your mill.

Traditionally, wicker apple baskets were used to collect fruit in, but they are limited in size and bulky to store, so woven sacks are preferable. Hessian or canvas sacks are better for collecting apples in because they allow the bag to breathe. They have the natural advantage of being porous and so allowing moisture and air to pass though them, meaning fruit can be stored in them for longer without rotting.

It's quite common to see many people collecting apples in thick plastic sacks that don't allow the apples to breathe. If this is all you have, then the apples shouldn't be in them for more than a day or two unless they are really unripe. Sealing moist ripe apples into a sweaty plastic sack will induce rot and all the backache will be for nothing. There are various apple collectors available on the market such as a small hand-pushed device or larger brush-sweepers that work from a tractor. These will also often collect grit, stones, twigs, leaves and grass – all of which will need removing before milling.

Top tip

"Visit your local microbrewer who'll have lots of malt sacks he has no need for. Make sure they're woven ones, then rip out the plastic inner and turn inside out – voila! -apple sacks!"

Matt Veasey, Nooks Yard Cider

Fruit selection

Ripeness is so important. It sounds very obvious but many newcomers make the mistake of pressing apples too soon, while they are still very starchy and hard.

A decent amount of colour on the skin in the form of a rosy sunburn from having direct sunlight on it is always a good indicator, as well as the hardness of the apple when the skin is pressed in by the thumb. The best way to get to know the stage of ripeness of your fruit is to bite deep into it and suck the juice from it and chew the flesh. You need a balance of sweetness and sharpness either in a single apple or within a batch of apples that will be milled and pressed together.

Apples aren't all the same – they can be divided into several categories. At one end of the spectrum we have plump, juicy, sweet dessert fruit that we find in the supermarket and at the other we have small, hard and bitter wild crabs or crab apples. In the middle, between the two, you will find cider fruit that ideally offers us a little bit of each of the flavour profiles, which is important to cider production. If you try to make cider with just dessert fruit you may be disappointed. Typically, traditional ciders have a good proportion of tannins in to help balance out the flavour and add interest in terms of bitterness and mouthfeel, but it's not always the case. There are popular ciders that are crafted from dessert fruit in UK and also all over the New World where cider fruit is rare, it's just important to be aware of the differences. Crabs and cider fruit contain high amounts of acids and tannins that really help to give the juice flavour/complexity (the same things found in wine) and they also help with preservative qualities.

CIDER APPLES

Apples for cider making can be divided into four types according to the relative proportions of acid, tannin and sugar found in each.

As your only ingredient, it's really important to understand the nature and balance of what makes cider fruit so essential to real cider production. Cider can be made with any fruit but, in reality, the best ciders are made using cider fruit because it contains three essential components:

1. Sugar

Apples are naturally high in sugar (approximately 12.5% on average, but the amount varies enormously) and these sugars are used by the yeast and converted into alcohol. No sugar means no alcohol, high levels of sugar means high levels of alcohol. The two main sugars typically found in apples are fructose and sucrose, although there are small amounts of glucose too. Different varieties contain different amounts of sugars but, to complicate things further, the weather during a crop also has an enormous influence over how much sugar levels can vary annually.

2. Acid

Acidity is the second key component of apples and cider. Of the acids in an apple, approximately 90% is malic acid, which is responsible for the classic appley taste: zingy, fresh and sharp. It occurs in all apples in varying amounts, as does quinic acid, which has a slightly bitter taste. Acids play a crucial part in determining not only the final flavour of the cider but the ability of it to ferment well and aid in the prevention of infection. Acid levels can vary seasonally too, so also need measuring if you want to maintain some control.

3: Tannin

Tannins are a group of substances that are responsible for both bitterness and mouthfeel/texture of cider. They are found in the apple skins and are released into the juice during pressing, and are technically known as 'phenolics'. The levels of tannin found in the skin are what make cider apples distinct from dessert fruit.

In terms of cider and flavor, tannins come in different intensities and these are described as:

'**soft**': astringent and furry feeling (contributes to mouthfeel)

'**hard**': very bitter tasting (contributes to flavour)

Tannin levels in cider fruit can vary quite considerably year on year, even by ±50%. Increased nitrogen (from feeding trees) has the effect of reducing tannin levels, dictating that nutrient-deficient trees, or at least ones with restricted feed regimes will produce a more tannic result. Measuring tannin levels is complex and expensive, so the best method in most cases is to taste the fruit and the juice.

Top tip

"When using dessert fruit make sure you:
1) only use fruit good enough to eat;
2) don't store it too long in tank – four months is your absolute max and;
3) blend judiciously – a top tip for all cyder makers, no matter what fruit they ferment from."

Henry Chevallier Guild, Aspalls Cider

CIDER APPLE CLASSIFICATION & COMPONENTS			
Type	Acidity %	Tannin %	Sugar (%)
Sweet	Low (< 0.45%)	Low (< 0.2%)	Largely determined by the weather, sugar levels in apples can vary from 17% in a good summer to < 10% in a bad summer (on average ±20% annually!).
Bittersweet	Low (< 0.45%)	High (> 0.2%)	
Bittersharp	High (> 0.45%)	High (> 0.2%)	Storing fruit can increase starch conversion (SG).
Sharp	High (> 0.45%)	Low (< 0.2%)	
FINAL CIDER	~ 0.45%	~ 0.2%	15% ≈ SG 1.070 (8.6% abv) 10% ≈ SG 1.045 (5.4% abv)

Cider apple types

▲ Taylors.

SWEETS

These apple are relatively low in both acid and tannin and are best used as part of an overall blend to boost sugar levels. They are often large and juicy and great to eat on their own, but for use in cider they offer little in terms of flavour and aroma. Examples include:

Berkeley Pippin, Court Royal, Eggleton Styre, Killerton Sweet, Morgans Sweet, Northwood, Sweet Alford, Sweet Coppin, Taylors, White Alphington, Woodbine

◣ **Morgans sweet.**

▲ **A blend of sweets.**

BITTERSWEETS

These give a quintessentially British flavour to the cider. Some of these varieties have been used for hundreds of years because they work so well in terms of final flavour. They are subdivided further as mild, medium and full bittersweet depending on their relative proportions of acidity, tannin and sugar. Some have an unbelievably high amount of tannin but, generally, the acidity is lower than other apple types so the sweetness and bitterness prevail. Examples include:

Mild: Ashton Brown Jersey, Broadleaf Norman, Doux Amer, Dove, Ellis Bitter, Tremletts Bitter, White Jersey,
Medium: Bedan, Binet Rouge, Broadleaf Jersey, Brown Snout, Bulmers Norman, Dabinett, Notted Kernal, Harry Masters Jersey, Michelin, Red Jersey, Royal Wilding, Yarlington Mill
Full: Chisel Jersey, Major, Medaille d'Or, Reine des Pommes, Royal Jersey, Strawberry Norman

▲ Tremletts Bitter.

▲ Bulmers Norman.

▲ Brown Snout.

▲ Dabinett.

▲ Harry Masters.

▲ Yarlington Mill.

▲ Fillbarrel.

▲ Vilberie.

SHARPS

As their name might suggest, Sharps are predominately higher in acidity. Acidity is helpful for flavour profile as it helps maintain a fresh, crisp and refreshing mouthfeel. It also helps fermentation, and some producers will always add particularly acidic apples, like Bramleys, to help with acid levels (many culinary apples have this characteristic). They are subdivided into medium and full sharps. Examples include:

Medium: *Backwell Red, Bloody Turk, Crimson King, Gatcombe, Lady's Finger, Langworthy, Yeovil Sour*
Full: *Browns Apple, Fair Maid of Devon, Frederick, Hereford Redstreak, Ponsford, Colemans Seedling, Winter Stubbard, Yellow Styre*

BITTERSHARPS

These are high in both acid and tannin levels, and so are valued for their contribution in making real cider (although possibly it could be argued don't have as much variety in flavour as the full range of bittersweets). They are also subdivided depending on the proportion of sharpness to bitterness (full bittersharps being more bitter than medium bittersharps *etc*). Examples include:

Medium: *Cherry Pearmain, Cowarne Red, Dymock Red, Kingston Black, Lambrook Pippin, Porters Perfection, Stoke Red*
Full: *Cap of Liberty, Duffin, Foxwhelp, Haglowe Crab, Joeby Crab*

Essentially, if you want to make a full-flavoured, complex cider, you need a wide variety of fruit to call upon for a wide variety of flavours. For many people, it may be that true cider fruit (the type of apples ideally required for cider making) is difficult to source, and in this case it may be necessary to add tannins from another source such as oak shavings, new oak barrels or even an additive from your local homebrew shop.

Saying that, some cider makers choose to make cider from single apple varieties, and while they may not match the flavour profile of a full-bodied blended cider, they offer an interesting point of difference which many of us enjoy. It is possible to make a good cider from dessert/culinary fruit; however, it will always be trickier as there is less taste dimension, most notably in the amount of tannin to blend. Nevertheless, makers in Kent, Norfolk, Suffolk and generally the East of the UK, away from traditional cider-apple-growing regions, do a good job. This style is sometimes called Eastern Style cider to distinguish it from the more tannic Western Style.

▲ Bloody Turk.

▲ Browns.

▲ Kingston Black.

▲ Stoke Red.

▲ Foxwhelp.

Single variety vs the blend

So is it best to blend apple varieties or can you make good cider from them separately? Ask a group of cider makers that and most will say blended is best, but one or two will always come to the defence of single varieties.

The debate over whether a single-variety cider (containing only one specific apple variety) can ever really compete with a blended cider brings out strong opinion because no apple varieties are the same. Ask yourself how likely is it that one single variety has enough of the 'correct' flavour components in it (sugar, acidity, tannin *etc*) in the exact proportions to create a balanced drink? Compare it to a cider that is produced by the hands of an experienced cider maker by blending a multitude of varieties, each with differing amounts of the flavor components. When you think about bittersharps, bittersweets, sharps and sweets and so on, they each bring their own bit to the final flavour profile, having their own specific mixes of sharpness, bitterness and sweetness. Cider

makers choose the proportions they want of each to shape and style their cider accordingly.

So, in reality, a single variety can't compete, although some do pretty well at coming close – the most notorious being the *Kingston Black*. A blended juice offers the cider maker the chance to measure and control each component and can therefore massively increase the opportunity to create balance and consistency year on year. Apples can be blended before pressing, juice can be blended before or after fermentation, and the cider itself can be blended before or after racking. Not only can apples or juices be fermented separately but because they are, they can be fermented using different yeasts and/or different techniques, only to

be blended at a later stage. So we see the convenience of a blended approach. Having said that, single-variety ciders have several redeeming features that offer both cider maker and cider fanatic an opportunity for something different. Common sense dictates that blending is the best method and it is therefore favoured by most, but because of that, making single varieties can be seen as taking an interesting approach and that is something to be celebrated. They often make a lovely and unusual alternative to the 'balanced' cider. You can achieve a greater understanding of how each variety tastes post-fermentation and I speak as someone who samples many different ciders regularly. Personally, I find them fascinating because they are almost playful by design so they are to be enjoyed and encouraged.

Another reason for liking them is that when judging cider-making skill, you can compete more closely within the limitations of single varieties. Ten ciders from ten makers from different parts of the country all using the same one variety will give you ten different ciders and ten different approaches to cider making. Tasting them allows you to judge the cider makers' skill and process more closely. Equally, apple varieties

and therefore flavours vary all over the world. The USA, for example, has its own particular heritage apple varieties and in this instance, a single-variety cider may offer us something really unique and special that you would never get the chance to try elsewhere.

The clue is in the name: '*single*' because it's just one type of apple, and '*variety*' because that's exactly what you get when you put it out there against a blended cider. Single varieties take you into new and often unusual directions in terms of flavour. It may be dorky, but it's a significant point of difference and enjoyment.

Despite the debate raging on, single varieties are as popular as ever. Britain in particular has some classic apples that many cider makers use for single varieties. They include Dabinett, Kingston Black, Yarlington Mill, Redstreak, Stoke Red and Slack-Ma-Girdle. Some more unusual apples that can make excellent single varieties ciders include Breakwell's Seedling, Porters Perfection and Tremlett's Bitter.

▼ The 22-apple blend that goes into Les Noyers 'Templar's Choice' cider.

36 Classic varieties for making great cider

These cider apples really are classics; their use is well known and respected. They are generally grown for blending, although some are suitable for use as a single variety. Despite this list, there are hundreds of cider varieties that you can use.

Apple varieties tend to have a geographical persistence, so always ask about which varieties are local to you, particularly when it comes to cider. Each county has its own traditional varieties and these can impart a lovely, local flavour into your cider and make it very distinct indeed. Some of them do better in other parts of the country and on different soils and sites than others, so see what's growing well and is popular locally. If you're after something really different, you can try to include

foreign varieties. For example, French cider apples are similar in overall composition although, as a bunch, they appear to offer a slight increase in floral aroma and acidity. Good varieties are: *Frequin, Binet Rouge, Reine des Pommes,* Douce Moën, Rambault, Petit Jaune… but there are hundreds more.

If you were to plant an orchard from scratch, try to include many of these plus pollinators (eg crab apples) and acidity regulators such as Bramleys, which are also useful for bulk.

Cider apple types are sub-divided thus:

Sweets:	= low acidity & low tannin
Bittersweets: mild bittersweet	= low acidity & mild tannin
med bittersweet	= low acidity & med tannin
full bittersweet	= low acidity & high tannin

Bittersharps:	medium bittersharp	= med acidity & high tannin
	full bittersharp	= high acidity & high tannin
Sharps:	medium sharp	= med acidity & low tannin
	full sharp	= high acidity & low tannin

36 APPLE VARIETIES FOR GREAT CIDER JUICE

Name (& type)	Season of a) flowering b) harvesting c) milling	SV	Typical SG approx (UK av)	Total Acid	Total tannins	Juice qualities & characteristics	Growing habits & notes			
							Scab Resistance	Mildew	Self-fertility	Other
Court Royal (sweet)	a) b) early Nov c)		1050	0.21%	0.11%	sweet, fast fermentation	bad			fruit rots quickly
Sweet Alford (sweet)	a) mid b) early Oct c) mid		1052	0.22%	0.15%	sometimes mild bittersweet, slow–med fermentation	good	OK	bad	often magnesium deficient
Sweet Coppin (sweet)	a) late b) mid oct c) mid-late		1052	0.20%	0.14%	pure sweet, seasonally mild bittersweet, slow–med fermentation	OK	bad		prone to canker in wet conditions
Slack-Ma-Girdle (sweet)		Yes	1052	0.24%	0.14%	rich, full-bodied, good aroma, great blender				
Taylors Sweet (sweet)	a) late-mid b) early-mid Oct c) mid		1053	0.18%	0.15%	best used for blending, good flavour and aroma but light on body				useful pollinator for others, unusual weeping habit
Dove (mild bittersweet)	a) late b) Nov c) late		1049	0.22%	0.31%	slow fermenter, good body, soft tannins, slow fermentation	OK			regular and heavy cropper
Major (full bittersweet)	a) mid-late b) late Sept c) early		1050	0.18%	0.41%	full bittersweet, great quality juice, slow fermenter	OK	good	variable	difficult to grow, gets silverleaf, does well in poor soils

36 APPLE VARIETIES FOR GREAT CIDER JUICE

Name (& type)	Season of a) flowering b) harvesting c) milling	SV	Typical SG approx (UK av)	Total Acid	Total tannins	Juice qualities & characteristics	Growing habits & notes			
							Scab Resist-ance	Mildew	Self-fertility	Other
Tremletts Bitter (med Bittersweet)	a) mid b) Oct c) Mid	Yes	1048	0.27%	0.34%	hard, bitter tannin, low sugar, slow fermentation, great for blending	bad	OK	bad	biennial, random growth habit, good pollinator, difficult to grow but useful to include
**Yarlington Mill (med bittersweet)	a) mid-late b) early Oct c) mid	Yes	1052	0.22%	0.32%	medium bittersweet juice, good aroma & sugar, med–slow fermentation	bad	OK	good	
Brown Snout (med bittersweet)	a) mid b) late Oct c) mid		1053	0.24%	0.24%	mild–medium bitterness, soft tannins, good colour, moderate fermentation	OK	OK	good	prone to narrow angled branches (needs pruning to open it up)
**Harry Masters Jersey (med bittersweet)	a) late b) mid/late Oct c) early mid Nov		1056	0.20%	0.32%	med–full bittersweet, soft astringent, good quality, med–slow fermentation	OK	OK	good	often magnesium deficient
Michelin (med bittersweet)	a) late-mid b) early Nov c) mid		1050	0.25%	0.23%	soft tannins, high yield, reasonable juice	bad	bad	good	heavy cropper (very fertile), prone to canker
Somerset Redstreak (med bittersweet)	a) mid b) early Oct c) early-mid Oct		1055	0.19%	0.28%	mild to medium Bittersweet, soft astringent tannin	good	bad	good	whippy, floppy growth, requires light pruning, biennial
**Dabinett (med bittersweet)	a) late b) late Oct/ early Nov c) late	Yes	1057	0.17%	0.29%	soft, well balanced, full bodied great for blending, excellent juice	OK	OK	good	can be potash deficient, prune & keep a strong central leader, wet intolerant, needs good winter dormancy
Nehou (full bittersweet)				0.17%	0.6%	full bittersweet, astringent, full bodied juice	bad	OK	OK	soft fruit, rots quickly
Ashton Bitter (full bittersweet)	a) mid-late b) early Oct c) mid		1060	0.2%	0.4%	full, juicy bittersweet, good aroma, useful for blending	good	bad	poor	
**Medaille d'Or (full bittersweet)	a) late b) early Nov c) late		1053	0.27%	0.64%	full bittersweet, sugary, fruity, (v.bitter)	good	good	good	biennial, brittle branches
**Ashton Brown Jersey (med bittersweet)	a) mid-late b) end Nov c) late		1054	0.14%	0.23%	Full-bodied, soft, medium tannins, excellent juice, slow–med fermentation	Very good	OK		large tree, heavy crops when happy
Binet Rouge (med bittersweet)	a) late b) mid-late Nov c) late		1064	0.26%	0.24%	classic juice, mildly bittersweet, aromatic				
Chisel Jersey (full bittersweet)	a) mid-late b) late Oct c) late		1059	0.22%	0.40%	full bittersweet, full bodied, astringent tannin, aromatic, slow-med fermentation	bad	bad	v. poor	prone to boron deficiency
Reine des Pommes (full bittersweet)	a) early-mid b) Nov c) late		1056	0.31%	0.44%	bitter and full-bodied, slow to ferment				apple ripens late and keeps well

36 APPLE VARIETIES FOR GREAT CIDER JUICE

Name (& type)	Season of a) flowering b) harvesting c) milling	SV	Typical SG approx (UK av)	Total Acid	Total tannins	Juice qualities & characteristics	Growing habits & notes			
							Scab Resist-ance	Mildew	Self-fertility	Other
Breakwell's Seedling (med bittersharp)	a) b) early c) early	Yes		0.64%	0.23%	medium bittersharp, thin body	good	good	good	soft fruit, rots quickly
Kingston Black (med bittersharp)	a) mid b) mid Oct c) mid	Yes	1061	0.58%	0.19%	well balanced, full bodied, great for blending, slow to ferment	bad	OK	poor	difficult to grow (benefits from spraying)
Porters Perfection (med bittersharp)	a) mid b) mid-late Oct c) mid-late	Yes	1054	0.82%	0.25%	quite acidic, blends well, good body	good	good	OK	keeps well
Dymock Red (med bittersharp)	a) mid b) mid c) variable		1052	0.62%	0.22%	good body, great juice, slow fermentation				vigorous growth & good cropper
Lambrook Pippin (med bittersharp)	a) mid-late b) very late c) very late		1055	0.58%	0.24%	good sugar levels/body, excellent juice for flavour and aroma	bad			
Stoke Red (full bittersharp)	a) late b) mid c) mid	Yes	1052	0.64%	0.31%	well balanced juice, good aroma. Slow to ferment	good	bad	good	soft fruit, bears fruit from a young age and crops regularly
Foxwhelp (full bittersharp)	a) mid b) mid Oct c) mid	Yes	1050	1.91%	0.22%	good juice, distinctive flavour and aroma, very sharp	good	OK	poor	soft fruit
Cap of Liberty (full bittersharp)	a) early-mid b) mid Oct c) mid	Yes	1055	0.92%	0.3%	excellent juice, great alone or as a blend, slow to ferment, rich and fruity	bad			prone to scab, irregular cropping
Bramley's Seedling (full sharp)	a) mid-late b) mid-late c) late		1048	1.7%	0.10%	very low ph, low tannin, high acid juice, very useful for blending/acidity regulation	good	OK	good	vigorous, prone to calcium deficiency
Browns (full sharp)	a) mid b) end Sept-Oct c) early-mid		1048	0.72%	0.13%	sharp, aromatic, fruity, low sugar, v. mild bitterness	good	OK	good	vigorous, big cropper
Frederick (full sharp)	a) mid-late b) early-mid Oct c) mid		1048	1.02%	0.09%	fruity, high quality juice, slow fermentation	good			reluctant cropper, prone to canker in wet
Backwell Red (med sharp)	a) early -mid b) early c) early		1051	0.70%	0.13%	good blending ability, good for an early variety				small tree
Tom Putt (med sharp)	a) early b) early c) early		1052	0.65%	0.13%	useful for adding sharpness, clean, pleasant flavour				prone to apple sawfly
Fair Maid of Devon (full sharp)	a) mid b) early Oct c) mid Oct					light body/low sugar, fast ferment, high yield				fruit rots quickly
Herefordshire Redstreak (full sharp)	a) mid b) mid c) mid					good flavour and aroma				can be cankerous, good cropper

**Names are an indicator of 'vintage quality' apple varieties generally accepted as producing the best quality juice for cider making. These varieties have been selected for a combination of reasons: high acidity, high tannin (or both) and are generally best used as a blend although there are ten that can be used as a single variety (SV) too.

16 PEAR VARIETIES FOR GREAT PERRY JUICE

Name (& synonyms)	Season of a) flowering b) harvesting c) milling required within..	SV	Typical SG approx (UK av)	Total Acid %	Total tannins %	Citric acidity levels	Juice qualities & characteristics	Growing habits & notes	
								scab resistance	other
Blakeney Red (Painted Lady; Painted Pear; Circus Pear; Red Pear)	a) mid b) late Sept–early Oct c) 7 days	yes	1056	0.42%	0.13%	low	medium acidity and tannins, fruit must be mature when milled		heavy and reliable cropper
Butt (Norton Butt)	a) mid b) early Nov c) 4–10 weeks		1056	0.54%	0.32%	low	useful for boosting acidity and tannin, its sharp and fruity, slow-fermenting juice can precipitate tannins during storage. Needs macerating	ok	heavy cropper, biennial,
Coppy	a) mid b) mid Oct c) 7 days		1067	0.28%	0.05%		mild fruity juice, full bodied & pleasant so useful for lowering acidity and tannins	bad	
Gin	a) mid b) mid Oct c) 3–5 weeks		1052	0.42%	0.15%	med-high (>0.3%)	good all rounder	good	good cropper but can be biennial
Green Horse (White Horse; Horse Pear)	a) mid b) mid Oct c) 3 weeks		1050	0.75%	0.11%		Useful for increasing acidity without increasing tannin too much	bad	regular cropping
Greggs Pit	a) mid b) early Oct c) 7 days		1055	0.57%	0.11%		med acidity and, mild tannins, it's astringent and juicy to taste	bad	large vigorous tree
Knapper (Napper; Knap Pear)	a) mid b) early Sept c) 5 days		1051	0.46%	0.08%		medium acidity and low tannin	bad	very early variety, fruit will rot quickly
Moorcroft (Malvern Hills; Stinking Bishop)	a) mid b) end of Sept c) 2 days		1066	0.5%	0.17%	low	medium acidity and tannin, sharp and of good quality. Useful for boosting sugar levels	bad	light-med cropper
New Meadow (Lintot; Yokehouse)	a) mid b) Oct c) 3 weeks		1062	0.53%	0.06%		mild fruity juice of good body and medium acidity	bad	low cropping
Oldfield (Ollville, Oleville, Offield, Awrel, Hawfield)	a) mid b) end Oct c) 3–6 weeks	yes	1065	0.73%	0.15%	med-high (>0.3%)	medium-high acid, med tannin, vintage quality	bad	prone from canker
Red Pear (Sack, Black Horse, Red Horse, Aylton Red, Blunt Red)	a) late b) early-mid Oct c) 2–3 weeks	yes	1055	0.29%	0.09%	low	low acid and tannin juice	OK	good cropper, biennial
Rock (Brown, Red, Black Huffcapp, Uffcap, Mad Pear, Madcap)	a) late b) end Oct-early Nov c) 8 weeks	yes	1086	0.51%	0.98%	low	very high tannin & sugar content, of excellent quality. Needs macerating	OK	regular, medium sized cropper
Taynton Squash	a) early b) late Sept c) 2 days		1058	0.45%	0.13%	med-high (>0.3%)	medium acidity and tannin	bad	heavy cropper, biennial
Teddington Green (Teddingtons)	a) late b) mid Oct c) 7 days		1063	0.80%	0.33%		useful for increasing acidity and tannin levels	good	heavy cropper, biennial
Thorn	a) early–mid b) end Sept c) 7 days	Yes	1062	0.57%	0.10%	low	medium acid, low tannin juice of good quality	OK	heavy cropper, biennial, compact growth
Yellow Huffcap (Chandos Huffcap; Black, Brown or Green Huffcap, Kings Arms, Yellow Longdon, yellow Longlands)	a) earl–mid b) early-mid Oct c) 7 days		1064	0.62%	0.10%	med-high (>0.3%)	Good all-round juice, fruity and full flavoured	OK	heavy cropper & biennial. Shake fruit from tree before ripe (or it may rot on tree)

NB: Some high tannin/high acidity level pears are included here as good all-rounders. The synonyms are here too as it's so important to know what varieties of pear you are using.

CHAPTER 3
STARTING OUT

Cider-making equipment

Equipment can be broken down into several types when making cider – the essential kit that every cider maker needs; scale-related equipment that depends only on the size of your cider making; expendable materials that can only be used once and need replacing frequently/annually; and finally, equipment that is just useful and makes your life easier.

Essential kit for all cider makers:

- Hydrometer
- Test jar
- Airlocks
- Notebook
- Food-grade plastic or metal measuring jug
- Food-safe shovel/scoop
- Food-safe collection juice tub
- Cleaning products

Essential scale-related kit:

- Woven sacks for collecting apples
- Mill/apple crusher
- Press
- Fermenting vessels
- Spray unit (hand held or rucksack) for disinfecting/sterilising
- Siphon tubing
- Tubs or buckets with sealable lids
- Pump
- Cleaning brush
- Long-handled spoon

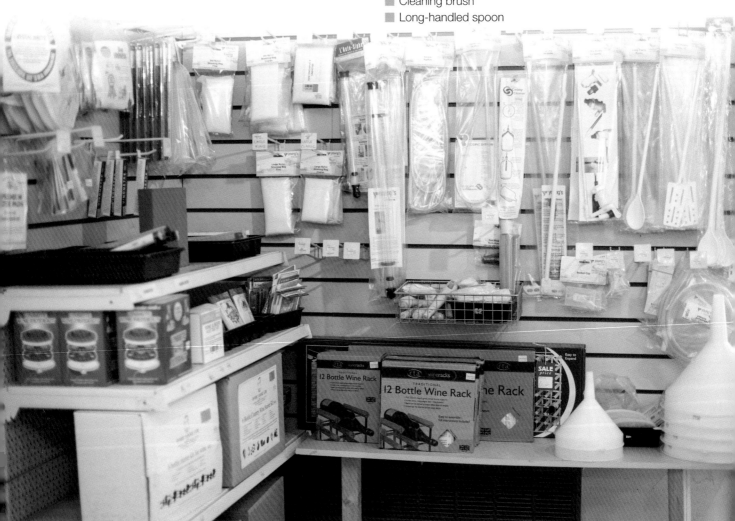

- Thermometer
- Yeast
- Yeast nutrients
- pH meter/pH papers
- Sodium metabisuphate
- Large scoop or food-grade shovel (for moving pomace)
- Milking apron (waterproof and washable)
- Wellies
- Gloves

APPLE MILLS

To remove as much juice as possible from the fruit, you need to prepare it for the press by crushing it and turning it into pulp. As a novice, this and the pressing stage is the most inconvenient if you don't have the right kit – but they are essential! The mill and the press are the most expensive pieces of equipment, but these days we have various options available to us. Our choice of mill depends on both the volume of apples you expect to press and also your budget.

LOG AND BUCKET

The most primitive way to crush your fruit and also the cheapest. This is certainly how it would have been done in times long past, before proper mills were commonplace. Basically, the apples are put in a half barrel or bucket in batches and then pulverised in a giant mortar and pestle action. Pummeling them with the end of a bulky log means it doesn't take long for them to be mashed. When squashed, the pulp would be placed onto the press.

JUICER

The best of modern juicers will make light work of whole apples while extracting the juice with reasonable efficiency, so these are a real alternative to traditional methods in that respect. They have the added convenience of only needing to invest in one piece of kit rather than two, as they both crush the fruit and extract the juice. I haven't done any trials to analyse the quality of the juice but it wins for convenience! High-quality juicers can take whole apples and take a lot of the messy, bulky work out of juicing. It definitely offers you the most ease, but it's not such a quick method because the juicer will need cleaning out quite quickly after each batch, and it does put it through its paces. Provided it's clean, it's worth a go if you are on a very limited budget. A small basket press costs quite a lot, can only be used for pressing fruit, and only once a year for a few days or even less. Juicers offer you the reward of being able to juice anything you want at any time of year, but be warned that a domestic machine might not quite be man enough for the job if you have a lot of apples to juice. While far from ideal for the serious enthusiast, it's a simple starting point and many homes already have a small juicer. They're a reasonable price to buy, very simple

to use and you get everything out of the apple with just dry pulp and pips left behind. The quality of the juice isn't the same as traditional pressing, however. Much like a grape, the sweetest juice in an apple is not in the core, it's in the bulk of the flesh between the skin and the core. If you use a juicer, you are taking all the juice and may notice a difference in the quality, although you will get a higher yield. Modern belt presses that are set up to extract the most out of the apple will have a similar effect, although not quite to the same extent. Traditional presses may only work at an efficiency of about 65%, but the quality of the juice is superb as it often leaves behind the flavour components around the tougher, starchier core material.

VIGO PULPMASTER

This Vigo product is basically a blade attached to a drill bit. It's a simple design to be used by pushing down onto apples within a bucket and slicing through them as it spins into pieces/pulp. It offers a very cheap solution but is best used on very ripe fruit in smaller batches.

▼ A Vigo Pulpmaster.

BUCKET TOP FRUIT CRUSHER

These sit over a bucket and apples are poured into the hopper over some drums with teeth. As these are turned (by hand) the apples are crushed and pulped into the bucket below. They are surprisingly expensive! Straightforward hand-cranked mills can be bought and placed over a bucket/barrel and apples poured in. Larger apples need to be chopped by hand first so that the teeth can grab them.

DIY BUILD YOUR OWN!

There are various designs on the Internet for making your own mill (see the example on page 159). Most are based around two cylinders with 'teeth' on them that are hooked up to a motor. A hopper rests over the top into which apples

are poured, as they fall in between the teeth they are crushed and minced before falling out into a tub at the bottom. Any homemade equipment must use food-safe/food-grade materials. For example, pine is a soft wood and, not only could it leave a resinous flavour in the juice but it's also a weak wood and could snap easily. Metal parts need to be stainless steel as other metals will taint the juice irreparably. The acids found in apples will eat into the metal and corrode it. In the 17th and 18th centuries, Devon Colic was the name given to an affliction that plagued rural communities in Devon. It later turned out to be lead poisoning, from the lead they lined their presses with! Motorised versions are quite popular and commonplace. It must be stressed that most metal can contaminate your cider and the point at which metal first comes into contact with the fruit is in the mill. It will often cause a discoloration of your final product as well as taint the flavour. Food-grade stainless steel is safe but iron and copper will certainly oxidise and spoil the cider – so please be careful about the metal you use.

SHREDDER/CENTRIFUGAL MILL

Designed like garden waste shredders, these long-neck motorised machines make short work of the fruit and chuck the pomace out into a waiting tub below. You can just switch them on and keep pouring the apples in and collect the pulp at the bottom. They work very well and take a lot of the effort out. Being modern in design they use food-grade parts and can work at quite a pace (up to 600kg an hour). They have a motor sitting at the base of a funnel into which the apples are poured and because they mill the fruit so well, they help to increase the efficiency of your press.

Larger, built-to-order models are used by larger-scale producers. These modern marvels are designed to make mincemeat of your fruit and can cope with a high volume (1000kg per hour) and so are perfect for anyone wanting to set up a small cider-making business.

◀ Basket presses.

▼ A rack and cloth press.

PRESSES

Basket press and cross-beam press

The basket press is a traditional design that's been used throughout Europe for hundreds of years. Cross beam versions are stronger and probably slightly more efficient and long-lasting, although overall the efficiency of such presses is probably only 50% at best. They're quite commonly available and come in an array of sizes from 5 litre to 45 litre and probably larger if you buy them outside the UK. For the size and volume of juice they produce, they are still expensive items and can set you back several hundred pounds. They are good for small-scale cider making and are suited for volumes of 25 litres or less. They're not particularly efficient, so you may need more apples than you initially plan for.

Traditional press/rack and cloth press

These two press types are similar in principle, the main difference being that the rack and cloth press is a modern version of the traditional square-bedded cross-beam press. Traditionally here in the UK we used thatching straw (or horse hair mats) to hold apple pulp in. It was then wrapped up into a square cushion shape before stacking a few others up on top of it and squashing under a heavy board with a beam pressing down on it. As the pressure increased, the juice would run free from the 'cheese' and could be collected. As technology developed, the straw was replaced with cloth mats and hydraulics took over from hand-screwed beams. This design became the rack-and-cloth method and is still used by many small-scale cider producers throughout the world. There are various versions out there to buy and they are more efficient at extracting juice. A press of this design normally suits serious but small-scale cider makers.

◣ A traditional beam press.

▼ A rack and cloth press on tracks.

▽ Loading a hydropress.

▲ Juice running from a hydropress.

Bladder press

At first glance, these look similar in appearance to a basket press, but inside they have a bladder that fills with water to press the fruit against the exterior cylinder under pressure. They are simple to use, around 50%–60% efficient and once set going allow you to carry on with another job (like milling more fruit) while they build pressure and squash the juice out. This kind of feature is great for one-man-band operations because it saves time. They also have the advantage of being easy to use and clean. One point to note is that when used in conjunction with a bladder press, the fruit needs to be milled well and to a particular consistency to get the most out of it. People will often invest in a matched mill and bladder press, to make the most of its potential efficiency.

◀ A hydropress set up: apples, pulp, press, juice collection and a wheelbarrow to collect the pomace.

▲ A small belt press.

▲ A squeezebox press.

Belt press

A belt press is something more and more cider makers are using, as they can be very efficient in removing juice and offer businesses a reduced labour cost. There are a series of rollers and a wide, very strong belt onto which the pomace is dropped constantly. As it passes though the system of rollers, each squashing the pomace further, the juice drains into a collecting tray in the bottom, and the dry pomace is removed automatically at the far end.

The biggest can process 6000kg of fruit an hour and so are efficient presses, but they require significant investment and some routine maintenance.

Squeezebox

This is a modern concertina design where apple pulp is poured into each slot that contains a bag hung over a frame. When full, the press is started and the ends come together using hydraulic arms to compress the slots together.

Industrial press

These beasts are not for the faint hearted! These types of machine are used by large commercial enterprises to extract their juice.

▼ An industrial fruit press.

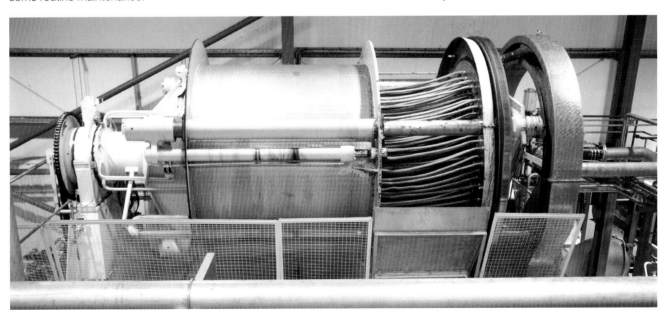

DIY – make your own!

You can pretty much guarantee that anything thought of as 'expensive' will spawn various engineering minds to ponder designs for homemade alternatives, and the cider press is no exception. Most of these are based on rack-and-cloth press designs, and a quick search online will bring up a plethora of designs based on car jacks, hardwood frames and buckets etc – all different types and sizes. Again, as it's for cider production, any part of it that comes into contact with the apple pomace and/or the juice should be food grade and inert. There is no reason why a well-executed homemade press shouldn't last for years. It's quite a job to do it well, but it will prove cheaper and allow for specific modifications – like the ability to undo it and pack it away for storage when you've finished with it for the season. See page 162 for more information on building your own.

Cleaning

Presses should be cleaned before and after use, washed under some pressure before use to remove any dust, cobwebs, insect life etc and some people will go so far as to sterilise the parts that will come into contact with the pulp. If the press was cleaned properly the previous year and stored under cover, it may be that a good rinse will suffice.

FERMENTERS

As sanitation is paramount from this stage on, your fermenters are very important, regardless of their size. They should

be made of inert food-grade plastic, glass, stainless steel, fibreglass or hard wood such as oak and can vary from 1 gallon demijohns to 1000-litre IBC tanks. It's important to understand that you need the same volume to rack into as you're about to rack. For example, if I have 10 barrels of cider, I only need 11 barrels in total. I'll rack from one into another, wash the one that had the original cider in, then rack the next full one into that newly-cleaned one. The idea of having an extra fermenter/fermenters of up to equal volume is so that you always have space ready to use.

Fundamentally, it doesn't matter what you use to ferment in so long as it is clean, sterile and sealable with an airlock. It must be inert, so as not to impart a flavour into the liquid. Ensure the shape of the vessel allows liquid to ferment and you have the means to store and move it.

Plastic

High-quality food-grade plastic is probably the most convenient way of fermenting. It's also one of the cheapest, because the plastic is cheap to produce and can be made in small sizes, from 5 litres upwards. If buying secondhand kit, avoid using containers that have held something odorous such as garlic or citrus fruits as these flavours can leech into the plastic and will be released back into the cider. The last thing you want is garlic-flavoured cider!

Black 1520-litre fruit juice containers are quite popular with small or medium farmhouse cider makers as they are made of tough plastic, can be sterilised easily and are easy to move about.

1000-litre IBC tanks are widespread commercially and used for many purposes, but primarily for transporting liquid safely. They are strong, lightweight and inert, and fit onto a pallet so they are popular.

Wood

Traditionally wooden barrels are used and they will impart their own flavour into the cider. Good wooden barrels work very well indeed but bad ones will ruin the cider, so make sure they are in good condition, they don't leak and check what has been stored in them previously. Wooden barrels are more popular with serious enthusiasts who have committed to a sizeable scale of production as they are large, bulky and heavy.

Aging cider in wooden casks that have contained something other than cider or water will mean that for the first year or two, some of the previous inhabitant's flavours and character will be imparted into the cider. It could be colour, taste or aroma – there is no real way of telling what exactly it will change without some experimentation but it will nearly always have an effect. Ex-whisky and rum casks are popular with many people these days but others shy away from any cask that hasn't had fruit-based liquids in it previously; port, sherry and brandy casks are popular with cider makers of this persuasion.

Barrels are useful if you plan to make a lot of cider traditionally. They can be bought fairly easily, when looked after they are sturdy and yet can be moved reasonably easily. It's traditional to mark up each one with its specific gravity (SG) and date it using chalk on the end.

▼ 52 gallon wooden barrel, also known as a hogshead.

Stainless steel

Stainless steel is great because it's easy to clean, tough and ensures a clean flavour – but it's expensive, so unless you decide it's vital to use, choose a more value-friendly option.

Fibreglass

Vats and tanks are more popular (and therefore available) on the continent but are harder to find in the UK.

Bottles

It's important to be aware of the pressure contained within bottle-conditioned drinks such as cider, beer and wine. If the gas produced during the fermentation isn't released, it dissolves and goes back into solution until such time when the pressure is released. If you decide to bottle your cider, the bottles need to be of sufficient strength to contain those forces. Proper beer and champagne bottles only should be used, as they are designed to withstand higher pressures. More about this later.

Considerations

Whatever kind of cider you want to make, the basic principles are the same. Even though it's a simple process (virtually the same as making wine), it can get complex, particularly if you run into problems or want to try some more advanced techniques. With the benefits of science and access to additives, there is more choice and precise control than ever before in creating the cider you want.

These days you can make your cider taste however you like by adjusting it, but as you increase the use of additives and environmental controls, you move further away from a traditional product. To a certain extent, most cider makers will practise some form of intervention as a matter of course. It serves them well to offer a consistent product, of high standards and with traditional values. While using preservatives is important for many, some cider makers want to make their cider as pure, raw and traditional as possible. However, cider made 100% traditionally can be very inconsistent, and for the newcomer it may often be as terrible as it is wonderful. So these days, the best ciders tend to come from producers who respect both approaches, using whatever science they need while respecting a traditional approach, and not interfering unnecessarily. Cider-making traditions and techniques have been honed over centuries, and with that amount of history and passion behind it, makers have got pretty good at straddling the fence between the traditional and the modern methods.

Whatever approach you take, you should have a clear, guiding philosophy that will help steer you through the uncertainties of the first years. If you are unsure as to which philosophy suits you, I urge you to try different methods, not only to help you decide more clearly which approach you prefer but also to increase your experience in half the time. After pressing your apples, split the batch in two (or more) and try a very simple traditional approach alongside a very modern one. Tasting the two side by side in early summer the following year will give you some idea of your preference. You only have to do this once or twice and you'll know.

One issue you'll encounter is that everyone does it differently, and as a beginner that can lead to confusion. Basic cider science is introduced in this section and many useful tables are provided for reference throughout. These may seem a little complex to a novice, but as your familiarity with the subject increases, so will your understanding of them.

STYLE

Ask yourself: *'What type of cider do I want to make?'* It sounds obvious, but it really helps to have some idea of where you want to go before you start. It's like setting out on a car journey – if you don't know where you want to go, you may be disappointed when you get there. Sometimes describing it on paper helps you formalise the kind of cider you want, or perhaps modelling it on a cider that you already drink.

Having a strong idea about the style you want to make at least gives you something to aim for, even if it does turn out to be a little different, which is likely for the first few times. Thinking about the ciders you drink and what it is you like about them will certainly help. Your answers will give you a basic criterion of what to aim for. Considerations can be made along the following lines:

- How sweet/dry do you like it?
- Do you like it sharp and crisp, or mellow?
- How tannic (bitter) do you want it?

■ Do you want a simple, clean cider or do you want to take a walk on the wild side?

■ Do you want it carbonated, or are you happy with still?

Another consideration is what fruit do you have available to use? This scenario is more likely for people who don't grow their own apples and have to rely on what they can get. A lot of newcomers manage to get hold of excess apples from their neighbours, friends and family the first time they want to make cider, because the apples may be wasted otherwise. I would argue that for a novice, despite being a great way to get started, it's more difficult to make a really interesting cider using no cider apples (although certainly not impossible). One benefit from this approach is that it's often easier to source the fruit as cider

apples can be hard to come by in non-cider producing regions.

Whatever your particular sensibilities for cider are will determine how you interpret the cider-making process. At one end of the spectrum you have the choice of making a straight-up traditional, still, farmhouse cider. At the other you have a clean, controlled and 'modern' cider. The different styles require different approaches, each have their advantages and disadvantages. Most experienced cider makers operate somewhere between the two approaches, relying on enough science and technology for reassurance and control, while respecting as much of the traditional values and practice as is possible. Where you choose to draw the line between the two can be a difficult balance to find at first, but it does get easier with experience.

Just get the juice!

The first cider I ever made was using a household juicer at home in the kitchen – it was all I had (that and a demijohn with an airlock!) so I thought I'd give it a go. I'd managed to find some abandoned cider apples so was off to a flying start in that respect. My juicer overheated frequently and I had to stop, clean up and start again.

The simplest method I have used to extract juice from apples was for the second batch I ever made. I had been given a sack of top-quality cider fruit out of the blue and was totally unprepared to make cider. They were at peak ripeness, I had no cider-making equipment at the time, was very busy with work and had no time to organise myself properly. I opted for a crude, experimental approach to see what I could get and it actually worked fairly well. In a stainless steel bucket, I cut 8kg Brown Snout apples into 2.5cm chunks and crushed them slightly using a sterilised metal potato masher. I added about half a pint of tapwater and a packet of champagne yeast and covered it with a muslin cloth. I mashed it daily, each time crushing the fruit slightly more than the last and I left it for seven days in all. Afterwards, I strained and squeezed it though a clean muslin cloth, collected the must via a funnel into a demijohn, and added an air lock bung. Another week later it had fermented significantly and tasted very dry, so I racked it (leaving the sediment behind) and added 500g caster sugar along with 350ml of fresh Dabinett juice.

After another racking and some bottle conditioning, this went on to become a lovely, small batch (4.5 litres) of a 9% sparkling cider, with a strong but juicy bittersweet characteristic. Because the process was so unconventional, it had a lovely bright orange hue, it was hazy, but it tasted ruddy, tannic, tangy and refreshing and remains very strong in my memory as one of my most successful early experiments. It was the first time I had hybridised my

approach to cider making – although I had added a packet yeast, the pre-existing natural yeasts weren't suppressed by the addition of any sulphites, so they too contributed to the overall flavour. It worked fine and was a very tasty cider indeed, albeit the tiniest batch I've ever made!

What I'm trying to demonstrate here is that it doesn't matter how you crush the fruit or get the juice, as long as you can. After that, providing you are careful with sanitation, things get a little simpler.

Sulphites

As modern as this sounds, we've been using sulphur-based additives or methods to preserve cider in one form or another since the 17th century, so in terms of being a traditional or a modern practice, it's somewhere in the middle.

The addition of a correct amount of sulphites to fresh juice will inhibit or stop most harmful microbial activity (both bacterial and fungal) as it releases sulphur dioxide. Sulphites come in the form of powder or tablets of sodium or potassium metabisulphite. If you dose your cider up using the maximum permitted amounts, you'll kill everything inside, but using too weak an addition will accomplish very little. The right amount will have the effect of removing enough of the undesirable microbes without affecting yeast performance. To a certain extent, the amount you want to add is entirely up to you, but the maximum legal limit of dissolved SO_2 in Europe is 200 parts per million (ppm). If you choose to use sulphites in one form or another, the pH of your juice will have a direct bearing on how much you need to add. See the Juice Analysis Table in Chapter 4 for further guidance and recommended usage amounts.

This step is discretionary, many cider makers abhor the idea of killing off what is already living naturally in their juice, and may have been making cider for two or three decades successfully without any sulphites. Novices be warned however, the exclusion of any sulphites after pressing can be a point of no return should things go bad, so even a small measured addition of SO_2 will help prevent some issues.

If you prefer the idea of controlling the fermentation more carefully, you should consider 'knocking out' the juice with some sulphur dioxide by adding sodium or potassium metabisulphite. For that to work, you need to understand how acidity levels will affect your decision.

Adding metabisulphites in the form of Campden tablets is the most common way of adding sulphites to your juice. Each tablet is typically formulated to give you 50 parts per million (ppm) of sulphur dioxide when dissolved into a gallon of liquid, but it must be stressed that you should always read and follow manufacturers' guidelines when using chemicals as they may vary. Sodium metabisulphite has the advantage of being dual purpose in practical terms. It is not only used for protecting the cider and preventing infection but also for sterilising equipment, although this latter use in no longer permitted in commercial cider making.

PURIST APPROACH

For the most part, the traditional approach to cider making will always give you 'real cider' and while producing some of the best ciders in the world, it's also capable of producing some of the worst too. As with all traditional approaches, it is a case of keeping things as simple with little or nothing being added or taken away. Cider-apple juice fermented with its own wild yeasts is about as simple as this process can get. It is one of the most satisfying ways to make cider, because

it's pure. However, without intervention and the control offered by science, you have to accept the risks you take and the limitations of this approach. When done well, with a combination of passion and skill, the traditional method will give you some wonderfully complex ciders, full of life, and will give you a taste of the past.

MODERN APPROACH

Alternatively, a modern approach to cider making involves using food-safe sulphites, such as Campden tablets, to eliminate anything living in the juice (good and bad); introducing a laboratory cultured yeast; testing levels of sugar and acid; controlling the fermentation and carefully conditioning. In some ways, it's a less exciting and safer approach, but in other ways, you really get to understand what's going on at a microbial level – which appeals to many people. When learning to make cider, a good degree of this is wise and will serve to give you valuable experience should any problems arise in the future. You may opt to do less and less of it as your experience grows and keep only what you deem essential through experimentation. This approach offers much more certain results.

HYBRID APPROACH

By being aware of the advantages and disadvantages of each method, yet also aware of the science behind the fundamentals of cider making such as acidity levels and fermentation *etc*, you can (to a certain extent) use your skill as a cider maker to handpick elements of each to your advantage. When done carefully and considerately, it offers both increased security from spoilage and quality of cider, so the idea behind this approach is to use the best of both methods. However, you still have alternatives within this approach as the beneficial wild yeasts already present in the juice will survive, so you can either add low levels of SO_2 or just introduce a cultured yeast as well (which will ferment quicker and more smoothly).

By adding low levels of sulphites to the fresh juice straight after pressing, some of the bacteria and yeasts present will be 'knocked out', but the beneficial ones will remain. In a semi-sulphited (low SO_2) juice, wild-yeast scenario, when left in a fermenter under an airlock for about ten days, those present will start to reproduce and ferment the juice into cider. You have a further choice of still introducing a cultured yeast if you want to.

If you don't like the idea of using any sulphites at all, you could also introduce a cultured yeast a day or two after pressing without knocking out the wild yeasts present, so they work side by side until the alcohol level kills weaker strains of yeast and bacteria naturally anyway. This has the advantage of allowing the wild yeasts present to work at their own pace and makes for a more interesting flavour right from the start. What tends to happen is that the cultured yeasts

Cider kits

They may be convenient but they're not as cheap as you think – the pack itself before any other equipment costs work out at over £2.66 a pint and the flavour will be nothing like a 'real cider' made from fresh cider apples.

start to take over after the wild yeasts have had a chance to work.

So you can see, it's not a black-and-white process. It has much to do with personal choice, which is why cider is made in so many ways. The following summary, balancing advantages with disadvantages, probably does little to help you decide! Personally, I prefer a hybrid approach because it offers benefits from both methods while reducing the risks too. Ultimately it's a personal choice and the best way to decide what suits you is to try all of them, then you can make an informed and experienced choice.

In any case, you'll benefit from a suitable level of acidity to initiate a healthy fermentation plus clean, sterile equipment, air-locked fermenters and careful note-taking.

	Advantages	Disadvantages
Purist approach No sulphites No yeast added (RAW and WILD)	More complex flavor	Higher risk of infection/ spoilage
	Simpler process	Difficult to be consistent
	Cheaper process	Longer fermentation
	No chemical additives	Can ferment bone dry
Modern approach Sulphites added to kill everything living in the juice Yeast added	'Cleaner' tasting	More homogenised (less unique)
	Reduced infection risk	Generally less dynamic result
	Fewer problems generally	Not as fun (less risk!)
	Better storage potential	Involves sulphites
Hybrid approach Low levels of SO_2 used, wild yeast ferment OR cultured yeast added, multiple yeast ferment	Improved flavors	Can involves sulphites
	Less risky	Less predictable fermentation
	Greater control	

Methodology and scale

Cider making is a simple process involving a series of stages, each needing a dedicated period of time, various pieces of equipment as well as operational and storage space to work in. As your methodology and scale changes, the time and space dedicated to your cider making will change also.

SIZE AND OPERATIONAL SCALE

Before we get stuck into the actual process proper, there are some considerations regarding the scale of your operation, the appropriate equipment you need and the approach you want to take, that need to be thought about and decided upon.

Some of the equipment you need is dependent on the size and scale you aim to operate at – and your aspirations! Some people may just want to make a few gallons from the trees they already have on their property, while others want to make enough to last them for a year or may even be considering making cider as a small commercial enterprise. The principles of creating real cider are pretty much the same whatever scale you intend to work at and some of the equipment is essential to everyone. Deciding on the scale you want to work at is a decision made more difficult when you realise however much you make initially, you always want to make more next time because you know you can! Cider making takes a lot of effort, and first-timers who want to do it in order to create a cheap, acceptable cider generally get a shock when they realise how much effort is involved with getting it right. The point at which you realise quite how involved the whole process is, is the point when you start to consider increasing next year's production. The answerless conundrum is when do you stop increasing production? For some, storage and production space are often limiting factors, and after that it's often the duty limit – 7,000 litres in the UK. However the usual contenders that limit your potential as a cider maker are time available to make it and fruit availability. Busy people with families who want to make cider need to try and involve the family right from the start. Growing apples and cider making can be an enjoyable, social and active practice suitable for all ages. If you were to add up the time taken in the process and think about what you'd expect to earn in return for that time in a job, you'll relate more closely to what I'm saying. Cider making becomes a lifestyle choice – people do it for the love of it. The availability of fruit is nearly always limiting unless you grow your own or know someone who grows it and will sell it or donate it.

In regards to scale, that decision is rarely ever fully made, and the hardest initial dilemma is committing to a certain scale of equipment that'll be enough to learn on, but easy enough to sell on whenever you decide to upscale. After investing in kit, you become somewhat committed to that scale and its limitations. Mills and presses aren't cheap so it does need careful consideration.

HOW MUCH SHALL I MAKE?

The best question to ask is: how much *can* you make? After that, other practical considerations are about how much time you can realistically dedicate to it? How much space do you have to make and store cider? How many cider apples can you get hold of? Do you have space for an orchard? How much can you afford to spend, *etc*? It can all start to feel a little negative, because these are the main prohibiting factors that stop you doing it.

Physically, it's not that difficult and it will contribute to part of an active lifestyle, but you do need to be reasonably able-bodied and a certain level of basic fitness helps. Cider making grew from traditional farming. It involves picking up apples, lifting full sacks, pushing, pulling, gripping, standing around on your feet – so for people who struggle physically day to day, it could be another limiting factor.

One thing worth considering at this stage is that, whatever size of operation you decide to aim for, you will need at least as much storage capacity than the volume of cider you intend to make. If you want to make 20 litres, you will need 40 litres of total storage, as the batch will need moving from one vessel to another of the same size. Alternatively, think about it as: if you want to make 30 litres, you could rack the cider from a 30 litre container into 3 x 10 litre containers. It doesn't have to be the same type of vessel but does have to equate volumetrically, and all of that equipment needs storing somewhere.

The press should be linked volumetrically to the scale you intend to work at: too small and it will drive you mad; too large and you will have wasted your money on something that exceeds your needs. Many cider circles share equipment with other enthusiasts, but the convenience of having all your own equipment and knowing how clean it is and what condition it's in makes a real difference.

The equipment available will differ from manufacturer to manufacturer slightly, and what you decide to use will mean you may do things slightly differently from someone else. As a cider maker, you have to decide how best to link the stages of the process in a way that suits you, your ideals and your equipment.

STARTING UP – SMALL-BATCH SET UP

Neatly dubbed (although technically incorrect) '*homebrew*' is a popular approach to cider making, and the place most people start. It's a great scale for curious beginners and allows space for learning and experimentation before committing to the cost of scaling up, or not. There is some set-up cost involved but careful planning, scrupulous second-hand dealing and borrowing what you can will all help. Talk to your local homebrew shop proprietor. They are enthusiasts – it's probably why they opened their shop. You may pay a bit more for kit from them than online, but you'll also get advice and contacts in the local area. Some kit is essential while other kit is useful; the more flexibility you have in your arsenal, the more choice it gives you, and the easier the production becomes. Beg, steal and borrow whatever kit and ideas you can from anyone you know who has previous fermentation experience. At home, as a hobby cider maker,

you have the choice of starting with as little as one gallon (a single demijohn), right the way up to however much you think can get away with in your house! Some people have enough extra space to increase their production up to 1000 litres or so, other lucky people even more, but as you increase in scale, it gets more expensive, gets more serious and takes more time.

At home, if you only want to produce a small amount, you don't need a large mill or press. You may even decide you don't need one at all and do it by hand – and although not recommended, it can be quite good fun. Something like a 20-litre press would serve well and should you give you approximately 7 litres (12 UK pints) of juice per pressing. Similarly, a 30-litre basket press will yield about 9 litres (16 UK pints) and a 45-litre version about 15 litres (25 UK pints).

A SMALLHOLDER'S SET-UP

Usually, as a smallholder you are either going to drink cider consistently throughout the year, or you will make it to sell or barter with. For these volumes you will need a larger orchard, a larger press, more kit and more storage so it requires slightly more investment and enterprise In terms of scale, You need to approach it like a farmer did traditionally,

which means having dedicated space for apples, production area and storage facilities.

For some, cider is something you make every year and you aim to make enough to last the season. When making cider on this scale, people tend to use hogsheads (a 52 gallon barrel) or plastic IBC (intermediate bulk container) tanks that can hold 1000 litres.

If I had five acres of classic cider varieties grown as standard trees (40 per acre = 200 trees in all), they should yield about 25 tonnes/25,000kg of apples, which should equate to approx 14,000–17,000 litres of juice per season when established. To cope with that volume, I would use a motorised scratter (apple mill) to pulp the apples, such as a modern centrifugal mill that can pulp about 1000kg of fruit an hour and will make short work of it.

The equivalent modern rack and cloth press would be a hydraulically-driven swivel bed press that can press 600–1000kg of pulp an hour (depending on the pressure requirements). I think you'd need about 18 IBC tanks/75 hogshead barrels for use as fermenters (I have included extras for racking), as well as the usual supporting kit – pH meter, thermometer, hydrometer, measuring jugs, spray units, airlocks, food-grade hoses and a pump *etc.*

Theoretical examples

Here are three different examples of cider making. Not only do they each vary in size, equipment and fruit requirements but also in approaches to making different styles of cider. Studying the differences between them will give you some idea of what kit you need to start cider making, how it varies depending on scale and style and also the timescales involved.

One of the most confusing things to a novice cider maker is just how differently people produce their cider – the more you ask, the more variety you will encounter and these three different examples highlight that. They aren't recipes as such but could be used as a guideline. Each one is done with a slightly different method to introduce the approaches (traditional and hybrid) at a practical level and they range from a small 200-litre batch to a 1000-litre batch. I have assumed that the fruit is fully ripe and the acidity is low (more on acidity and pH testing later.) I have also allocated extra apples in these examples to compensate for fruit spoilage, loss during initial fermentation, racking, back-sweetening etc. If you decide to base a recipe on any of these, the volumes, equipment and techniques should be altered accordingly to suit your scale, intended style and approach.

EXAMPLE 1: HYBRID METHOD A

Makes 200 litres of bottled, medium, sparkling cider.
This is a small-to-medium size batch using low levels of sulphites to reduce the risk of infection while leaving enough native wild yeasts in the juice to ferment a tasty and more complex cider. It also instructs when to stop a fermentation for a medium cider and bottling, and is made using a hybrid approach between modern and traditional techniques.

Fruit requirements:

500kg of mixed cider fruit should be plenty for up to 200 litres of cider.

Kit

- Food-grade shredder/centrifugal mill
- 40-litre hydropress
- 2 or 3 x 40-litre collection tubs
- 3 x 100-litre fermenters
- 3 x airlocks
- 20 x Campden tablets
- Siphon tubing
- Hydrometer
- Thermometer
- 265 x champagne bottles, caps, corks and/or cages etc
- Original gravity: 1.058

Process outline

Apples are washed and milled, the pulp is placed into a sterilised bucket/bin and then covered and allowed to macerate overnight, before being pressed in the hydropress. The juice is put into fermenting bins and a sample is taken for its specific gravity and acidity levels. If the Original Gravity is below 1.058, add sugar to achieve that level of gravity. In this hybrid approach, I would use only 35-45% of the full sulphite dose, so as to knock back anything bad living in the juice. In this case, add 20 campden tabs, less than half the recommended 44, then it should be covered/air locked.

Fermentation should occur naturally and start within ten days to two weeks. It may only take two weeks after that to get down to a gravity of 1.015, when it should be racked (although it could be longer). At a gravity of 1.010, it should be racked again into sterilised bottles. If you pasteurise the bottles at this stage, you will have a medium cider. If you don't pasteurise the cider will continue to ferment (ultimately to dryness) in the bottles, slowly building up a level of carbonation (also know as 'condition'). You can drink the cider any time after bottling, the sooner you do the sweeter it will be and the lower the level of carbonation you can expect. Leaving it longer will result in a drier and more highly carbonated (more fizzy) cider.

1st racking gravity:	1.015
2nd racking:	1.010
Final gravity:	1.007-1.000 (depends when drunk)
Final ABV:	6.8%-7.7% (depends when drunk)

EXAMPLE 2: HYBRID METHOD B

Makes 455 litres of medium, still cider.

This second medium-to-large size batch offers a slight alternative to the hybrid approach, in that it doesn't use any sulphites but does introduce a yeast to work alongside the native yeasts. It's a more simple approach, as it is intended to create a more traditional, flat cider.

Fruit requirements

700kg of mixed cider fruit should be plenty for up to 455 litres of cider.

Kit

- Food-grade shredder/centrifugal mill
- 90-litre hydropress
- 2 or 3 x 40-litre collection tubs
- 3 hogsheads (52 gallons each) inc. taps
- 2 x 7g packets of champagne or cider yeast
- 4.5-litre jug
- Airlock
- Siphon tubing
- Hydrometer
- Thermometer
- 30cm funnel
- Original gravity: 1.057

Process outline

Apples are washed and milled, pressed and the juice collected and analysed. Put the juice into fermenters as per usual and secure with an air lock. As soon as you know the wild fermentation has started in the barrels (bubbles moving through the airlock) press another 4.5 litres juice and add the manufacturer's recommended dose of yeast nutrients and 2 x 7g packets of selected champagne or cider yeast. This needs covering and leaving covered overnight. When the starter has obviously come to life, equal amounts of it need adding to the fermenters. As no sulphites have been added but some yeast has, both the wild yeasts and the introduced yeast will work on the juice individually.

When the gravity is down to around 1.020, it can be racked – and again at about 1.015 before a final racking at 1.010 when some Campden tablets may be added to discourage further fermentation. Racking is a good way to keep cider in hogshead barrels sweeter and in good condition for longer as it results in a cider that continues to ferment very slowly. This doesn't result in any dangerous build-up of pressure because most barrels are not particularly airtight. It does, however, mean the cider will retain some sweetness for longer, and adds a blanket of carbon dioxide over the cider, which helps prevent oxidation and spoilage of half-empty barrels – for a certain amount of time at least.

1st racking gravity:	1.020
2nd racking:	1.015
Final gravity:	1.010 (Campden tabs added)
Final ABV:	7.6%

EXAMPLE 3: PURIST METHOD

Makes 1000 litres of dry, farmhouse cider.

This is the largest batch example, the most traditional in approach and uses the simplest method of production. If you wanted to make 1000 litres of cider, you need the following sort of kit.

Fruit requirements

2000+kg/2 tonnes mixed cider fruit. If you want to make more, use this as a guide and scale up accordingly.

Kit

- Food-grade shredder/centrifugal mill
- 3 or 4 x 40-litre collection tubs
- Hydraulic swivel-bed rack & cloth press
- 2 x 1000-litre IBC tanks or 5 hogshead barrels with taps
- 2 or 5 bungs & airlocks, depending on vessels
- food-grade pump
- hydrometer
- thermometer
- Original gravity: 1.062

Process outline

Apples are washed and milled, the pulp is placed into a sterilsed tub/bin and then covered and allowed to macerate for 3–4 hours before being pressed. After the juice has been strained, collected and analysed it should be moved into the fermenters, which should be airlocked or have their bung holes covered loosely to prevent anything entering. Within ten days to two weeks, yeast plugs should start rising from the barrels in the form of white, curly foam. Ambient temperatures will have the greatest effect on the yeast progress – smell for excessive 'egginess' coming from the airlocks and add yeast nutrient if it gets too much.

1st racking gravity:	1.010
2nd racking:	1.005
Final gravity:	0.998
ABV:	8.7% *

* In cases where this is too strong (*eg* in terms of duty payable) the cider may be diluted using water to reduce the overall ABV. However, if diluted much more than 10%, you will start to notice an impact on the flavour. In this case, if you were to add 100 litres of water to the fully fermented batch, it should reduce the ABV to approx 7.9%).

NB: Beware UK HMRC production limits on quantities – you may produce 70 hectolitres (7000 litres) annually without paying excise duty. Any more and the whole quantity becomes dutiable. This can change annually, especially during these austere times, so it's worth checking what's current and keeping an eye on it. In a commercial situation, if the ABV is over 8.5%, it is classed as an apple wine and subject to a much heftier rate of duty.

Note-keeping

Note-taking is REALLY important. When you are learning to do something, it's important to track the facts that affect your decision-making so you understand what makes something good or bad, what may have caused it, when it started and why. If you ever get to a stage where you sell your cider commercially, then it is required by law to keep records. I still have the notes from my first batches of cider and it's fascinating reading through them now. You need to record the basic details, dates, ingredients, quantities, temperatures, reaction times, tasting notes, and even your ideas for next time.

It may feel laborious or even unnecessary, but in two years' time when you are looking back, you won't remember the details and you'll wish you had a record of them. Use a book or a file and record everything in the early years, and then hone what information you need to collect. Don't forget each season is different and notes help you look back from the future if you are trying to determine a cause or reason. The more thorough they are, the more useful they will be. It's important to experiment with your apples, yeasts, techniques etc, so meticulous notes are vital for understanding both the success and failures that happen. You can copy the 'Batch record' template on page 183 or create a version of your own based on it.

▼ 1000lt IBC tank

Essential preparation

Assuming the apples are happy and ripening in the autumn sun, the process for cider making itself begins by checking everything thoroughly. Best practice dictates that you inspect all the equipment you need *before* starting. Six to eight weeks ahead of harvest, any livestock should be moved out from the orchard and preparatory work should begin on locating, checking and gathering all necessary equipment you will need for cider making. Bags for collecting should be clean and dry, fermenting vessels inspected, re-cleaned and sterilised if necessary. The 'use by/best before' dates on any expendable materials such as chemicals used for sterilisation should be checked and they should be replaced if out of date. Rubber bungs should be checked to make sure they haven't perished. Glass demijohns should be checked for cracks, *etc*. Basically, anything that might slow down or halt the process of cider making in the middle of pressing should be discovered and dealt with prior to starting. It's boring but essential, and if you don't do it, you will regret it!

SANITISATION, CLEANING AND STERILISATION

Cider making is a messy business. We're pressing fruit for sugar, so we have sticky liquid that we then grow yeast in for weeks/months. We move it about from vessel to vessel to bottle through pipes, hoses and funnels *etc*, so inevitably it gets everywhere, and consequently we have to be thorough when it comes to cleaning up.

Cleaning is about removing obvious and unwanted physical matter that may harbour bacteria. If you clean something well and regularly, bacteria don't get a chance to build up and so you are preventing potential infection as a matter of course. *Sanitising* is about reducing and maintaining negligible levels of unwanted bacteria/microflora and *sterilising* is about killing and removing all forms of life. The three terms go hand-in-hand and if you want to sterilise your equipment and really know it's safe, you need to understand that all three are important. Prevention is easier than cure. Cider makers use hurdles at various stages to prevent infection from spoiling their product and the most important one is hygiene.

Equipment needs to be both clean and sterile to minimise the risk of infection months down the line. I cannot emphasise enough the importance of this – speaking from personal experience, it's heartbreaking when you develop a mould or bacterial infection and you just have to pour your cider away.

There is no doubt that one of the benefits of modern science is our ability to both clean and sterilise using food-safe chemicals that can dissipate and oxidise, or rinse away easily. Even if you don't want to sulphite your juice, using chemicals to clean and protect your equipment before and after its use will serve you very well. Soaking/spraying with fresh running

▶ Cleaning: before and after.

water and scrubbing well with a brush or scourer will in most cases be enough to remove the visible debris of cider making. After that, equipment should be soaked in a 1% solution of sodium metabisulphite to sanitise it.

If you hope to keep your chemical use to a minimum, another alternative is steam. For a larger-scale operation, steam cleaners are a good investment as they produce high temperatures fairly easily that once sprayed into a barrel or fermenter (or onto a mill/press) for a calculated measure of time, will not only blast-clean them at a high temperature but will pasteurise an enclosed space in preparation for fermenting/conditioning.

LESSON 1: HOW TO CLEAN

I don't mean to patronise but, if I were teaching anyone how to make cider or beer, this would be their first lesson, because if you get this wrong, everything that comes after it is futile. There's no point in even picking up an apple if you can't get this bit right - its <u>crucial</u> to every drop you make. Never underestimate the importance of cleanliness.

▼ Soaking equipment can be useful for deep cleaning and sterilising equipment.

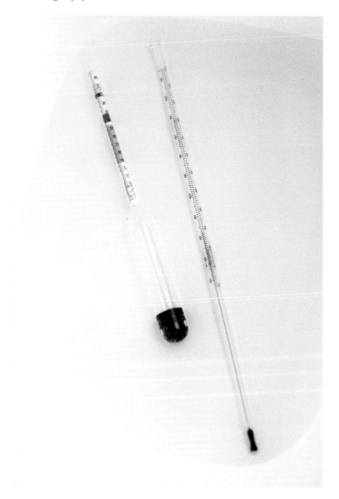

Rinse it

The first thing to do is rinse it, whatever you are trying to clean off. This will always remove anything loose and allow water to start the penetration process that softens anything solidified or firmly stuck on. Increase the water pressure to help blast any stubborn crud.

Soak it

If something is hardened and dried on, and a rinse isn't working, it's worth soaking to soften it – even for a few days before trying again with a scourer.

Scrub it

A good scourer will work wonders but may leave microscopic scratches on the surface of things, so be careful you're not making the surface rougher by scrubbing too hard.

Be methodical

Start at one end and work slowly over each section of surface, being sure to cover everything. Don't miss any section out.

Rinse thoroughly

If you are using harsh chemicals to clean with (like a bleach) then you need to rinse them thoroughly. They have a viscous, oily quality that means they cover everywhere they're supposed to. When you are satisfied everything has been entirely treated and scrubbed, all traces of the chemicals should be hosed off using pressurised water from a clean spray head. Again, being methodical, work slowly from the top to the bottom allowing everything to drain off and not forgetting to blast up or into small spaces/gaps that may hold or catch things. Allow run-off to drain away.

Repeat. Twice

Once dry, it is ready to be *sterilised*.

SUGGESTED CHEMICALS

Campden tabs are probably the most widely used of the multi-use chemicals by amateur cider makers and homebrewers. They are measured doses of sodium metabisulphite and act as both sterilant in a strong mix (*ie* five crushed tabs to one pint of hot water) or to offer general protection if you want to 'knock out' your juice before fermentation and prevent oxidation at bottling/racking *etc* (*ie* one crushed tab per gallon of juice).

No-rinse, acid-based sanitisers (such as Star San) are very popular and are an effective approach to sterilising equipment that comes into prolonged physical contact with the cider. A solution should be prepared according the instructions and sprayed thoroughly onto equipment – such as a hydrometer or inside a fermenter. It can be used in a 'bath' in larger quantities to submerse things such as siphon tubing, an airlock *etc*.

VWP is a popular chlorine-based disinfectant available from all homebrew shops. It is a cleaner and steriliser that you make up at home, simply by adding water to it. It's particularly useful for a more thorough, deeper clean by soaking things in it for extended periods of time. It really softens any built-up material, allowing you to blast it off with some running water after a good scrub. It can also remove staining, but be sure to rinse it well. Chlorine-based chemicals tend to feel slippery on surfaces so if something is still slippery after a good clean, you haven't rinsed it thoroughly enough. You can also usually smell the presence of chlorine if it hasn't been rinsed sufficiently.

Iodophor is very good to spray on kit that's too big to soak. However, the raw chemical is very dangerous and extreme care must be used.

Alternatively, heavy debris can be removed with normal household detergents like washing-up liquid and highly diluted bleach, and can be used in succession on plastics, stainless steel and glass after a good soak in water. Beware of heavily perfumed products as they can leave a residual aroma and always follow manufacturers' instructions. Everything should be rinsed thoroughly, **three times**, under fresh running tap water.

As a matter of course – before putting cider or juice into any container – sniff it. Aroma is one of our keener senses and alerts us to problems that our eyes can't see. If in doubt, clean it.

Chemicals have a best-before date and should be replaced seasonally. Old chemicals may become ineffective and ruin your cider if used. All chemical cleansers and other additives need to be stored appropriately – out of the way of young hands, and where they won't get damp or hot.

STERILISATION

Although this is a part of sanitisation, it's not the same. Sterilisation involves understanding cleanliness risks on a microbial level and how to prevent infection from bacteria *etc*. It should always be carried out after equipment has been thoroughly cleaned and completed just before it is to be used.

NB: VERY IMPORTANT!

Follow manufacturers' guidelines on each product and never risk using old, inferior or sub-strength chemicals for use in your cider. Remember, you're going to drink this and give it to your friends and family, and so appropriate caution must be taken when preparing, handling and storing them. Many are harmful in the wrong hands!

How to make a solution of sodium metabisulphite

One of the first jobs to do at the beginning of each cider-making season, sometime in early autumn, is to prepare a large batch of strong sulphite solution that can be stored and used throughout the remainder of the season. If stored properly in a strong and airtight container, a strong solution (around 10%) will remain viable and inert for months and you will benefit from having it ready to use. A weak solution (around 1%) can be used to soak things and work as a slower treatment, for treating stains or for general preparatory cleaning, or before storage. This solution will store less well – *eg* a 1% solution should be used in a week or two.

1% solution of sodium metabisulphite
($1\% \ Na_2S_2O_5 + 99\% \ H_2O$)

To prepare a 1% solution of sodium metabisulphite (which equates to 10,000ppm) place 15.6g of sodium (or potassium) metabisulphite in a measuring vessel and add sufficient water to make a total volume of 1 litre. This is useful as a bathing solution to soak equipment that will come into direct contact with the juice/cider. For larger objects, the solution can be sprayed on using a spray unit and left to evaporate.

5% solution of sodium metabisulphite
($5\% \ Na_2S_2O_5 + 99\% \ H_2O$)

As a general-purpose stock mix, a 5% sulphur dioxide (which equates to 50,000ppm) can be made up by placing 78g of sodium (or potassium) metabisulphite in a measuring vessel and adding sufficient water to make a total volume of 1 litre. It works as a faster, more intense sterilant than the weaker solution, as it incorporates a greater amount of SO_2. This can also be used to 'knock out' the apple juice prior to fermentation if you want to be sure about preventing any bacterial growth, and can be used at a rate of 1ml per litre (equivalent to 50ppm of SO_2). See Juice Analysis table for more information.

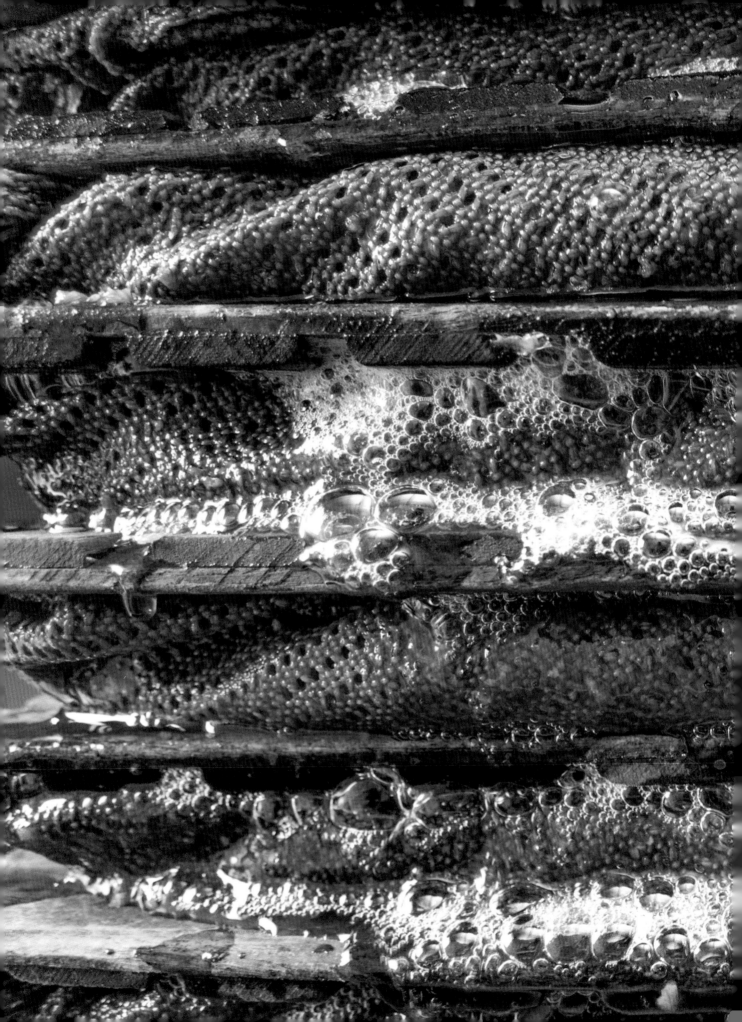

CHAPTER 4
THE CIDER-MAKING PROCESS

Outlined here are the fundamental stages involved in making real cider. All of these stages are essential for the production of any cider although, having already covered apple growing and harvest, we continue by considering the actual cider making itself.

Traditionally this is done once a year when the apples are ripe in late autumn and can continue through until as late as Christmas. In some parts of the world, apples are put into cold storage and kept at perfect temperatures allowing the cider makers to take apples out for pressing at their convenience. More generally though, the apples arrive straight from the orchard, are washed and ready to be milled.

This section assumes your apples are picked, ready and ripe, and that your equipment is all set up, clean and sterile where necessary.

Cider-making path

All real cider making is done in the same basic way, much like a wine. Beginning with the apple harvest, the following stages of the cider-making process are:

- Apple harvest
- Apple washing
- Milling and pressing
- Juice assessment
- Fermentation
- Racking
- Storage/packaging

Apple harvesting and sorting

Collecting apples is best done as a group, so ask for some help. Cider making in general is a very social activity, and having an extra pair of hands or two can certainly help with the efficiency of picking and pressing, as it often means that things aren't hanging about and so the process can continue smoothly. If livestock have been grazing in the orchard, they should be removed a month or two before harvest to reduce the risk of bacterial infection (and eating all the fruit!).

Fruit needs sunlight and warmth to ripen so any sheltered, shadier trees (or orchards) might need a little more time to ripen fully. It's essential to not collect fruit too early. When it falls off the tree naturally, you can collect it with ease and it's probably ready to mill – a quick taste test will let you know. The apples should be selected and gathered with care, then placed into breathable sacks or put gently into crates ready to transport to the mill. Sometimes they are gathered together and allowed to 'sweat'. 'Sweating' the fruit involves letting the apples ripen further still to turn as many starches as possible into sugars. The fruit will get softer (which helps pressing) but don't let it get too soft or start to rot. Where possible, store them in well-ventilated areas so the air can move around the sacks or crates. On the flatter areas of the orchard floor, the traditional 'tumping' of the apples into piles in between the trees allows them to ripen *en masse*. Cider makers these days often gather apples into sacks or crates and leave them at the base of trees in the orchard or in the yard against a wall for a similar effect. Warmth and gathering fruit together will always speed up the ripening process, so beware about doing this for too long.

Cider is made from apples, not leaves, sticks, mud, stones, insects *etc*, so all of these need to remain in the orchard. As apples are collected and just before they are milled are the two opportunities to decide which ones are suitable to use and which ones aren't. You don't want anything rotten or black, but bruised and dented is fine. Ultimately, fruit quality is a very personal choice and you will get some people using fruit that others would not. It's worth remembering that whatever you put into your cider will determine what comes out. Bruised fruit can actually contribute positively to the final flavour and may be used so long as it's not obviously infected (mouldy) or dirty (has mud stuck inside the apple). As long as a fruit isn't more than a quarter brown, it can be used. Affected parts can be cut out if needs be but this becomes impractical after a while. Ciders that only use 'perfect' fruit' are often slightly less dynamic in final flavour.

It's worth mentioning, that your fruit selection may in itself determine further choices available to you, just like sulphiting your juice, or adding yeast. Conversely, a decision not to sulphite the juice may affect the criteria on which your apple selection is based.

If you visit a cider farm in the pressing season and look at the fruit going into the mill, often you can see just what does make it in. You have to draw the line somewhere so it's a case of each to their own. Apples are difficult to collect and the more of them you have, the more juice you can collect, so think twice before saying no.

WHAT TO WEAR

Cider making can be a cold, messy and sticky business, often undertaken in unheated sheds or open barns. By the time apples are picked and bagged, the cider making commences and there are usually frosts at this time of year. Good warm clothing, a decent pair of wellington boots and an apron are essential. A plastic dairyman's apron is good as it can be hosed down. But it will get wet and sticky with all the pomace. Waterproof trousers are a very useful addition and clean easily. A pair of household washing up gloves can also help.

▼ Apples are 'tumped' on the orchard for to ripen further

Washing

Assuming you have your apples ripe and ready, they need to be cleaned before you press, usually by rinsing them in water. Again, it sounds obvious but it's another classic mistake newcomers make. Apple picking is a messy business, so apples can be covered in natural detritus like leaves, grass and twigs but also mud, stones and even animal faeces, and efforts must be made to remove all of these before the fruit enters the mill.

Just before washing is the last opportunity to check for unwanted material and remove it. Depending on how carefully it was gathered, there will be varying degrees of unwanted extras in your apples that need removing. Essentially, just the apples should make it to the mill, so anything non-fruity needs removing and the quickest way to do this is in a water bath or watery channel of some kind. Allowing the apples to soak in moving water will loosen anything encrusted on them, and bobbing them up and down against each other will remove most of the unwanted material. Mud and grit will loosen and sink but grass, leaves and sticks will float, so after rinsing they will need roughly filtering to catch these. After that, they should be rinsed briefly with clean water before being milled. If you are doing it by hand, this is simple enough, many people use a

colander to pick up the apples before pouring them into a mill of some kind. Small-scale producers will often use an old bath filled with water to rinse the apples. If the apples are particularly dirty, a hose can be left to trickle feed cleaner water through at one end. If they have just been soaked, sometimes they will be hosed off with fresh water before draining and milling.

Larger production houses will often use a water trough with a sluice at one end. As the apples make their way down the channel, through the trough, they are caught in a basket that allows the water and heavier solids to pass through. When the apples are moved onto a conveyer or similar, they are rinsed quickly and dropped into a mill. This is normally done on the same day, but prior to pressing. When clean, the apples are ready to mill.

HOW MANY APPLES DO I NEED?

Most people don't need to know how much they can make from the apples they have – they just make as much as they can. But it is handy as a novice to have a rough idea of how much juice you're likely to collect from your apples to help you prepare enough fermenting space. As a rule of thumb, you can estimate 25kg apples will yield roughly 15 litres of juice. This will vary drastically when you consider ripeness, season, press efficiency and so on – but you have to base your calculations on something! Understanding this can help you decide on how much fermenting space you need, or how many apples you need to fill it.

APPROXIMATE VOLUME OF JUICE FROM APPLES BY WEIGHT			
Juice volume		**Apples weight (±12%)**	
Metric (l)	**Imperial (gal)**	**kg**	**tonnes**
0.57	0.13	1	
1	0.219969	1.75	
2	0.439938	3.5	
4.55	1	13.92	
5	1.09	8.75	
9.09	2	15.91	
14.25	3.13	25	
22.73	5	39.78	
25	5.49	43.75	
50	10.99	87.5	0.08
289.56	66.04	508	0.5
579.14	127.25	1016.05	1
1000	219.78	1750	1.72
1158.28	254.5	2032.09	2
2857.14	627.91	5000	4.91
2895.6	636.94	5080	5
5000	1098.9	8750	8.61
5,791	12,725	10,160	10
7,000*	10,773	11,700	11.5
100,000	219,969	175,000	172.24

This is a comparative table that compares the volumes involved with cider making (as both metric and imperial) and also the rough quantities of apples needed to reach those volumes.
NB: Press efficiency, apple types, seasonal changes and crop management will make a big difference on these figures (±12%).
UK Duty limit (70Hl)

BLENDING APPLES

Some cider makers blend apples during the washing process before entering the mill, others will do them all separately and blend them later, so whatever you choose is up to you. The art of blending apples for cider is essentially that of flavour and component balance. Not only do you need to consider the right mix of sugar, acidity and tannin

for flavour but you need the right pH and nutrient levels to ensure a safe and strong fermentation. (A lower nutrient level may be beneficial to a slower fermentation.) Some cider makers will start by making base cider from which they can make adjustments to create further batches of slightly different cider later on. A bulk blend should really contain some bitterness and some sharpness, and you can get this from blending bittersweets with sharps. This will offer the cider maker the greatest amount of flexibility and dynamism from which to tweak subsequent batches.

Other, smaller batches such as single-variety ciders, batches fermented with different yeasts, or those that employed different techniques or have been racked earlier, can be used to create different final ciders when added to the base blend. It may be that a cider maker requires more fruitiness, more sharpness (acidity) or more tannin, so other (single-variety or blended) batches can be used to certain proportions to change the flavour. Some will also back-sweeten fermented ciders with fresh juice that has been pasteurised and stored. It's not something that everyone does, but some people do and it works well for them.

To make a base blend, you want to use a good mix of apple types to bring about the qualities you want from your cider. Aside from acidity that is essential for a healthy fermentation and a pleasing sharpness, the other taste components are tannins and sweetness. The more apple types you use, the greater diversity of flavours, aromas and textures you will have in your cider although some base blends will just be a mixture of whatever apples are ready at pressing time.

A bit of research on cider apple types will explain individual apple flavors in greater detail and enable you to make a more informed decision. If you hope to make a decent base cider, you need to think about all the apples you have available to you, what types they are and how many you are likely to get. It could be that you decide to separate out some of the higher tannin varieties to ferment alone and blend back in later and use everything else in one big batch. Or you may want to make a mellow, lower-tannin cider so decide to ferment non-cider apples separately from the cider fruit with a view to blending it to suit your taste at a later date. A bulk blend could constitute anywhere from 40 to 70% of your final cider, so balancing the acidity at this stage is the most important factor. One of the most practical exercises a new cider maker could do is press and ferment all varieties separately and upon tasting them, decide how best to blend them (in what proportions etc) at racking time. However, it's risky fermenting pure bittersweets as they are high pH/low acid. With careful measuring and note-taking, you will be in a much better position the following season to think about what varieties blend best in what amounts, so they can be blended at milling time.

Milling and pressing

These two stages are done very closely together, usually on the same day, but not in all cases. Assuming your apples are ripe, clean and free from detritus, the next thing to do is to break them down using a mill. As they are small, hard fruit and in order for the press to be able to get the greatest amount of juice from them, it needs help in the form of crushing the fruit. It's about surface area to volume ratio – you're breaking the apple up so the inside of the flesh is exposed and the juice in the cells has less distance to travel out of the flesh.

MILLING FRUIT

This can be done anyway you choose, but the best way will always be with a motorised mill made of food grade materials. A small home-scale mill is a worthy investment that could be shared among a few people and will make the process much more enjoyable and efficient. Alternatively, you can ask a local cider maker, but then you need to think about how to move your juice. This can be a problematic and laborious stage if you try and 'wing it', so have a good think about how best to do it. The size of your mill is dependent on how much cider you hope to make, which is a question of commitment. If you know you want to make cider every season from now on, investing in a decent mill will make all the difference. Crushing the fruit is essential and because of the sheer volume of it, efficiency becomes important.

PRESSING

The juice now needs extracting and separating from the pulp, and for this we use a cider press. Various press designs are available, modern and old, of varying sizes and efficiency depending on your space, requirements and finances. Again,

these are a good thing to part-own as you benefit from the economy of scale with something larger and you already have a ready-made 'cider team' to work it all if you share ownership.

Press efficiency is not to be underestimated; a press with an efficiency of 50% will extract 50% of the weight of the fruit it presses as juice. When you consider that something like 95% of the weight of an apple is juice, it means a lot of juice is left un-extracted from the pomace. Having said that, it's rare for a press in a non-professional environment to exceed 70% efficiency.

Whatever press you end up with, each manufacturer will have their own set of instructions, so be sure to read these thoroughly and follow them carefully.

For more on press types see the Presses section.

Used pomace

After pressing, the dry pulp left behind can be discarded but it may still have a use. It can be fed to livestock (pigs, cows, chickens, goats *etc*) or used as soil conditioner for acid-loving crops such as blueberries, or as a fertiliser.

Pressing

USING A BASKET PRESS

Basket presses are simple to use. You will need a sterile juice collecting container ready and waiting at the base of the press before you start filling it, to collect the 'free run' – juice that leaves the press before pressing has started. Some people will also use a straining bag, colander or similar to collect any larger material that makes it through the press. This will prevent any bits (skins, chunks, pips *etc*) from entering the fermenter and clogging up its taps or hoses. Keep an eye on the collecting vessel so it doesn't overfill and become too heavy or cumbersome. When ready, it's a case of filling the basket with the milled pulp using a scoop and placing the two half-moon blocks over the top. When these are placed on and pressed slightly by hand, they should sit flush with the top of the basket edge. Several sets of wooden blocks need to be stacked perpendicular to each other (the bottom ones across both half-moons). These are to increase the height over the half-moons, in order to prevent the ratchet system colliding with the basket as it lowers under pressure and leaving unpressed pulp in the base of the basket. Holding the blocks, secure and tighten the ratchet so that it holds them in place. Start applying pressure slowly. Pressing is best done in stages, so when you increase the pressure in the ratchet, stop for a minute or two, rest and let the juice run free from the pomace. As the trickle slows, the pressure will ease so you need to increase the pressure again. Taking more time to press the juice will increase the efficiency of the press and allow more juice to run from it, so don't rush. The slower your pressing, the more efficient your juice extraction will be. This is repeated until all the juice is out and the pomace stops running.

When you feel the pressing is complete, release the pressure on the ratchet, move it up slightly and remove the blocks. When the ratchet is off, you can remove the half moons and then the pins that hold the basket shut. This will allow you to access the compressed pomace more easily.

USING A TRADITIONAL PRESS – HOW TO BUILD A 'CHEESE'

A 'cheese' is the name given to the stack of pulp that has been wrapped in cloth or straw in preparation for pressing. It is the traditional method of holding the crushed apple as it is pressed, allowing the juices to run free from the pulp while containing the solids. It is a technique that benefits from experience but can be done, if a bit more slowly, by anyone with the correct equipment, a few pairs of hands and a sensible head!

I will outline the process using straw, as it is the more difficult of the two options – the other method uses purpose-built square cloths that are more straightforward. The straw used is thatching straw that has a longer stem and is better because of it. Ensure that all the equipment is clean, checked for correct motion (not stuck), the apples are milled, the straw is ready (**see photos A & B**). It's sensible to have a collection vessel ready to catch juice before you start as it often runs free before the actual pressing begins and there is no point in wasting it.

1 The former (the square wooden frame) should be placed centrally on the flat bed at the base of the press with a layer of straw over the it. All the stems should run parallel to each other. Using your hands push the straw against and into the frame to bend it so the ends start to stick up in the air – they don't have to go straight up, just bow up slightly. Overlay a second layer with the stems running at 90 degrees against them (the other way) and repeat the gentle pressing until both layers criss-cross each other and the straw ends entirely surround the press base on all sides. In the flat middle section of the straw, lay the pulp in the centre and spread it out evenly, **(see photo C)** and continue until you have enough. You don't want too much or the straw won't cover it enough. Similarly, you don't want too little as it becomes ineffective; 2–3 inches (or nearly the depth of your former) should be ample. Make sure the pulp is in the corners and you have an even distribution. An uneven base will mean the whole cheese is wonky, so get this right!

2 When satisfied, gently fold the straw over the top of the pulp so it lies flat on it **(see photos D, E & F)** and secure it with your other hand. Repeat all around the former until all of the straw is bent over the pulp, using one bit to hold another down. Where all the ends of the straw meet in the centre, place a dollop of pomace on top to weigh them down. Spread another, much thinner, layer over the top to secure all the straw. **(see photos G & H)** The former can now be lifted off **(see photo I)**

3 The pegs should now be used by locating them into the first layer of pulp securely. They should be high enough to rest the former on and hold it steady and flat **(see photo J)**. They should be fitted two per edge on opposing sides (two on the left of where you are standing, two on the right) and the former placed on them. Make sure it sits straight and neatly onto them to establish the next layer. If not, relocate them more suitably until it sits true.

4 Start by laying a new batch of the straw one way, and then the other over the former (as per the original layer) **(see photos K & L)** making sure to keep it neat and square. Stability will become more important as the cheese gets higher and weighs more.

5 Repeat steps 2, 3 and 4 **(see photos M, N, O, P & Q)** until you have a full cheese.

6 On the final layer, cover with some extra straw **(see photo R)** before placing a substantial flat wooden board (or boards) **(see photo S)** squarely over the top to secure the cheese and distribute the downward pressure of the press evenly.

7 Secure the board by bringing down the beam and holding it. Pressing can now start. Lower the beam according to its design, and you are ready. Often, particularly with a large, full cheese the stack was left to sit and compress under its own weight before pressing itself began. This is certainly an option and is best judged in situ for each particular case. **(see photo T)**

8 Turning the screw and bringing the beam down onto the cheese will increase the pressure and juice will start to run fairly quickly **(see photo U)**. It's worth letting the flow decrease somewhat before applying more pressure, so as not to put the structure of the cheese itself under undue pressure, causing it to slide or even break. It's quite a slow process that involves a regular increase of pressure that often took a few days in the past. Each cider maker has their own preferred method and it's something that experience teaches you about more than I can!

If the cheese is uneven, it will start to show as the pressure increases. If this happens, sometimes you can force it by pushing back to where it should be as evenly as possible but it's not easy. It's much better to build a stout, square one in the first place.

The juice that runs from the front of the press was traditionally collected in a half barrel **(see photo V)** and then transferred into fermenting barrels via buckets. These days most people will run a hose from the front into individual barrels or some kind of holding tank. The juice can be tested and adjusted if necessary, but most people who employ this method prefer their must/cider unadulterated and raw!

USING A RACK-AND-CLOTH PRESS

Rack-and-cloth presses are popular with many small to medium cider-making businesses because they come in various sizes and offer a reasonable efficiency. The basic design is the same as a traditional beam press with the stack being built up in a very similar way using a square former, although slatted wooden racks and square cloths are used to hold and secure the pulp, rather than straw. NB: As with a traditional press type, it's sensible to have a clean collection vessel ready to catch juice <u>before you start</u> as it often runs free before the actual pressing begins and there is no point in wasting it.

1 In the middle of the square base, place a slatted rack centrally and then the square frame known as the 'former' on it **(see photos A & B)**.
2 Over these, lay a square cloth at a 45° angle **(see photo C)**.
3 Using a scoop, add (and spread) the pulp into the centre of the cloth so that it sinks down, filling the former **(see photos D, E, F & G)**.
4 When full (but not overfull), fold the edges back over the top neatly **(see photos H & I)**.
5 The former can now be removed by lifting clear of the 'parcel' **(see photo J)**.

6 Another rack can be sat squarely on top of it **(see photo K)** before the former is replaced and the process begins again **(see photo L).**

7 Place another cloth over the former in the same way as you did before **(see photo M)** and fill with pulp **(see photos N, O & P).**

8 The process is repeated until the 'cheese' or stack is big enough to fill the press area **(see photo Q).** Then, a strong flat board is placed over the top cloth and, if needs be, chocks are placed on top of that, before the whole lot is pressed under a hydraulic arm. This ensures an even distribution of weight and makes for a more efficient pressing.

9 When ready, activate the downward pressure – note the compression of the cheese and the increase in juice running **(see photos R & S).**

10 Many presses of this design have a rotating bed that allows the cidermaker to build a second cheese while the first is being pressed **(see photos T & U).**

11 When the collection bucket is quite full, **(see photo V)** remove it and replace it.

12 The juice can now be moved into a fermenter either using a jug **(see photos W, X & Y)** and it is often best having a spare cloth to filter any bits.

13 When the pressing is finished **(see photos Z & Zii)** the cheese can be broken down, the pomace collected and the process begun again.

Assessment and intervention: Juice analysis

Apples are about 95% juice, and the most important component of that juice is the sugar. The job of the cider maker is to ensure yeast ferments those sugars into alcohol. Apart from sugar, the juice also contains acids, tannins, pectin, minerals, nitrogen compounds, vitamins and other living matter. In terms of a *successful* fermentation, or preventing problems, the other components become much more important.

At this point, you have a decision to make. The juice already contains wild yeasts, moulds, bacteria (and probably the remnants of the odd fly or worm). The yeasts are both beneficial and important, the moulds are only really a problem if the fermentation gets a delayed start, but the bacteria can cause trouble. So do you leave it to ferment in a traditional manner, or intervene and control it to some degree?

Many people will simply put their raw juice into a fermenter and leave it. Given the right conditions, the natural yeasts will start to work and make use of the natural sugars to bring it to life. Cider has been made this way since its inception. It is the original method, the first cider ever made by man was made this way because there was no other way then. As such, it's a bit of a gamble at times but can produce the most delightful cider you've ever had. But, because of the bacteria present, it can also go wrong, and quite easily if your hygiene standards aren't high or you don't keep a watch over it. This kind of approach has as much potential for greatness as it does for disappointment. It requires regular attention, will benefit from a good degree of experience from someone who has a firm understanding of the processes involved and the conditions surrounding fermentation but is also influenced by the season, your instinct and some luck! When you realise this, your main objective becomes to encourage the development of beneficial yeasts while preventing other troublesome organisms from spoiling the fermentation.

If you want to improve your chances using a bit of (sympathetic) science, there are some good practices that you can employ to give yourself a fighting chance – primarily, measuring the acidity. High acidity (a low pH of 3.2–3.6) will significantly hinder the action of bacteria while not affecting yeasts, so testing the juice with pH strips is really useful. Another consideration is using sulphur dioxide (in the form of sodium metabisulphite) to reduce the chances of spoilage. To get enough juice to make cider you will have expended a lot of energy by this stage, so to many it's worthwhile to empower yourself further when possible. SO_2 will inhibit bacteria and yeasts, but in high doses will kill them and render your juice inert. SO_2 has obvious benefits but it's an approach that doesn't suit everyone. See MLF on page 129.

ACIDITY

Knowing the total acid level (also known as 'titratable acid') and the pH of your juice is useful at least, and important at best! Acid is present in sufficient quantities to be advantageous to the cider maker in a few ways, providing the juice is made from the right blend of apples. Strictly speaking, it's not necessary to measure acidity – it's only in the 20th century that we have the widespread ability to determine acid levels at home. Many traditional cider makers won't bother and trust Mother Nature to work her magic, which for the most part she does. However, taking the time to analyse the acidity in your juice will inform you if you're on track for the cider you want, or not.

Measuring acidity

Why? Acids are very important structural components of cider and there are two reasons for this – the first one being that yeasts need an acid environment to work effectively in fermentation. High levels of acidity protect the cider from unwanted bacteria. Below a pH of about 4, bacteria find it more difficult to survive and so allow the yeast to thrive unabated. The second reason is about flavour. In terms of taste, the perceived acidity we feel in our mouths dictates sharpness. Too much and it tastes too tart and sour, too little and it's bland and insipid. After pressing your juice, the pH should be checked and, if necessary, adjusted. Sharp drinks tend to offer a cutting, quenching satisfaction to thirsty people and drinks with higher levels of acidity also work well with fattier food as the acids will cut through the fats, refreshing the palate. We can increase and decrease acidity in various ways and to whatever degree you as a cider maker find pleasant and refreshing. The best way is by using fresh juice from very acidic apples, although packets of granular malic (and/or citric acid) are also available from homebrew suppliers and could be used as an alternative. Both types of acidity need measuring for different reasons:

pH

Knowing the pH of your juice is important as it sets the parameters in which certain processes are more likely (or not) to occur, such as bacterial infection. A lower pH (more acidic) juice is safer from bacterial infection as bacteria struggle at high acidity levels, whilst yeasts are less affected. Having a low pH juice before fermentation creates more favourable conditions in a wild-yeast scenario as the juice may not have been sulphited. However, a juice that is too acidic (<3pH) may be too sharp for many palates as a finished cider, so ideally you are looking for a pH somewhere in the range of 3.2–3.6.

Using pH strips and a pH meter

The pH strips are bought in packs and can be torn off and dipped into a solution. The acidity in the juice alters the colour of the strip and it is then compared to a colour chart on the pack that determines an approximate pH. They're not always as accurate as you might hope for but they are better than nothing! A taste test is always a good idea right from the start.

Modern digital pH meters are reasonably cheap and easy to use. Turn it on, place one end (or the probe) into the juice/cider and wait for the display to tell you what you've

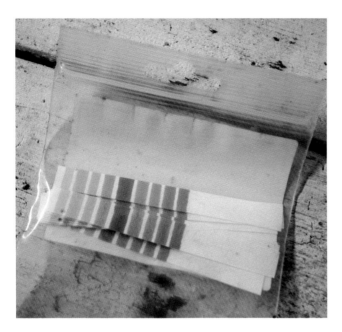

got. However, they do need calibrating from time to time and should be stored in a buffer solution so can be a bit of a pain, but they are generally accepted as being more accurate than the pH strips.

Total acidity (TA)

Total acidity, or TA, is the term we use when referring to the perceived acidity levels in taste, rather than the actual pH. Knowing the TA is really important if you want your cider to taste nice. A cider that isn't sharp enough is really unsatisfying. If the TA is too low, the cider will lack fresh crispness and taste insipid. Alternatively if the TA is too high, it will be too sharp and also unpleasant to drink. An 'ideal' amount of acid in our juice is of course subjective, but for most people, an amount of 0.3–0.5% of malic acid is a safe area to aim for.

Acidity is measured by titration testing and a titratable acidity kit can determine the amount of malic acid in a solution. It is expressed as either a percentage or as grams per litre (g/L) – obtained by multiplying percentage TA by 10. For example, a TA reading of 0.7% becomes 7g/L. Some kits aimed at winemakers are based on sulphuric acid, so the results need converting to malic acid by multiplying them by a factor of 1.4; some kits return a result in tartaric acid units, the results from which need to be multiplied by 0.89 to return them to malic acid units.

Titration kits are available from decent home brew and winemaking stores, online or in the high street and are simple to use. Samples need shaking well because the kits usually involve mixing liquids and adding measured doses of a compound until there is a significant color change. Each kit will have its own set of instructions that need following carefully.

Some really experienced farmhouse cider makers who know their fruit well and how they want their cider to taste will just scoop some fresh juice into their mouth with their hands after pressing to determine if the acidity is 'right.' Such techniques are never scientific but it does seem to work for them and serve as well by adding to the alchemy of cider making.

Altering the acidity and other acids

A pH reading over 3.8 will mean your cider is much more likely to be susceptible to microbial infection, so you are advised to increase the acidity but, in reality, if you have made a good fruit selection, this shouldn't be necessary. Various acids can be added to contribute to the final acidity of your cider.

If I need to add acidity to my cider, I'll use a really sharp apple juice (like pure Bramley juice which has a pH of less than 2.8) to help maintain the apple fruit character in my juice as well as boost acidity levels. In this case, the best option is to increase the acidity of the juice enough to reduce the overall pH as far as it needs to go.

Some producers will add malic acid (and even citric acid) to increase the acidity but by doing this step away from a traditional approach. An addition of crystallised malic acid, approx 1g per litre or as per manufacturer's instructions should do it, although you may need to add more in drastic cases. Adding citric acid will also have an impact on the flavour and can cause problems for your cider at a later stage.

Should the pH be too low (less than 3), you can decrease the acidity with calcium carbonate (precipitated chalk), following the manufacturer's guidelines. Any addition to increase or decrease acidity should always be left for long enough to let the juice readjust before reanalysis.

Top Tip

"I offer three golden rules for good clean cider making.

1 **Measure the pH and ensure it's no higher than pH 3.8 by blending acid fruit with the less acid sorts (principally bittersweets). Higher than that, you run the risk of nasty bacterial off-flavours and you will have an unbalanced cider that is too low in acid to enjoy.**
2 **Use an SO$_2$ level appropriate to the pH, before fermenting. Or at worst, use one Campden tablet to the gallon (50 ppm). This helps to keep the nastiest micro-organisms at bay.**
3 **After fermentation, keep air away from the cider at all costs."**

Andrew Lea, cider professor

JUICE ANALYSIS TABLE

pH	Approx Total Acidity (% malic acid)	Microbial Activity	Fermentation	Flavour	Advice/ Action Required	Approx SO$_2$ (if required)					
						Purist Approach (fully wild & no SO$_2$)	Hybrid Approach (partial knock out)		Modern Approach (cultured yeast)		
							(SO$_2$ as ppm)	Campden tabs per gallon	(SO$_2$ as ppm)	Campden tabs per gallon	
< 3	>1.2			Flavour too sharp	Increase pH (add calcium carbonate)	Not required	Not required		Not required		
3	1.2	Unwanted microbial activity unlikely				-	-		-		
3.1	1.1		Good fermentation	Becoming too sharp		-	-		50	1	
3.2	1		Good fermentation			-	-		60	1	
3.3	0.9		Good fermentation	Sharp			50	1	70	1	
3.4	0.8	Optimum range for minimum microbial activity	Good fermentation			-	60	1	85	2	
3.5	0.7		Good fermentation	Optimum range for desired sharpness (is subjective)		-	70	1	100	2	
3.6	0.6		Good fermentation			-	80	2	125	2	
3.7	0.5		Good fermentation	Not quite sharp enough		-	90	2	150	3	
3.8	0.4	Safer from unwanted microbial activity	Good fermentation			-	100	2	185	3	
3.9	0.3			Bland /watery tasting	Reduce pH with addition of fresh 'low pH' juice or malic acid	-	150+	3	200 (max allowed within EU)	3	
4	<0.3	Unwanted microbial activity likely		'Off' flavours from bacterial activity start to appear	Reduce pH						
4.1		Unwanted microbial activity likely	Fermentation starts to slow down		Reduce pH	pH too high for SO$_2$ to work effectively, pH needs reducing significantly by the addition of fresh (highly acidic juice) or other additives (such as malic acid)					
4.2		Unwanted microbial activity likely			Reduce pH						

MEASURING SUGAR & SPECIFIC GRAVITY

The level of naturally occurring sugar in your fresh apple juice is the next important thing to measure. Without it, there will be nothing for the yeast to live on and consequently no alcohol. The natural amount of sugars present in apples will vary from season to season (hotter seasons providing sweeter fruit) and levels may vary as much as ±20% year on year. An accurate measurement taken at the time of pressing will give you a good idea of the potential alcohol your juice has, an important fact. I tend to favour making a stronger cider because it lasts longer and if I haven't used any sulphites, the stronger it is, the safer it is from bacteria. I also like a small amount of residual sweetness. To have both those features in your cider, a high original gravity works in your favour. Determining specific gravity also allows you the chance to make any necessary alterations or adjustments before the next stage, using chaptalisation – the addition of sugar.

Measuring sugar levels in your juice is done using a hydrometer. Ideally, you want juice that reads over 1.045 and under 1.070.

A hydrometer is a blown glass device, with a bulbous bottom half containing tiny weighted beads. The long, thin top half has measurements along its stem. When floated into a sample, it determines the density of sugar dissolved in your juice that will determine the gravity by coming to rest at a given level – depending on how high or low it sits in the juice. The sugar dissolved in the juice makes it more dense, so the hydrometer floats higher in the liquid. An example of an unusually high original gravity would be 1.080 (a more typical one would be 1.045–1.055, a mid-fermentation gravity will be something like 1.020 and a very dry final gravity would read something like 0.997.

Knowing both the original and subsequent specific gravities of your juice is important because it determines how much sugar there is to ferment and lets you know what to expect on a microbiological level. Measuring it before and during fermentation determines what's happening and allows you to track and control yeast activity. It allows you to approximate the potential alcohol your juice has before yeasts start working, and also determines if fermentation has stopped (or should be stopped). It should always be measured as fresh juice and regularly throughout the process. When in doubt, measure it!

There are various models available on the market, some expensive and some cheaper alternatives. I believe it's a case of you get what you pay for so, again, a high-quality hydrometer will serve you well. Beware – they are very fragile and replacing them can be costly! Hydrometers are also calibrated for different purposes, and the measurements on the side need to fit in with your plans as a cider maker. It's pointless buying a hydrometer that works outside of the range (amount of sugar) you expect from your apples and hope to work within. Something like a range of 0.995–1.080 would suffice for most people, although if you want to use it for making wine too, you may want to increase that, or buy two that cover the range between them.

How to use a Hydrometer

Using an appropriate-size sample tube, siphon off enough cider to fill the tube about two-thirds full and place it somewhere flat. This is the sample that you will test to see how much sugar it contains.

It's important to use a hydrometer in conjunction with a thermometer, because hydrometers are calibrated to be most accurate at a certain temperature, usually 20°C, or 15°C if it's an old one. An accurate temperature reading using a sterile thermometer is the first thing to do – note the temperature for any necessary adjustment following the hydrometer reading.

Gently lower the hydrometer gently into the juice or cider, it will bob and wobble for a second before resting still. Check for tiny bubbles clinging to the side of the glass and ensure they are shaken free with some gentle motion – give it a gentle spin between thumb and index finger when it stops. It is now ready for reading. All along the top half of it, inside the glass 'stem', will be a calibrated measurement with numbers

on. These numbers are calibrated to correspond with the specific levels of sugar dissolved in the juice in comparison to water. Accuracy is really important here, so be careful and don't rush it. Measure your reading from bottom of the meniscus, not the top. Cold samples may need warming slightly, but you can use the adjustment table instead if needs be. The reading can be adjusted using a hydrometer correction table.

If you have a very small batch of cider and don't want to waste a drop, you will need to sterilise the hydrometer, remove the airlock and place it directly into the fermenter. Placing anything into the fermenter by removing the airlock does increase your chances of infection, so it's not an ideal scenario. It's much better to draw a sample off, which is tested and then discarded. You can always taste to see how things are developing, but returning the sample to the fermenter is risky and messy. The first time you do this, after pressing and before any fermentation you will have the highest reading. This is known as the original gravity (OG).

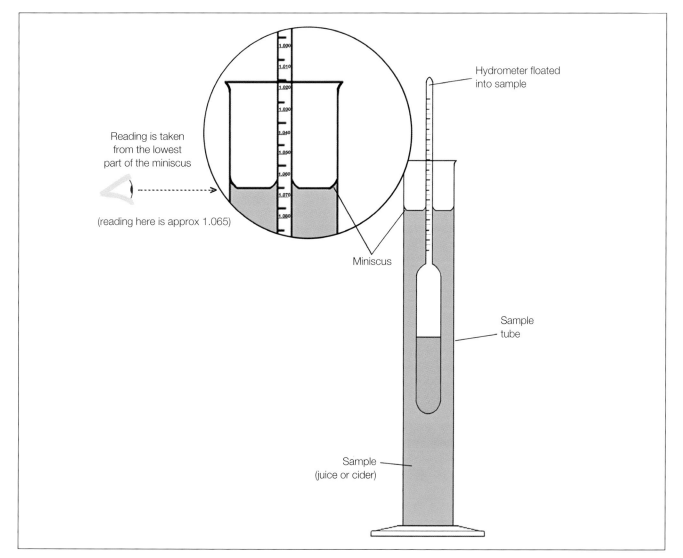

Reading is taken from the lowest part of the miniscus

(reading here is approx 1.065)

Hydrometer floated into sample

Miniscus

Sample tube

Sample (juice or cider)

HYDROMETER TEMPERATURE ADJUSTMENT TABLE

Temperature °C	Correction
10	-2.0
11	-1.8
12	-1.6
13	-1.4
14	-1.2
15	-1
16	-0.8
17	-0.6
18	-0.4
19	-0.2
20	0.0
21	+0.2
22	+0.4
23	+0.6
24	+0.8
25	+1

% Alchohol by volume

A calculation of the alcohol can be made at any stage of the fermentation. Note the loss of the decimal points in the gravities:

(original gravity – specific gravity) x 0.1285 = % alcohol by volume

Example: (1063 – 1012 = 51)
51 x 0.1285 = 6.5% abv

An original gravity reading of 1.065 that is allowed to ferment fully to a final gravity of 0.997 will give you an approximate potential alcohol of 9.1%.

When taking gravity readings at temperatures above or below 20°C, with a hydrometer that is calibrated to 20°C, small adjustments should be made to the reading depending on the temperature of the liquid. The above table shows you how much to adjust it by.

For example, if I measured the gravity in a sample that was 12°C and it showed a gravity of 1.0225, I would have to adjust the reading by subtracting 1.6 from it, therefore the true gravity would be more like 1.0214.

What happens if my gravity seems a bit low? (chaptalisation)

Low original gravities are always a bit of a disappointment, but it's not the end of the world. If the original gravity is above 1.045, you can ferment it really dry and it should be safe. The problem this will create for some people, is that it you may not want a dry cider, in which case your alternative is to add sugar – a technique known as chaptalisation. If the gravity is under 1.045, and you don't want a dry cider, you really have no alternative but to add some sugar or risk fermenting a weak cider (< 6% abv). This will be much more prone to infection and will severely limit the natural shelf life unless pasteurised. Plain white household sugar can be used for this purpose, although darker sugars may offer some extra flavour and can add some pleasant vanilla and caramel characteristics. They are best dissolved into the juice by stirring it thoroughly before retesting it.

POTENTIAL ALCOHOL: COMPARATIVE % ABV AT DIFFERING FINAL GRAVITIES

Original gravity	Final gravity			
	1.020 (Sweet)	1.010 (Medium)	1.003 (Dry)	0.997 (Very dry)
1.076	7.2%	8.5%	9.4%	10.2%
1.073	6.8%	8.1%	9%	9.8%
1.070	6.4%	7.7%	8.6%	9.4%
1.067	6%	7.3%	8.2%	9.3%
1.064	5.7%	7%	7.8%	8.6%
1.061	5.3%	6.6%	7.5%	8.2%
1.058	4.9%	6.2%	7.1%	7.8%
1.055	4.5%	5.8%	6.7%	7.4%
1.052	4.1%	5.4%	6.3%	7.1%
1.049	3.7%	5%	5.9%	6.9%
1.046	3.3%	4.6%	5.5%	6.3%
1.043	2.9%	4.2%	5.1%	5.9%
1.040	2.6%	3.9%	4.8%	5.5%

NB: These figures are guidelines only and although reasonably accurate, they are approximate. Percentage alcohol was calculated with gravity readings in the formula shown at the top of the page.

Fermentation

When you consider just how reliant both bread and alcohol are on yeasts, and what they mean to mankind, you realise just how miraculous yeast is. I'm sure I'm not alone when I say how grateful I am for the blessings it bestows upon us. Fermentation is a natural process that coverts sugars into alcohol, and part of your job as a cider maker is to control the outcome as much as possible. As such, it is also a potential minefield. Although the phenomenon is a complex everyday occurrence that happens in the wild, in a controlled fermenting scenario the aim is to simplify it and reduce the numerous micro-biological pathways it can take.

By influencing or controlling the conditions of a fermentation through acidity levels, sugar levels, temperature, sulphites, yeast choice *etc*, we not only gain much greater control over steering the outcome towards where we want it to be but we can also reduce some of the risks associated with fermentation, and these tend to come from experience.

Careful, accurate notes should be kept, and all hydrometer readings should be measured and recorded. Both acidity and sugar level measurements should be taken prior to any fermentation activity both as a precautionary measure and for control purposes. Assuming the pH of your juice is between 3 and 4 and your hydrometer gives a specific gravity reading over 1.040–1.045 (ideally higher) then your next step is to start a fermentation.

Wild yeasts should already be present in the juice if you don't knock them out with sulphites, so the process has probably already started by the time it's in your fermenter. One tip you learn early is not to overfill fermenters; if you do, they overflow and make a mess as the yeast kicks off.

Initially, the process has a slow start, followed by a sudden boost that can get vigorous. For this reason, it's best to leave 10% headspace to accommodate the floating debris, and many cider makers only loosely cover the outlet until it dies down. It's always best to actually airlock the cider and if you leave enough space in the fermenter it shouldn't overflow. As the surge dies down, you can top it up with some fresh juice and place an airlock over it. At this stage, temperature is one of the most important factors to consider. Traditionally cider is made in the autumn, when the temperatures in the cider shed are perfect for yeast activity – not too hot and not too cold – between 10°C and 12°C. In my experience of a home scenario, these temperatures are fairly easy to find too.

SULPHITING

The use of sulphites in cider is part of a contentious and never-ending debate depending on who you ask about their benefits and drawbacks. It's the jumping-off point at which a purist, traditional approach differs dramatically from a modern scientific approach, as their ideals separate fundamentally.

Sulphur is a preservative and has been used for centuries to protect beverages from infection and help prevent spoilage, so it's no new idea, although the modern-day understanding of it and its applications are. In cider making, sulphur compounds such as sodium metabisulphite ($Na_2S_2O_5$) or potassium metabisulphite ($K_2S_2O_5$) can be added to the juice in the form of powder or measured tablets, such as Campden tablets, for the same purpose. They work by releasing sulphur dioxide (SO_2) that inhibits the growth of damaging bacteria, yeast and mould by excluding oxygen from their environment. Some people, in very small numbers, are particularly sensitive to them – such as some asthmatics – and need to be careful when handling them, but as many of our packaged foodstuffs and most of our alcoholic beverages already contain sulphites their use is widespread and they are difficult to avoid on a daily

basis. When used appropriately during cider making, the levels are very low (they are measured in parts per million) and serve to benefit the cider maker by preserving freshness.

When used, they are primarily added prior to fermentation to kill or reduce bacteria and bad yeasts at a microbial level, but they are often also used (at lower levels) during racking, conditioning or packaging for their antioxidant preservative qualities.

The amount of suphites to add to your juice prior to fermentation varies, and primarily depends on the acidity of the juice after pressing, and the approach you wish to take (see Juice Analysis table). You should decide on your preferred approach prior to pressing.

If you plan to totally 'knock out' the indigenous population of yeasts and bacteria using sulphites, the correct time to do it is after pressing and before pitching a commercially available yeast. Sulphiting the juice at the appropriate level for the pH by allowing the juice to mix with the sulphites as it enters the fermenter (or stirred in after it's full) should render the juice inert and preserve it for the time being. The cider should of course be covered and air-locked until access is needed again. It's recommended that you leave the juice for 24–36 hours before trying to pitch a cultured yeast, as the sulphites will inhibit its growth and development. This will give you ample time to start a yeast culture growing, which you can add to the main fermenter.

If you plan to use the native yeasts in the juice, these should bring about fermentation usually within 24 hours, but it can take up to two weeks. Initial signs are a foamy gathering at the top of the fermenter, with tiny bubbles appearing from beneath. This will develop further into a brown, yeasty head (or plug) that quite soon may try to escape from the fermenter. Typically a loose covering is placed over the top (rather than sealing it) to let any initial rush of foam leave the fermenter naturally rather than blocking up an airlock, but again use caution so as not to introduce infection. Avoid windy/draughty situations, or allowing anything not sanitised to come into contact with the juice.

Temperature is often underestimated in terms of how much it affects the behavior and final flavour of a fermentation. As a rule of thumb, for every 10°C increase there is in temperature, the rate of reaction approximately doubles. Low and slow is best, but too low and the yeast will stop, or too high and you will get some really odd and not very pleasant flavours. Temperatures of 12–15°C are best, and non-sulphited juice should spring to life within 48 hours. If it was sulphited it may take a few weeks.

Ideal fermentation temperatures are usually found in a cool room – although many cider makers leave their fermenters outdoors or in an unheated shed and still manage to get fermentations going in November.

Commercial yeasts tend to ferment fairly fast and steadily and may be done within two weeks, depending on ambient temperature, its voracity and its ability to withstand alcohol.

© Nicole Owen

YEAST: WILD VS CULTURED

I am a passionate advocate for the use of native, wild yeasts that are already present in the apples for fermentation. Any comparable aroma and taste tests will immediately show just how much more complexity you get from a potent set of indigenous yeasts when compared to a single-strain cultured yeast that you buy in a packet. It's quite common for many cider makers to come round to the idea of using wild yeasts after a few seasons, because the results will speak for themselves. However, the extra hassle and risks associated with a wild yeast fermentation mean that many people prefer a simpler approach and use a cultured 'packet' yeast. In the warmer, drier regions of the world (that may offer us great environments in which to live) the availability of suitable wild yeasts are sparse, so it's important to understand both approaches.

It's foolish to underestimate the influence yeast has over the final product. It's an important decision, and you will benefit more if you experiment with various strains. Ask any baker or brewer about the importance of their yeast and why they favour their particular one. Some even go so far as to culture and harvest their own that they use with each batch for extra consistency – a practice that has yet to be adopted widely in the cider world. Asking about and discussing yeast choices with cider makers will help steer your decision. Ask them what they use and why they prefer it. Luckily, for the home cider maker, a traditional orchard should provide you with a wonderful selection of all the yeasts you need.

Wild yeasts

The main aim of a wild-yeast, naturally fermented cider is to increase complexity of flavour. In all the traditional cider-producing areas in the world, we are surrounded by wild yeasts. They thrive particularly in mild, moist regions such as those offered in the traditional apple-growing regions in Europe. In natural growing conditions, like an unsprayed traditional orchard, there will be many types of wild yeast present on a single tree. Traditionally, we wait for our fruit to ripen and allow it to fall naturally onto the grass beneath the tree before we collect it some time later. This sitting around brings the fruit into direct (and damp) contact with wild yeasts that inhabit our orchard floors and allows them to thrive. It's worth considering that in a hand-picked scenario, the amount of wild yeasts present on the fruit may be significantly lower to the point that it affects the fermentation to some degree. If you want to initiate a wild yeast fermentation, it's best to let as much of your fruit fall naturally when ripe, and collect it from the orchard floor.

When fermenting using wild yeasts it is important to understand that you are using a concoction of yeasts that actually work on the juice in succession. In this scenario, the initial fermentation is carried out by lemon-shaped apiculate yeasts (*kloeckera, hanseniospora etc*) that are present on

and in the fruit. These initial yeasts are succeeded by the *saccharomyces* family (*bayanus* working earlier and *cerevisiae* predominating towards the end), but other genera such as *candida, pichia* and *brettanomyces* are also present. The amount of naturally occurring yeasts present on and inside an apple already can be up to 45,000 cells per gram of fruit, so a 'crush and go' method is very easy in that respect. As soon as fruit is crushed, the sugars are released and available for the yeasts already present in the juice to take advantage of. Therefore, the traditional way of fermenting cider is to crush the rinsed fruit, press it, put the juice into a fermentation vessel like a barrel and leave it. After an initial lag period, it starts 'working', bubbles can be seen to form and rise, and a yeast plug forms at the top which is often seen coming out from a fermenter.

When allowed to prevail, multiple strains work in succession to ferment and influence the cider, each bringing its own characteristics to the juice as it develops over time. Overall, their effects combine to give a more complex, multi-dimensional beverage with an increased perception of aroma, taste and mouthfeel. However, it is a slightly trickier approach as their action is less predictable, so wild-ferment cider makers must learn to watch the progression of their cider carefully.

As such, the action of the yeasts can (and should) be a little slower and less vigorous than a cultivated, single-strain yeast that may have been selected for its vigour, alcohol tolerance or flocculation properties.

Cultured yeast

Cultured yeast use is a modern way of fermenting cider. It often involves killing or reducing the indigenous yeasts already contained in the juice and replacing them with a lab-grown strain of a single yeast that has been cleaned up and packaged. Adding a decent commercial yeast is a sure-fire way to get fermentation going before bad bacteria spoil the juice, as the process of fermentation and creation of alcohol acts as a disinfectant. The resulting flavour is likely to be more simple and clean tasting and in ideal conditions, the yeast is likely to work fairly quickly and consistently, often dropping 1–3 degrees of specific gravity per day. Providing the juice has been sanitised to some

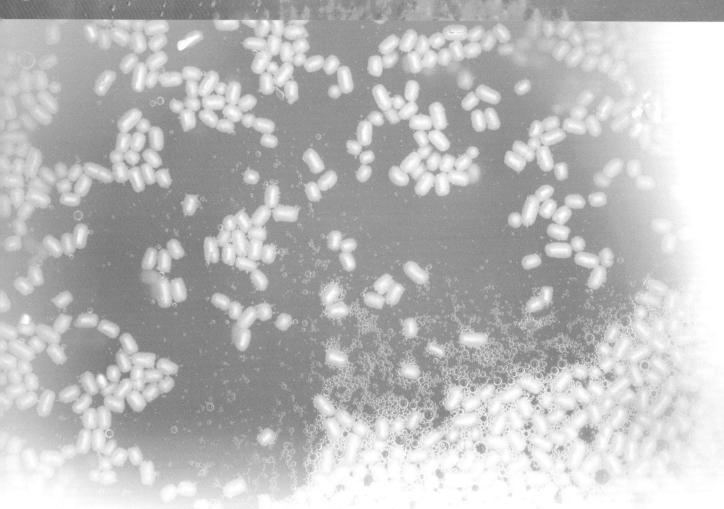

extent, the predominant organism in the fermentation is the single yeast strain introduced by the cider maker. The results are more predictable and reliable strains are therefore popular with many commercial enterprises. Recommended yeasts are those used for making wine or champagne, and there are some cider yeast strains for sale these days, although many are simply re-labelled wine yeasts.

Different strains have different habits that influence the cider (or perry) in specific ways. Some will work rapidly, others will tolerate higher amounts of alcohol, some will leave a more fruity sweetness in the flavour, some will flocculate better – the list goes on. Most manufacturers will detail the nature of the various yeasts they sell. Each strain should be considered for its benefits and chosen on the merits that suit the cider maker best. Please note, if you are planning to keeve your cider it's better to do so with a less-vigorous yeast, otherwise it can be harder to control and may overtake the keeve, making it unsuccessful.

Modern cultured varieties that are currently available on the market and popular include, White Labs English Cider yeast, Lalvin EC118 Wine/Champagne yeast and Lalvin DV10.

FERMENTATION CONDITIONS

Yeast is a living organism and as such requires, and is limited by, certain needs and conditions. Anything you can do to promote its activity will serve you well and help with a clean,

simple fermentation. As mentioned, the process itself acts to preserve the juice, so it's a good idea to get this happening as quickly as possible. Important conditions for fermentation are:

- A temperature of about 12–15°C (as even as possible is best)
- Sugar – to fuel alcohol production (8%–15% = 1040–1070)
- A pH of 3–3.8
- Sufficient supply of nutrients to live off
- Sufficient oxygen in solution for yeast replication in the early stage

It's a critical stage of the cider-making process, so great care should be taken to prevent infection and spoilage – the juice is now at its most vulnerable. In warm, unprotected conditions, it can spoil very quickly as 'sweet, aromatic and wet' appeals to just about anything that lives – insects and bacteria alike.

So, whenever you don't need direct access to the juice itself, it must be covered and sealed with an airlock somewhere cool. Once the yeast has taken hold of the fermentation, the risk starts to subside (although it never truly goes away), so a good start to a healthy fermentation really is a bonus. For those wishing to add a cultured yeast, it's worth making a starter culture in preparation of the pressing. This involves pitching a packet of yeast with some yeast nutrient into some juice sulphited at least 24 hours previously, and protecting it from the air until it starts to obviously ferment – usually within 24 hours. Alternatively, you can take 250ml of boiled water that's been allowed to cool to just below body temperature (so it feels tepid), add a couple of teaspoons of sugar, one of yeast nutrient and pour the packet yeast in. Stir and leave for a few hours. This starter is then added to the main fermenter and acts as a booster to kick-start the main fermentation.

If you are hoping to start a wild ferment, I think it's worth milling some ripe cider apples and leaving them covered in a clean and sterile tub somewhere warm (around 20°C) overnight before pressing them, mixing in some yeast nutrient before returning it somewhere warm for another 24 hours. When obvious activity has started (bubbles appearing, a fizzy appearance) pitch the mix into your main fermenter to encourage the fermentation to start. Although it will still be a longer, slower process overall this should help, unless you want to keeve!

No matter how you want to ferment, if you want to make up a starter culture, how much you need to do is determined by the size of the main fermenter – the larger it is the more you should do. For a 5-litre batch, I would aim for about 250–500ml of juice (which equates to approx 5–10%) for a healthy start.

In fermentation, there are three phases to be aware of:

Lag phase

This name is given to the period of time between pitching yeast (or completing the filling of the fermenter if you aren't using cultured yeast) and when you first start to see signs of yeast activity (bubbling, frothing etc). During this time, the yeast is acclimatising to the juice by taking in amino acids, protein and other nutrients, but it appears as if nothing is actually happening. This is normal as it's preparing to reproduce and consume large volumes of sugar, but the wait can cause some concern to the uninitiated. The length of the lag can be quite variable, and wild yeast fermentations on some occasions, can even take a few weeks. If sulphites have been added to the juice, they will have an effect on yeast activity and will slow down the start. Assuming fermentation temperatures are 'correct', a cultured yeast should start within 24–72 hours.

Log phase

This is the stage that looks so impressive, and sometimes it's so vigourous at first that it spills out from the fermenter. The yeast is now reproducing rapidly and it's a time of exponential growth – a sight that delights any cider maker. Many of the important flavours and aromas are developed during this stage, and temperature has a significant bearing on these – different temperatures influencing the yeasts to produce

▲ **Log phase: the yeast is fully active and pushing itself out from the fermenter, a very reassuring sign**

different flavours. Cooler temperatures within the viable rage of yeast activity are generally favoured for the best results. This is the longest stage of fermentation too and it can take months in a cold, wild-ferment scenario.

During the log phase, it is important to track the specific gravity changes as the yeasts work their magic. Regular measuring and careful note-taking will give you a sound basis for records that will be useful for years to come. It's important to confirm that what you hope is happening on a microbial level is actually happening, and regular gravity readings will allow you to follow its path and anticipate its finish. Should the yeast stop (or change speed significantly) for any reason, a hydrometer reading will confirm this.

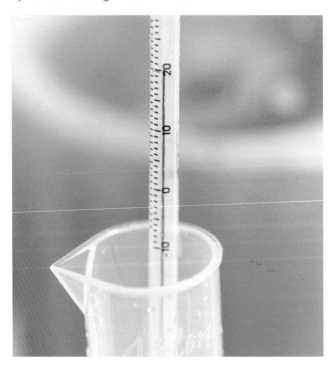

Stationary phase

This stage is where fermentation has peaked and the yeast activity slows significantly. The yeast can be seen to flocculate together and settle on the bottom.

Ironically, alcohol acts as a prohibitor for yeast reproduction so the more of it there is, the weaker the yeast will become. Most natural yeast fermentations will struggle to operate at beyond 10% ABV, but cultured yeasts are frequently able to cope at higher levels of alcohol. The liquid will start to clear, although not entirely, and various compounds will continue to be converted even after apparent activity has ceased, so it's important to not rush this stage and allow the yeast and cider to exchange flavours. Given enough time in the right conditions, all yeasts will eventually stop of their own accord when all the remaining sugar has been used up and there is nothing else left for them to convert.

If left too long in the cider, the yeast *may* start to autolyse (eat itself.) While this can be beneficial and introduce some desirable flavours, it's best avoided before the first racking due to the large amount of yeast present. Best practice is to allow autolysis after a second racking when maturing, or in a bottle.

Fermentation has been compared to a three-legged stool, where the legs are yeast, nutrients and sugar; the idea being that if you take a leg away, the stool collapses or fermentation stops. Pasteurisation will kill the yeast, micro filtering will remove it; successive racking or keeving will remove the nutrient, and allowing the cider to ferment to dryness will leave no sugar.

Temperature

As ambient temperatures drop, yeast activity will slow down. Traditionally, the winter period brought stillness to the cider house until the warmer spring temperatures would start it up again (see malolactic fermentation on page 129). Ambient temperatures really affect a cider maker's control over the pace of a fermentation both beneficially and negatively, depending on what you are trying to do.

For the novice, it's tempting to increase temperature so you can speed up initial fermentation as it starts to slow, but it's important to realise that it slows for a reason. A key influence over the flavors produced by yeasts during a fermentation is temperature and increased awareness of this will benefit you. Lower temperatures will produce slow ferments, and the final taste will be better because of it as the overall mycological profile is very different to that of a rapid alternative. Below 10°C, cultured yeasts tend to slow to a standstill, so a temperature of 12–15°C works best. Wild yeasts will work at lower temperatures and have a different fermentation pattern as there are more than one strain of them, and each have their own characteristics

and behaviours. Using temperature to slow fermentation is preferable because it's a natural, non-invasive control. Consequently, it has the disadvantage of starting up again once warmer temperatures return, providing there is still sufficient sugar left for it to eat. Slower ferments are also easier to control, and being in control can be very useful.

When you reach a desired gravity, a dramatic drop in temperature will cease the yeast activity and allow you to rack your cider into another fermenter, or bottle it when you choose to. This will have the effect of slowing down the yeast anyway, when upon returning it to optimum temperatures, it will continue its process, but at a much slower rate.

Here are a few tips on the practical requirements of a fermentation:

Space

If you plan to make five gallons of final cider, then you will need between five and six gallons of juice added to your fermenter, as you lose some through racking.

Airlock

Technically, airlocks should be fitted as soon as possible after filling the fermenter to prevent anything entering back in that will hinder the cider, eg air, microbes and insects. However, in the early stages there is a lot of frothing as the yeast comes to life, and during this stage it's best to cover the hole loosely in case an eruption spills into the airlock and blocks it. Something loose, like cotton wool balls that form a basic plug, will suffice. As soon as is possible after that, an airlock should be filled with a 1% sulphite or stronger alcohol solution (cheap vodka) and fitted.

In the silence of the cider shed or a cellar, one of the most pleasant sounds to hear is the regular, gentle emerging 'plop' of a bubble from the airlock as the yeast quietly undertakes its job. When this starts happening, it will bring a smile to the most hardened of cider makers – it's working! As such, it offers you a reassurance that your job is successful so far, but also allows you to track the pace of the fermentation. The closer the bubbles are together, the more activity there is. If it slows down, or stops, fermentation is finishing or struggling, at which time it's appropriate to do a gravity reading before going any further.

When does it stop?

If you want to make a dry cider with a final gravity around 1.000, you don't have to stop a fermentation, it slows down enough toward the end so you can it rack it. It's helpful to know you can stop it by reducing the temperature to around 5°C and storing it there for as long as possible to clear. Yeast, left totally unchecked will ferment all the sugar in the apple juice or cider until it's gone, at which stage the cider will be very dry – too dry for some!

Sweetness

Maintaining some residual sweetness to accentuate the fruitiness of the cider can be done in several ways. Actively stopping yeast activity earlier than its natural finishing point will leave some sugar behind and chilling the cider will halt the yeast significantly. If you follow this by multiple rackings while still chilled, you'll remove most of the yeast, some of the nutrient which will be bound to yeast cells and the lees, and it'll slow it to a virtual standstill. For a sweet cider, you could rack it at a gravity of 1.025–1.030 and again at 1.020–1.025. For a medium, the second racking should be done at 1.010–1.015.

Racking for a carbonated bottle-conditioned drink should be done at 1.010 and this will result in a dry, naturally sparkling cider (see racking section for further details).

Alternatively, you can ferment your cider completely dry and rack it carefully, then back-sweeten it with as much sugar (or sterile fresh juice) as you require. Do remember, though, that if you're bottling and relying on racking to stop a fermentation, you should choose bottles capable of withstanding the pressure that would be developed if ALL the sugar were to turn to alcohol. So only bottle cider at a maximum of 1.005 gravity if you are using beer bottles, and use champagne-style bottles with corks and wire cages for racked ciders up to a gravity of 1.010.

Fermentation can also be slowed to some extent by the addition of sulphites. Adding metabisulphite to the juice immediately after racking will help reduce the yeast action – but it almost certainly will not stop it entirely – but it will also hinder malolactic fermentation in the future, which may or may not be beneficial. Back-sweetening a fully fermented cider with some apple juice is a simple and popular technique. The sweet juice, blended with a fresh dry cider in the right proportions works well for many people, but the cider will almost certainly re-ferment unless no yeast is present in either and should be kept cool and drunk fairly quickly, or bottled according to the potential pressure the apple juice addition would achieve if it did fully re-ferment.

Homebrew shops offer all sorts of non-fermentable sweeteners to help sweeten ciders (saccharine, sucralose *etc*) but I believe 100% pure juice is a better approach all round. You have the option of doing it naturally by racking several times to reduce the nutrient levels and overall yeast amount (remember the three legged stool principle). Cider can be pasteurised by heat treatment but it can also cook the cider and alter the flavour significantly.

Another technique that is trickier but eventually allows for a greater degree of control of the fermentation, is keeving.

IMPORTANT NOTE: never rely on racking, the addition of sulphites, or the addition of potassium sorbate to prevent fermentation. They will all probably slow fermentation to some extent but are NOT guaranteed to stop fermentation in cider.

Properly carried-out pasteurisation is the only method that's (almost) guaranteed to prevent further fermentation of a cider that contains any kind of fermentable sugar in a small-scale cider making environment. This is only a problem if you try to bottle (or otherwise contain in a sealed vessel) a cider that still has the potential to ferment and produce a pressure beyond the design limits of the bottle you are using. The obvious danger is the bottle – or other sealed container – exploding. Serious injuries have been known to be inflicted by exploding bottles in particular, and always bear in mind that it might be a friend or family member who gets injured, so when choosing a bottle always make sure it is capable of withstanding the pressure generated if ALL the remaining sugar is fermented.

Blending

Blending cider is a good way of refining or enhancing a basic batch that may be good, but not yet great, and this is best done by taste. Many cider makers will ferment a base blend of apples that represent the bulk of their cider in volume. Aside from that, certain other blends, or single varieties that have been fermented separately, can be added to it. The advantage of creating separate batches of cider is that you can make batches more sweet or tannic to add to the base blend to alter and improve the final taste accordingly.

Indeed, it may be that a cider maker has fermented several batches of cider, some with a commercial yeast and others using wild yeasts, and wants to blend them for a more interesting final taste with less risk. Different yeasts will have different properties so fermenting separately with a view to blending afterwards gives you the advantage of controlling the proportions of each one in a final mix. Some will bring great aroma, different fruity characteristics, clarity, body, *etc.*

It's quite common to see measured mixing beakers in which cider makers will add proportions of various ciders to try out different versions of blends. Mixing of blends should ideally be done during or before the first racking, but in the case of blending a sweeter cider into a dry one into order to retain some final sweetness, it will have to be done after the second racking, then pasteurised, or residual yeast may start the fermentation up again.

Top Tip!

"During fermenting, sniff the airlocks every day and if you can smell hydrogen sulphide, add a bit of yeast nutrient. It helps keep the cider clean-tasting."

Andy Hallet from Blaengawney Cider

Racking

After the initial rush of yeast activity, the fermentation slows and will stabilise. The cider gets clearer as the yeasts drop out of suspension and settle. The gravity will be significantly lower and when the yeasts seem inactive, this is the time to think about racking.

Racking is essentially the process of moving the cider from one vessel to another while leaving behind the spent yeast, proteins and lees (general detritus) of fermentation *etc* at the bottom. This step is about reducing the amount of yeast and yeast nutrients in the cider with a view to slowing the fermentation and clearing the cider. It normally works best when the fermenter has stood un-agitated in the cold for at least a week, preferably longer. Both temperature and stillness will have helped pack the waste products of

fermentation into a reasonably solid sediment, and you want it to stay that way.

Knowing when to rack depends on the gravity of your cider. Different yeasts behave in different ways, so it's important to keep a close eye on your gravities and regular hydrometer tests will help tell you what's going on. Some yeasts are more vigorous that others and will need taming quicker, so should be racked earlier. What level of sweetness you want to retain in your final cider will also dictate when you need to rack. A

RACKING GRAVITIES			
Desired taste	**First racking gravity**	**Second racking gravity**	**Final gravity**
Sweet	1.030	1.025	1.020 (needs pasteurising)
Medium	1.020	1.015	1.010 (needs pasteurising)
Dry	1.010	1.005	1.003
Bone dry	1.010	1.000	0.997
Dry & sparkling	1.015	1.010 (Champagne bottled)	1.003

modern, cultured yeast might only take a few weeks and will need racking at a gravity of around 1.008–1.005, and in the northern hemisphere this could be done around January. As many modern yeasts tend to flocculate and settle heavily, racking early helps prevent autolysis and off-flavours. If you are using wild yeasts, this process may be slower and take longer, and so may happen later in the year. Traditionally, a wild-ferment cider made from the last of the apples and pressed just prior to Christmas, is left alone. It should be near completion by Easter, although it could be earlier or later. Around three months, the yeast has usually settled on the bottom of the fermenter.

Blending could be done during or before the first racking, as nutrient, acidity, yeast and sugar levels will alter and affect your fermentation. If you want sweeter ciders and decide to leave some residual sugar in your juice, you must remember that unless you pasteurise the cider, the yeasts will slowly continue to digest the sugar and bottles can become over-carbonated and explosive. Many cider

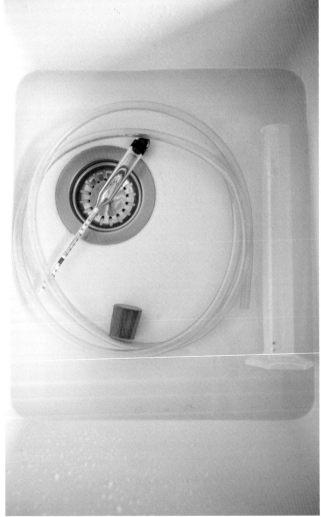

▶ **Ready to rack**

makers will rack later in the process, though it's up to you when you do it so long as you are aware of what batches have residual sugar in and what batches have been racked/sulphited/pasteurised *etc*.

It's important to have clean and sterile vessels of the total racked volume ready to move the cider into. So for example, one very full IBC (1,000-litre) could be racked into five 220-litre barrels. Each 220-litre barrel could then be racked into a couple of 100-litre barrels, or three 60-litre and a 30-litre one. Remember you'll lose about 5%–10% at each racking. When filling a second vessel, try and fill it as full as is sensible, to eliminate the presence of air on the cider. Although any continued yeast activity will produce CO_2 that 'should' sit over it (in between the cider and the air) it might not be producing enough to protect it fully. If sulphites have been added, it might not be producing much CO_2 (but shouldn't need any either). Racking doesn't remove all the active yeast that is still held in suspension, but it does remove a lot of remaining nutrient, so subsequent yeast activity will slow down if it is done at lower gravities.

Racking requires some careful handling and more thorough sterilisation, since it is an opportunity to introduce infection – heartbreaking at this stage! Using a sterile siphon tube or food-safe pump depending on your volume, slowly move the cider into its new fermenter, trying <u>not</u> to introduce any oxygen into it by splashing it about. Lie the outlet end of the tube into the new fermenter on the bottom to start with. Then, as it fills, keep it just below the surface to allow for a steady run, or lay it down the side wall of the new vessel to stop it splashing. At the same time you need to keep the inlet end just under the surface of the original cider, so it doesn't suck up or agitate the sediment at the base – you want none (or as little as possible) to move through. Some fermenters have a tap an eighth of the way up from the bottom. This approximates how much sediment is usually generated from the first fermentation, up to first racking.

Repeated racking will render the cider virtually, but not quite, stable. It's beneficial to have a very slow fermentation over a long period of time rather than a cider that ferments out quickly. Cider that has been racked two or three times should have slowed down enough for you to be able to store it safely – although bear in mind my earlier comments about bottling racked ciders. If you wanted it to add a bit more protection, the addition of sulphites at this stage will help, and prevent a natural MLF (malolactic fermentation).

If you intend to add suphites to the cider, they are best dissolved into a small batch of the cider you want to move first, in a jug or bucket. Then gently pour into the bottom of the new fermenter, before the remainder of the batch is allowed to

run into it, and mix. It should be used at about 50ppm of the total batch or one Campden tablet per gallon.

Racking is completed when the new fermenter is full and sealed with a fresh airlock, but another racking will be required once (maybe twice more) before final casking or bottling to remove any further yeast sediment. Minimising airspace in the new vessel is one of the tips to successful racking, as the cider is now at a stage where it is most vulnerable to becoming vinegar. So it should be topped up with another batch of cider or even with juice. Where possible, racking should be done during periods of high barometric pressure to aid the precipitation of solids while atmospheric pressure is at its greatest.

Gravity racking is done by putting one end of a clean and sterile siphon tube into a fermenter about an inch below the surface and holding it there. The tube is then primed by a brief gentle suck on the other end allowing cider to flow into the tube, which is rested on the bottom of the new (clean and sterile) fermenter that is lower than the original. The height difference will determine the speed at which the cider moves through the pipe – slowly and without splashing is best. Be careful that sediment from the bottom or yeast from the top doesn't get sucked into the tube and carried through. You can use a food-grade pump (hand or electric) for larger batches, so long as they can be cleaned and sterilised before and after use.

▼ Knowing when to stop means not dragging dead yeast through to the next vessel.

MALOLACTIC FERMENTATION (MLF)

Malolactic fermentation (or malolactic action) is a secondary fermentation that is brought about long after the initial yeast fermentation has completed. It involves the conversion of sharp-tasting malic acid present in the cider, into less sharp-tasting lactic acid and carbon dioxide, so has the effect of smoothing and mellowing the flavour. The process can also introduce new flavour notes in the cider, often referred to as 'buttery'.

It's a naturally occurring process that happens as the spring temperatures start to rise, and traditionally, when this has finished, the cider is ready. In some countries it is seen as a fault in cider, but in the UK, France and Spain it is both accepted and encouraged. The action of naturally occurring acid-tolerant *lactobacilus* are responsible for reducing the overall acidity of the cider, so any ciders that haven't been sulphited are likely to undergo some MLF as temperatures increase to 15°C–18°C. In the right conditions, it can be difficult to stop, as it can happen very quickly so if you don't want any MLF to occur, you need to sulphite your cider at the end of the initial yeast fermentation (first racking) to prevent it.

It does have its benefits – MLF in a bottled cider will serve to increase the levels of CO_2 in the bottle. This not only gives it a pleasant gentle sparkle, it contributes to preservation of the cider too and may be seen as yet another 'hurdle' the cider maker employs to protect his produce.

These days you can buy cultured MLF additions to add to your cider to recreate the effect if you decide you want it to occur. This is useful if you can only source acidic cooking or eating fruit and not enough cider-apple varieties.

MATURING

So when is it ready? Traditionally, you're not supposed to tap the cider until you hear the first cuckoo of spring, but it's always wise to do a bit of quality control to see how the cider is developing. Sharper (high acidity) ciders will store for longer and probably improve slightly for it. Some sound advice from an experienced cider maker to a novice cider maker would be 'drink it when it tastes good'. Yes, it might get better – but it might also get worse. You've put a lot of effort in, and waited a long time, so enjoy it.

PROTECTION AND LIFE SPAN

Sulphur dioxide is used to preserve freshness and when a measured dose is added to many of our daily foodstuffs, it allows them to survive for longer than ever. Not everyone likes the idea of them though. With regards to cider, the purists may often turn their back on the idea, as it interferes with the natural processes that give cider its unique character. However, it does really offer some control throughout the cider-making process, and when used in lower (measured) doses, it can still allow for enough of the traditional character

to shine through. Once fermented, cider is much more stable and so can be preserved in an airtight container for long periods of time. Cider stronger in alcohol will always last longer as alcohol is a particularly good preservative. Carbon dioxide is another useful substance that when dissolved into solution, helps protect against bacterial action, and a blanket of carbon dioxide will keep oxygen away from the cider so preventing surface film yeasts developing. Air (in particular oxygen) has a very negative effect on cider, so once something is opened and exposed, the microbiological clock starts ticking and its freshness starts to decline. Aerobic fermentation (a bad process using acetic acid bacteria) as opposed to anaerobic fermentation (a good process using yeasts) will mean the natural processes of fermentation follow a different pathway and eventually mean that the cider will turn to vinegar. This is normally a long slow process but in the right conditions can start quickly. With the exception of Spanish *sidra natural,* cider that tastes too vinegary will mean it has been exposed to the air at some stage in production through bad handling. It should always be kept free from air until it's absolutely unavoidable. One of the benefits of a bag-in-box packaging is that the bag collapses around the cider as it is drained and so preserves it longer, unlike a rigid barrel. Small amounts of volatile acidity, acetic acid – the predominant component of vinegar, can be considered good in some ciders but don't let anyone tell you that too much is acceptable – it is often down to poor production.

FILTRATION AND MICRO FILTRATION

Filtering/micro filtration of the cider is unnecessary as a home cider maker. It can remove so much from your juice that it actually alters the flavour so unless you absolutely have to have a perfectly clear cider, I believe its best to leave it as raw as possible. With a healthy fermentation and some careful racking, your cider will almost always settle bright and clear, free from any solids, and at worst just a little opaque.

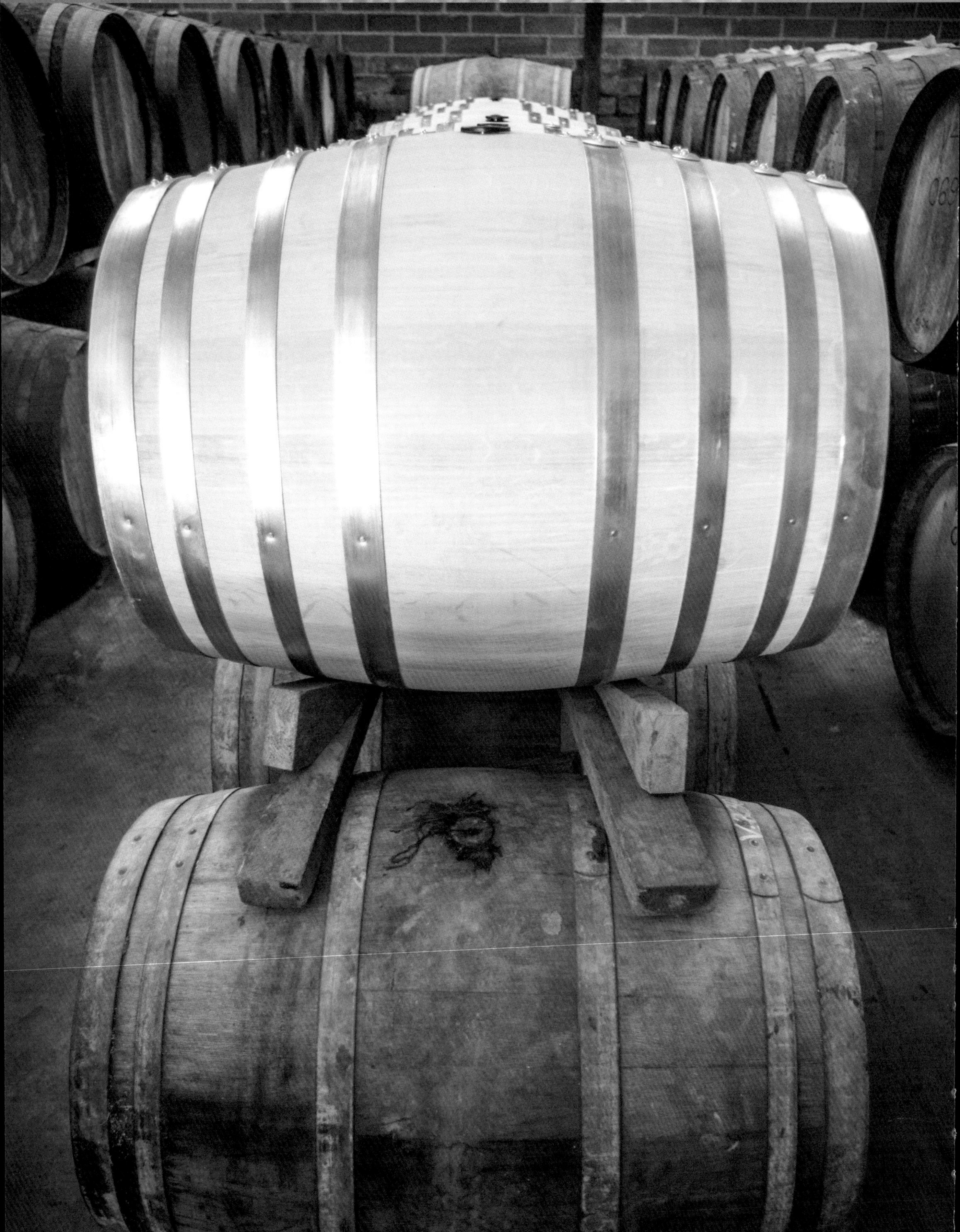

Storage & packaging

The dry coolness of a cellar is perfect for storing cider, so anywhere cider is to be left should try to recreate those conditions. Between 4 and 10°C will mean your cider can sit safely and improve with age. Temperature fluctuations will affect the aging of your cider and so cool and steady is what you want to aim for.

It's practical to bottle your cider as it can make storage easier, offers a convenient alternative and allows for some bottle conditioning. If you want to bottle, you need a good source of the right bottles, the right caps, cages and corks *etc*, as well as space to store them once filled. They have the advantage of making the cider easier to pasteurise if necessary. It's important to know the gravity and condition of the cider you plan to bottle at bottling time, and the safest thing to do is to test it for gravity and choose a bottle capable of holding the ultimate pressure should fermentation to dry take place.

As the pressure of fermenting in a bottle (even partially) can create significant levels of built-up CO_2, it's really important that you are careful to use the correct bottles that are designed to withstand the strong pressures involved. Being aware of your bottling gravities is equally as important and so it's advised that you do no bottle higher than 1.005 for crown cap beer bottles or above 1.010 for champagne bottles.

The only real exception to this is if you're making keeved cider, but it takes a cider maker with good experience of keeving to bottle at a gravity above the bottle's design limit with confidence. Even experienced exponents of the art of

keeving will often do preliminary tests by taking two or three bottles from the same batch and filling them two-thirds full, sealing them and leaving for two-to-three weeks at room temperature (approx 20°C). These can then be opened and sampled for taste, carbonation levels *etc*. If it's hazy and excessively fizzy, it's probably a little early to bottle it.

Making perry

"Next unto Cider, Perry claims the precedency, especially if made of the best juicy pears celebrated for that purpose."

John Worlidge, Vinetum Brittanicum, 1676

Perry making is the exact same process as cider making *most* of the time, but there are enough significant differences in the fruit that need to be taken into account if you want to increase your chances of success. There are two main reasons why more perry isn't made. Firstly, the trickiest thing about perry is finding enough fruit! Perry pears are not common and so in the few places where they are grown, the fruit is highly coverted. If you can get hold if it, you need to know what varieties you're dealing with. Secondly, perry making is regarded as more fiddly than cider and it's due to important compositional divergence from cider fruit. Because of this, it's a more prolonged and technical process that some people would go so far as to describe as an art form.

The habits of each perry pear variety can be quite individual so identifying your fruit correctly will give you a better chance of success. Although similar, the pears aren't classified in quite the same way as cider apples, many of them are more like sweets or medium sharps. Having said that, the ones that are higher in tannin and acidity (the bittersharps) contain very hard-tasting tannin (astringent and bitter) so the flavour/effect is more pronounced.

The quality of the fruit is paramount to good perry making. Perry pears have a habit of rotting internally before any outward signs become apparent so if you are ripening fruit, they need watching very closely. Samples from each variety should be cut open and checked as they all ripen at different rates. In some cases, they even rot on the tree before they fall naturally and so need picking. As this rotting introduces bacteria and because pears are less acidic than apples, there isn't the acidity to keep bacteria down and vigilance is paramount.

Sugar levels are often higher in pears, and an initial gravity reading may register at 1090 or more. Another unique factor about perry pears is that they contain a degree of non-fermentable sugars which will mean final gravity readings are also higher (1.010–1.020.) A non-fermentable sugar such as sorbitol found in perry pears will have the advantage of leaving some residual sweetness and will also contribute to a fuller mouthfeel. Some need to be left to mature/ripen to improve flavour/sugar levels, but others will need pressing very soon, often within a day or two of receiving or gathering the pears.

After milling, a maceration pause is essential for some varieties if you want your perry to clear. This is particularly important for high-tannin varieties – you'll know which these are because when you bite into the fruit, your mouth will feel extremely dry. In other varieties, it will destroy any body in the pulp. When using pears like *Butt* or *Teddington Green,* the tannin levels are often so high that the perry won't clear unless it has a chance to leach out during the maceration. Yet, encouraging tannin precipitation may result in the important wild yeasts present in the must being leached out too, compounding a fermentation lag, so they mustn't be macerated for too long and a yeast nutrient addition may be sensible. In addition, mixing different varieties can introduce a tannin or pectin haze, and often a particularly milky or cloudy perry will not clear.

Because of their softness, some cider makers use a different (more traditional) press to obtain the juice. Modern belt presses can clog more easily with soft fruit and they take longer to clean and reassemble than a simple rack-and-cloth press.

The acids found in pears are significantly different in many cases and need appropriate treatment. In some cases, citric acid is the predominant acid, giving a sharper taste. As if that's not enough, another characteristic of pear juice is that it is lower in soluble nitrogen than apple juice and so doesn't support yeast growth to the same degree. This can mean fermentation is typically slower to start and remains sluggish throughout, so many people will overcome this by adding yeast nutrients (ammonium sulphate or thiamine) to their juice which helps the yeast to produce proteins and amino acids from which to grow. Lower levels of nutrients also increase the risk of hydrogen sulphide – the yeasts are then forced to strip the nitrogen away from the amino acids and leave the sulphur behind making it very eggy smelling.

Higher levels of naturally occurring acetaldehyde in pears mean that, if you want sulphites to be effective, you need an increased dosage in comparison to cider. Acetaldehyde has the effect of neutralising the sulphites, so SO_2 should be used at the same dosage rates as for cider but with an added 50ppm on top (remembering not to go over 200ppm). When you add up these factors, you start to realise why perry making is a specialism and attracts a certain kind of mind. People get hooked on it!

There is a distinct lack of research and written material out there to learn from, although enthusiasts are gathering and compiling information, tips and data more than ever on the Internet. Online groups like the Cider Workshop (www.ciderworkshop.com) are invaluable for sharing data and experience, and anyone who wants to make perry (or cider) seriously is best off getting actively involved with such groups. Also, you can always ask the producers who make your favourite perry, although they're unlikely to divulge any real secrets!

SEVEN TIPS FOR BETTER PERRY

1 If possible, find out what varieties of pear you are using as they all behave differently.

2 If necessary, ferment single varieties (pick and press as they ripen) then blend later.

3 Be prepared to press at short notice (pears ripen fast)

4 Unripe pears = lack of flavour. Overripe = sloppy, slimy pulp and increased chance of bacteria from rotten fruit

5 Macerate high tannin pears to reduce milkiness and excessive bitterness (4 hours – overnight)

6 When blending high and low tannin perries, do so before storing

7 High tannin perries need storing/maturing to allow for increased tannin precipitation

Top Tip!

"Conditioning cider and perry *sur lees* in bottle, can lead to a very satisfying, gentle fizz with yeast autolysis, adding further complexity to an already characterful cider or perry. However, the usual constraints of yeast challenges apply in order to minimise hydrogen sulphide problems. I believe a good mix of varieties with very low nitrogen levels, from old trees is best. As the cider blend is being determined at pressing, selection of varieties is crucial, and trial and error over many years invaluable."

Tom Oliver, Oliver's Cider & Perry

Improvements and troubleshooting

Some people like to style their cider depending on their tastes and there are various techniques to do that. For the most part they can be included in the general cider-making process at the correct stage and in many cases, become routine. Some are more difficult than others and alter the outcome of the cider dramatically (in both flavour and volume), but are thought to be worth it by thousands of cider makers globally.

MACERATION

This involves leaving milled apples to sit for a period of time prior to pressing. Not everyone will leave the fruit to sit after it's been milled, but some cider makers choose to (for no more than 24 hours, but 6–12 hours is more usual). This 'pulp rest' introduces a different character to the juice, and can be done for several reasons. The process allows the fruit to oxidise slightly, which improves the colour by deepening it. It also softens the fruit and makes it easier to press. It allows for more pectin to be extracted, which is very useful for the keeving process, as well as increasing the juice yield from the pulp.

If you plan to macerate, you need to be extra-vigilant about hygiene during this time. If you are planning a wild ferment, the added time has the bonus of allowing the juice to take on more oxygen that the wild yeasts depend on in the early stages of fermentation.

Once milled, place the pulp into a sterilised, sealed tub or similar vessel, and allow to sit undisturbed overnight. During this time, oxidation occurs which both darkens the juice colour and increases leaching of pectin so that the next morning, when the pulp is pressed as normal, it is a deeper, richer red and is thicker in consistency.

ADDITIVES

A visit to your local or online homebrew shop will reveal an array of additives to 'improve' your cider that include finings, grape tannin, sweetener, colouring *etc*. However, on the whole, I believe less is best and a well-made real cider never suffers without them.

Yeast nutrients (for fermentation) will certainly help the yeast ferment the sugars in the juice, will keep the yeast working at a steady pace and speed up your fermentation overall. That being so, there are arguments for adding them to your juice, or not. Yeasts need a source of nitrogen, vitamins, phosphate and other minerals if they are to grow. Depending on the qualities of the juice – and to some extent how and where the fruit is grown – these will be present, in greater, or lesser amounts, and affect yeast growth accordingly. Some classic cider varieties are notoriously low in nitrogen and thiamine and so slow down a fermentation (see Cider Apple Varieties table on page 58). Single-variety ciders made from these apples will benefit from a nutrient addition.

Sometimes however, it's best to not include them initially as a slower fermentation is generally regarded as better than one that's too fast. In a multi-variety juice, adding nutrients may be unnecessary and can even speed up a fermentation to the detriment of the final flavour. But they are advisable to add in cases of slow or sluggish yeast action and can help when reviving a stuck fermentation.

▼ An addition of grape tannin being used in cider made from eating apples

Most of us will agree that nothing should be added to cider that isn't necessary, although what we deem necessary will differ widely. For instance – I'll never add anything to my cider to reduce the haziness of it, as using bittersweets in a sound fermentation and with careful racking, it'll normally drop clear, or nearly clear anyway. And in cases where it doesn't, I don't mind because traditional cider would be hazy, and in many cases my favourite ciders are. Whether it's a pectin or tannin haze, quantities of it are in every apple we've ever eaten so it does no harm whatsoever. It's possible that a haze can be bacterial, but with sufficient care, it's much less likely. However, in cases where people can't get true cider fruit (so the likelihood of a haze is increased) or when it really matters to someone that they have a bright clear cider, products are available to add.

KEEVING

Keeving is an ingenious method of stopping cider fermenting to complete dryness and creating a naturally sweeter cider. It's a technique that has been practised in France and the UK since the mid seventeenth century. Recent times have seen a revival of the technique here in the UK but in France, it has been the only method of making cider for hundreds of years.

The basic principle is to remove the nutrients on which the yeasts survive. This halts the fermentation, retaining the natural sugars and offers the drinker a sweeter alternative. The first requirement is the right kind of fruit. Traditionally, this is a blend of true cider apples harvested late in the season from mature standard trees. This kind of fruit is lower in nutrients while still high in tannin, and will offer the cider maker a decent

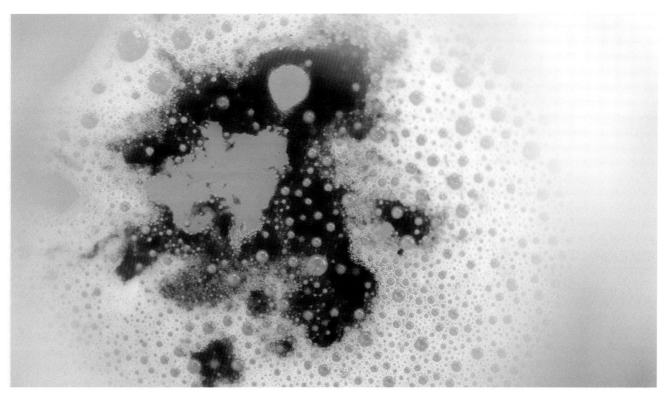

original gravity of 1055 or more. The acidity of the juice should be slightly higher than normal (3.6–3.8pH) and a greater proportion of bittersweets is better for encouraging this.

The next (and arguably most important) requirement is the maceration of the fruit. For a period of time after the apples are milled, they are left and allowed to rest while covered and protected. They can be left from as little as 4 hours to as much as 24 hours, but more often they're left overnight. This rest period allows pectin to leach out of the pulp into the juice and encourages the juice to oxidise slightly, deepening the colour. The pulp is then pressed, the juice collected and put into a fermenter as usual. A low ambient temperature (lower than 10°C, but higher than 5°C) is quite important, as while you want the yeast to start its work, you want it to have a slower start. The aim of keeving is to reduce the speed and strength of the fermentation enough to control it carefully, so it's also best to stick to a wild-yeast fermentation as a cultured yeast fermentation is generally too vigorous.

Natural enzyme reactions in the juice allow the pectin to cling to itself forming into a gel ball that floats up to the surface in the fermenter. Traditionally, French cider makers would add salt (NaCl) and chalk ($CaCO_3$) to encourage the formation of a thick brown 'head' on top of the juice. The modern equivalent is calcium chloride ($CaCl_2$), which combines with the available pectin in the juice to form a calcium pectate gel which is insoluble and floats. When successful, the main body of juice is now separate from the brown gel (know as the *chapeau brun* in France) and any sediment remains at the base. The pectin (or flying lees) traps much of the amino acids and vitamins that the yeast depends on to work on the sugar. While held there, the cider maker siphons off the juice from the middle section into a separate fermenter leaving behind the *chapeau brun*. The fermentation in the new vessel then continues as per usual, albeit at a slower pace. A successful keeve, followed by a combination of winter temperatures

mean the fermentation proceeds very slowly and is easier to control. When the gravity reaches 1.025–1.020, the cider is racked, which slows it further. If racked again at about 1.015 in low temperatures and bottled, the cider may undergo some MLF as it warms, but it will remain sweet for the most part, if lower in alcohol.

If you want to add calcium chloride to assist a keeve, it should be added at about 4g per 10 litres of juice soon after pressing. Unless used at low levels, the addition of sulphites will delay or prohibit a fermentation in which case a cultured yeast will have to be added that will probably overtake a keeve and it won't undergo any MLF either. Transparent fermenters are a big help because they allow you to see the split in the juice.

BOTTLE FERMENTING

Finishing a fermentation in a bottle will bring about a crisp refreshing sparkle to your cider or perry. Simply racking at 1.010 into a clean champagne bottle will do it well enough. After bottling, corking and caging, they need to be left somewhere cool and dark for at least six months. When you want to drink them, leave them upright in the fridge for a few hours to settle. When opening, uncork them carefully into waiting glasses and try to leave as much of the sediment as possible in the bottle.

This process will probably throw quite a sediment; it's harmless but not so pleasant to see in the bottom of the bottle. A second alternative is to allow your primary fermentation to ferment to dryness before racking in into bottles primed with approximately 7.5g per 750ml bottle of juice or sugar syrup before sealing it and laying it down for a month or so. During this time, any yeast cells in suspension should work on the sugars slowly and carbonate a fairly clear cider, leaving a much smaller degree of sediment.

To truly overcome the issue of any residual yeast, the

'champagne method' of bottle fermenting was devised. It's more involved and even more of a pain, but the results are worthwhile and it's definitely worth trying at least once, because it's exciting when you get it right.

This method starts in the similar way, by bottling a dry-fermented cider and initiating a small secondary fermentation in the bottle but differs by also introducing a small sample (approx 7–8ml) of fresh yeast alongside the dosage (12–18ml) of fresh juice or sugar syrup that is also added to the bottle. The bottles are then capped, and laid on their sides for up to 18 months. At that point the bottles are placed neck down in a special rack (*pupitre*) and turned a quarter turn frequently in order to encourage the yeast and sediment to collect at the thinnest part of the neck, just beneath the bung/crown cap.

After a period of anywhere between one and six months, the caps and necks of the bottle are frozen using a special freezer before the bottle is stood upright, the cap is removed, the sediment plug pushed out by the pressure inside the bottle and its final cork and wire applied. Sharper ciders tend to respond better to bottle fermenting and conditioning and high-tannin apples can make the bubbles taste more metallic.

AGING ON LEES AND AUTOLYSIS

Cider can be improved by being left to age on its lees ("*sur lie*") but this is not recommended before the first racking, where a large crop of dead yeast can leave a rough flavour. If left on a small amount after the first racking, the effect will be more subtle. After a ferment has finished, the yeast starts to autolyse (eats itself) which results in more pronounced flavours, in particular the aroma becomes more intense and the taste complex and pleasing.

LABELLING AND NOTES

Throughout the fermentation and racking processes, each batch of apples/juice/cider should be labelled with its origin, to relate it back to whatever orchard it came from. Gravities and dates should be marked on each fermenter to help keep track of what's going on inside. As you experiment and trial ideas more and more, this becomes even more important. In a 30-barrel fermenting scenario, there is no way you can remember which cider is doing what. Some will be fast and some will be slow; some will be different blends of apples; some will be dry; some will be sweet *etc*, so do yourself a favour and make it easier by being organised.

EXPERIMENTATION

The idea and the freedom of experimentation requires discipline but will, over time, yield better results and enable you to make the cider you want. Careful note-keeping throughout will mean you can track batches, ideas, conditions *etc* that have an impact on your trials. Many cider makers will ferment single varieties with a view to a taste analysis afterwards, and make appropriate notes. These can of course be used to blend and improve a final cider of mixed juices, offering the drinkers a more satisfying array of aroma, taste and texture. Therefore, experimenting is to be encouraged when a hobbyist feels he or she has enough confidence to push themselves, their ideas and techniques into unknown territory within the safety of prior experience and proper, established practices. One favoured technique I experimented with early on (which is safest to do with an acidic cider (low pH 3), is to not sulphite the juice but to chaptalise it and bring the starting gravity right up to 1.070 or more. After 72 hours (or when the wild yeasts are *definitely* working) you can add a small cultured yeast starter that was made at the same time. By then, wild yeasts in the large fermentation will have started to work, but the cultured yeast addition will take over and complete it. They will also cope much better in a higher ABV scenario and leave a cleaner finish. It should be noted that yeast doesn't like being in alcoholic environments and so pitching a packet of yeast directly into a semi-fermented juice will have limited effect. It's always better to get it started separately and then add it when it is powering!

▼ It's important to experiment. Use dessert fruit if it's all you have.

Common faults and problems

Prevention is always better than cure and never more so than in cider making! If you are strict about hygiene, processes, ingredients and conditions, then many common faults can be minimised or eliminated by default. The most common fault in cider making, the one that everyone does at least once, usually right at the beginning is getting lax on sterilisation.

The benefits of modern science empower us with the ability to remove the chance of infection when making cider, the principles are sound and the science is clear. What tends to let us down, however, is something that science cannot help us with – motivation! The more effort you put into your sterilisation the first time and every time you 'clean and sterilise', the less heartbreak you will have months after you've spent all the money, got all the kit and done all the work when suddenly infection appears. I can't emphasise enough how easy it is to let one thing slip and introduce unwanted bacteria into your precious juice. Cider making is nearly all cleaning at times.

Many problems are prevented by the use of sulphites in the early stages as these knock out the bacteria responsible. As such, it's probably the best reason for using them, even in low doses early on. Simple hygiene management such as fitting an airlock and cleaning transfer hoses as soon as is possible will also help prevent problems being introduced. Gently sniffing each airlock regularly will give you a good idea of what's going on inside the fermenter – bad smells are never a good sign. If you can detect something early on, it's much easier to contain.

MOUSE

Mouse is the name given to one of the more common faults you can find in a cider. Its name is taken from the mousey smell cider can have when it's tainted with certain strains of lactic bacteria and is most easily prevented by sulphiting the juice prior to fermentation. Our perception of mouse varies widely, while some people will never notice it, others are very sensitive to it. To increase your chances of detecting it, a small amount of baking soda and water mixed together and swilled around your mouth prior to tasting will lower the pH in you mouth long enough to make it more apparent if it's there.

ROPEY CIDER

The phrase used to describe something as 'a bit ropey' comes from this particular problem with cider making. Ropey cider is caused by a bacteria living in the cider that joins together and forms strands. When the cider is poured, it pours with a twisted, rope-like appearance. If your cider is sufficiently acidic, it's not normally a problem. It can also be prevented by using sulphites early on. If it does occur, it can be treated by the addition of metabisulphite, a good stir and a racking once it's settled.

ROTTEN EGGS!

This is a particularly unpleasant and alarming stink and the last thing you want to smell in your cider. It's caused by hydrogen sulphide (H_2S) and is common at low levels for many fermentations. It is caused by the yeast looking for a source of nitrogen, and if it's in short supply, the yeast takes nitrogen from cysteine (an amino acid found in proteins) which contains sulphur. As the nitrogen is taken, the sulphur is released as H_2S. It usually clears of its own accord as the process continues. If you notice the smell increasing during fermentation, yeast nutrient should be added. You can either add tiny amounts of copper sulphate to the cider, or rack it off the lees. It'll disperse eventually. It's just a very pungent gas which we can sense at extremely low concentrations, which is useful as it's poisonous!

ACETIFICATION

When cider gets infected with *acetobactor* it causes the oxidation of alcohol into acetic acid, slowly turning the cider into vinegar. It's very recognisable as it smells so strong. Exposure to air will almost certainly start the reaction so the best way to prevent it is with careful handling, particularly when racking. At low levels in the early stages you can treat with potassium carbonate, but at high levels there is nothing to do other than start making good cider vinegar – far, far away from the rest of your cider! See later in this chapter for more details on making vinegar.

FILM YEASTS
(CANDIDA, PICHIA OR HANSENULA)

These are yeasts that can very easily contaminate ciders made traditionally (that haven't been sulphited) but only become apparent during the final stages (after bottling, during storage *etc*) if they've been exposed to the air. One of the problems with fully fermented, dry cider is that no more carbon dioxide is produced, so the container doesn't form a layer of CO_2 above the cider to keep the oxygen away. They can be detected by the smell they give off (solvent-like, acetone), and eventually as a powdery skin formed on the surface of the cider. If the cider is infected with film yeasts, the film should be removed gently, the cider should be racked into a cleaned and sterile vessel and sulphur dioxide can be added (at 50ppm) to stop any further infection. The cider should also be topped up when possible so as little air as possible is left in the vessel.

STUCK FERMENTATION

A stuck fermentation is one of the easier things to fix when making cider – it's more like jump-starting a car, rather than having to replace the engine. The first thing to do if yeast activity stops (or doesn't even start) is to take an accurate gravity reading using a hydrometer, and including any necessary temperature adjustments. Providing you measured the all-important OG (original gravity) straight after pressing, you will have something to compare it to now. This will confirm if the yeast has or hasn't been working thus far and to what degree, and understanding this informs you if you need to pitch more yeast or not. Pauses or delays in fermentation are often down to temperature (*ie* too cold) and an extended 'yeast lag' (an initial delay after pitching yeast) is not uncommon. Some yeasts work much faster than others so always find out the facts first. Wild yeasts are slower to start and slower to finish, so bear that in mind. Measuring the specific gravity will allow you to track the progress of the fermentation and to confirm how much sugar is left in the cider and only a SG (specific gravity) reading (or a succession of them over a week or so) will tell you if the fermentation really is 'stuck' at a particular level, or is just progressing very slowly. By doing this, it'll help you understand if fermentation has stopped or is still going and what stage the cider has reached. Another cruder method is to taste for sweetness. In most cases, excluding simple temperature issues, preparing and adding a restart culture will fix the problem. Once you know what the specific gravity of your cider is, you can determine what the problem is. For instance, assuming your cider is in the viable temperature

range for yeasts to work, if the gravity hasn't changed at all since you started, the yeast may be dead, in which case it will need restarting. Does it smell bad? It may be that you need to use some yeast nutrient to boost the ability of your yeast to digest the sugars. If you had a very high original gravity (1.060+) and the fermentation has slowed or stopped, it could be that the alcohol levels are too high for the yeast. Temperature could be a factor – too cold and the yeasts will slow to a virtual standstill. Cider can be allowed to freeze over winter outside, and the yeasts will go into hibernation (some types may be killed) but whatever survives should then start up again when the temperatures increases.

RESTARTING A FERMENTATION

Reintroducing yeast to a fermenter is best done carefully and gradually. If you were using a wild yeast, it may be impossible to reintroduce the same mix unless you have a healthy batch from which you can take some. Otherwise, your best option is to inoculate a small amount of boiled, cooled sugar water to which has been added some yeast nutrient and lemon juice. The amount you need will depend on how large a batch you need to restart.

Per 250ml of boiled water, add 10g (two teaspoons) of sugar, allow to cool in a sterilised jar and add the 5ml of lemon juice and a pinch of yeast nutrients. When 27°C or below, add an appropriate wine or cider yeast and keep warm for six hours. You should see some activity by this time in the correct conditions. Add the same amount (250ml) of 'stuck' cider to the fermentation and leave for another six hours. When this is going well and the yeast is clearly working (and reproducing) it can be introduced to the original batch in the hope of kick-starting. If it is a particularly large batch, you may wish to add another 250ml of stuck cider to the new fermentation a few more times, before introducing it back into the original fermenter. A champagne yeast is often particularly good for restarting cultures.

CHAPTER 5
APPLE & CIDER DERIVATIVES

Cider derivatives

You can produce numerous products from the humble apple. If you grow apples for cider, you can pretty much guarantee some will be good for eating too, so you can sell some fresh apples. If you press apples for cider, you can leave some of it as delicious apple juice. If you ferment it, you get cider. If you go one step further and distill the cider, you get cider brandy, and so on.

Apple juice

If you can make cider, you already have the skills to make apple juice, although it will need pasteurising if you don't want it to turn into cider.

Classic dessert apple varieties are used for juicing normally and these ripen much earlier than cider fruit, so it's a chance to warm up the mill and the press before cider making commences. While some of the milder cider apples can be pressed for the bulk of the juice, some of the sharper ones can be used to cut very sweet juice and give it a more refreshing quality. Some classic apples for preserving as juice are Cox's Orange Pippin, Discovery, Ribston Pippin, Egremont Russet, Ashmeads Kernal, Worcester Pearmain and there are SO many more. All dessert apples will taste nice, although some of the more delicate flavours may get lost if blended. Ripeness of fruit is paramount so a good summer will make all the difference. Cleanliness and

sanitation is even more important because there is no alcohol produced throughout the process to counteract any nasties that appear – so be careful. To make sure it's safe from bacteria that can cause illness, make sure you only use unbruised fruit. In particular you want to avoid *patulin*, a mycotoxin commonly found in rotting apples, which would normally be counteracted by the fermentation process.

Once pressed, juice can be preserved by dissolving some ascorbic acid (vitamin C) at a rate of 500 milligrams per litre (5g per 10 litres) or half a teaspoon per gallon, and bottling. Heat the uncapped bottle in a water bath or deep saucepan to 75°C before capping and storing (screw thread is fine), and it should last for a year or so.

Distilling/Cider Brandy

"Civilization begins with distillation"
William Faulkner, *Nobel prize winning novelist*

The earliest record of cider brandy production in Britain is found in John Worlidge's *Vinetum Britannicum: Treatise of Cider*, published in 1676, although it was already well established in Normandy and Spain by then. The evaporative distillation of alcoholic beverages is a fun, but very serious business, which is why you need a licence to do it. It's done by heating cider to various temperatures where the component parts start to vaporise. As the different liquids vaporise at different temperatures, they are collected and cooled. One of the first to vapourise is the alcohol itself and as traditional stills are flame-based, you can see the potential for problems! Different parts – or fractions – of the liquor are kept, recycled or disposed of depending on which component they are and if they are deemed beneficial or not. Some of the distillates (*eg* methanol) are very dangerous and can cause blindness in large doses, others simply taste unpleasant. The traditional way to classify the distillates is into three parts: the heads, the hearts and the tails.

The alcohols with the lowest vapour points are the first to run out from the still and these are known as the 'heads'. These very volatile liquids have an unpleasant aftertaste. The 'hearts' is the good bit – this is what gets barrel-aged before bottling and is made up of a mixture of alcohol and other elements of the original drink. The 'tails' is made up from the remaining liquid and contains both some good and bad parts, so needs careful consideration. It is more aromatic in character but will also be more cloudy and also has some bitter tasting oils in it.

The art of the experienced distiller is knowing when to make the cut between these three stages. The temperatures and ingredients involved increase the likelihood of accidents, but when done carefully by a skilled distiller, it producers some of the most wondrous drinks ever consumed. The hearts are aged in barrels for as little as three years and for as long as people can hold on to it. In 2012 I travelled to a distillery in Normandy and sampled a Calvados from 1939! It takes two types of still to produce cider brandy – the traditional alembic pot still and the continuous column still – and it normally requires the cider from about seven tonnes of apples to make 500 litres of spirit.

The other, much cruder, method of distilling is freeze distillation (illegal in the UK). The basic principle being that alcohol has a much lower freezing point (-114 °C) than water and so when cider is left below 0°C the process will commence. It's a highly unsafe approach as the damaging components that would normally be removed in the heads and tails are left in the liquid that is drunk.

CIDER BRANDY

Most cider-producing regions will have someone distilling cider into a cider brandy, a spirit like any other brandy, about 40% ABV that has wonderful apple flavours and aromas. The first record dates back to about 1554 in northern France, although it's likely people were doing it before that. It's great for sipping after a meal and it's also popular for use in cooking and for cocktails. As part of the cider maker's arsenal it introduces a sense of permanence to your products as it takes time to age. It improves over time and examples can be found throughout France, the UK and USA.

When first run from the stills, it comes out as clear as tap water and is know as *eau de vie*, or 'water of life'. At this stage it feels hot and fiery, it has intense floral aromas but is lighter in flavour than you might imagine. Its use as *eau de vie* is for pickling fruit (such as cherries) or it is bottled alone and used for cooking and cocktail making, although some people do sip a glass of it. The majority of it though is put into oak barrels for ageing and turning into what we know as cider brandy. As any spirit ages in wooden barrels, it decreases in volume through evaporation in what is know as 'the angels' share' and consequently, the colour darkens and flavour concentrates

and mellows. The rich hues we associate with brandy are picked up from the cask itself, the flavours tend to soften and mellow and it loses some of the fieriness associated with *eau de vie* and younger brandies. Great skill and plenty of experience go into ageing cider brandies – aging spirits is an art in itself as each individual cask imparts unique properties to the liquor within. Some barrels are so unique they hold an immeasurable value to the distiller as their influence on their contents is difficult to replicate. Blending is also a key technique at this stage and regular tastings are undertaken to track and anticipate how each batch might be improved.

POMMEAU

Often mistakenly referred to as a fortified wine, Pommeau is actually a *mistelle:* a mixture of fresh sweet, acidic unfermented apple juice blended with a fiery young cider brandy and aged in oak casks to make an aperitif/digestif. It's mostly aged for at least two years to allow flavors to merge and develop further, but often longer. It comes out at around 17% ABV and is deep mahogany in colour. The taste is a wonderful combination of sweet, sharp, slightly musty, earthy apple juice and the intense concentrated flavours from the cider brandy. The ageing accentuates vanilla, butterscotch and caramel flavours, so it's popular to cook with in France and makes a lovely way to begin or end a meal. Traditionally, it's drunk in wine glasses and is a classic accompaniment to melon and foie gras, any number of chocolate or apple desserts, or with a soft cheese selection.

ICE CIDER/*CIDRE DE GLACE*

Pioneered in Canada (based on a dessert wine from Germany) this cider derivative takes influence from ice wine and is also now produced all over the world. In precise conditions, the apples are allowed to freeze. This has the effect of 'cooking' the juice, condensing its flavour when pressed as much of the water content stays frozen and will be separated in production. There are two methods of producing ice cider – cryoextraction and cryoconcentration. Cryoextraction is harder to do because it involves leaving apples on the trees to dehydrate and freeze before being picked, crushed and fermented for several months. Cryoconcentraion is far more widespread because it's easier to manage and guarantee. Ripe apples are picked and crushed, then the must is allowed to freeze to remove enough of the water. It's a process that makes ice cider more expensive, but a bottle of it makes a really special treat to share on special occasions.

VINEGAR

A by-product of cider production is vinegar and most artisan cider producers will also make good artisan vinegar. If a fermentation should fail or spoil, the best alternative is to aim for good vinegar. It's a popular and healthy product used in every household, though every cider maker I know houses the production of the two products as physically far apart as they can in case one should spoil the other! Good vinegar is a wonderful thing and great cider vinegar is a special find: dark, rich, sweet and complex enough to rival balsamic. Traditionally it's made slowly and the process can take months. It has a host of culinary and medicinal uses as it's beneficial for your digestive system, and also many people find it beneficial in their skincare regime.

Making vinegar

Chefs love good vinegar and will go to great lengths to select the best ones for their kitchen. Good cider vinegar is held in high regard. It's fairly simple to make if you have the patience and enough space to dedicate to it and is as fascinating a process as fermentation.

If you want to make cider vinegar, you will need to be both strict and to break a few cider-making rules. Apple juice, if left uncovered and exposed to the air, will always ferment naturally then start to turn into vinegar. It won't even be a nice vinegar, as it could contain a plethora of organisms that have no use to cider or vinegar production so if you intend to make cider vinegar, you should be using a cider that has been fermented properly and with care.

You need to do it in an area far from your cider production, somewhere out of the wind and cold where you can set up a traditional system. It's fairly simple but it can be a lengthy process to get things really moving.

THE PROCESS

Using a wooden barrel, fill it three-quarters full with a fully-fermented cider of about 6–7% ABV that hasn't been sulphited. In order for the cider to turn, it has to be exposed to the air so the bung hole is left unplugged to allow the air in. Covering it with hessian, sack cloth or a gauze is a good idea as it will keep the flies out. It needs to be exposed to the air so acetic acid bacteria (*acetobacter*) can access the liquid and work their magic. From the moment it is exposed to the air, the process will start. To speed it up you can obtain a starter culture from an existing vinegar – known as a mother – or even start your own.

MOTHER

This is the jellylike substance that floats on top of the liquid as vinegar is made. It is a gelatinous mat of cellulose that the *acetobactor* produce to hold themselves against the surface where the air they need is plentiful. Once this is established, you can make vinegar with greater ease and with more consistency by transferring the mother to a new batch of cider and repeating the process. It becomes a starter culture that you need to turn cider into vinegar.

MAKING A STARTER CULTURE

There are two ways to make a starter culture and both are fairly straightforward.

1 In an open jar, place a 75% cider/25% vinegar mix in a warm, dark place with a thin layer of hessian over the top for as many weeks as it takes for a 'mother' to form.
2 When cider making, collect some freshly pressed apple juice in a jar and keep it somewhere warm and dark for two weeks. The normal cider-making process will ensure it ferments naturally after which it will start to turn. When it starts to smell strongly of vinegar, it means the juice should now contain a significant amount of *acetobacter,* which are then added to a batch of cider or even spare juice.

Cider vinegar – the health benefits

Hugely fashionable in Hollywood as part of an uber-healthy lifestyle, cider vinegar is less appreciated as an aid to wellbeing in the UK. It is proposed to have an array of health benefits when included as part of a healthy diet or even taken daily as a general tonic.

Drinking a regular preparation is said to help improve (and in some cases totally remove) joint pain associated with conditions such as gout or arthritis.

Phenolics (from the tannins found in cider apple skin) have antioxidant properties when consumed and so are beneficial in helping prevent things like heart disease, diabetes and cancer. Traditional West Country real cider (100% juice) contains very high levels of tannin, so a good quality vinegar should be sourced from a traditional producer.

It also has uses outside the body to aid numerous skin and hair conditions too such as alleviating sunburn and treating acne.

Many people also use a cider vinegar to treat problems in their animals and it's popular with owners of horses, dogs and poultry.

Preparation:

For general everyday benefits, drink the following before eating food (up to 3 times a day.)
Mix 2 teaspoons of cider vinegar with 4 tablespoons of water.

For the treatment of more serious cases:
Mix 2 tablespoons of cider vinegar to 4 tablespoons of water.

Some honey can be added to either preparation to adjust the flavour if desired.

Keep your distance

Acetobacter are fatal to good cider so be absolutely sure to keep them well away from (and downwind of) any cider production you have going. They are, however, essential for vinegar production and so the potential for cross-contamination must be taken seriously. Be sure to thoroughly sterilise anything that may have been in both areas of operation. Never use the same equipment for making cider and vinegar or you will likely only end up making vinegar! If you want to move some cider in order to turn it into vinegar then rack it off from the fermenter/storage vessel (and you can do so without too much caution) into a separate vessel and then use that vessel as a temporary go between in which to move it into a vinegar barrel/production area so as to avoid cross-contamination.

Once set up, the bacteria should start to work naturally. The rule of thumb for conversion of alcohol to acetic acid is about 1% alcohol per week in warm conditions, so a 7% cider will take about seven to eight weeks.

When it is ready, two-thirds of what is in the barrel is drawn off for bottling and then replaced with fresh cider and the cycle is repeated again.

BALSAMIC CIDER VINEGAR

If you want to age your vinegar significantly and make something akin to the style of a dark rich balsamic vinegar, the process is slightly different and will need to be repeated annually for years to achieve something wonderful. Using the same mother each year following this technique, the vinegar will be darker, richer and more complex.

Imagine a cellar with about 20 barrels each containing vinegar, some of which is 10 years old and some of which was cider only a year ago. The traditional method to age and produce a balsamic vinegar is to top up the empty space in the oldest barrel (created by evaporation and also by drawing-off vinegar for bottling) by adding as much of the second oldest batch to it as possible, until it is nearly full. The third oldest batch is then used to top up the second oldest batch; the fourth oldest is used to top up the third oldest; the fifth to top off the fourth and so on, with the newest batch being topped up with cider vinegar or fresh juice.

The amount you draw off annually will determine how much you can use or sell, and it's entirely up to you. Too much and your process will lose some consistency, not enough and you won't have much to use, so for the first few years of production as little as possible will ensure a healthy stock for the future. However much you choose, there must *always* be some vinegar left behind to carry the process on, the oldest vinegar having the richest flavour and best aged qualities that you will want to carry over into the next batch.

In Modena, the home of Balsamic vinegar, this process has to be repeated for 12 years and then certified by a consortium of traditional vinegar producers before it can be sold as officially recognised traditional balsamic vinegar of Modena.

Their principal difference is the use of sweet, fresh grape juice that is boiled and condensed significantly prior to a fermentation, concentrating its richness and certainly making

a sweeter vinegar. The concentrated juice is added to a barrel in the same way a cider would be, and the mother from a previous/existing batch is blended into it to begin the process. Boiling fresh juice prior to starting vinegar making has the bonus of condensing the juice, but also of driving off any existing volatile acids (like acetic acid) and it will allow your mother culture to exert total influence over it. Non-volatile acids (such as malic acid) will remain. Another difference is the scale of production, as it requires the use of more barrels in which to age the must/vinegar. As it does so, the must evaporates and condenses further, so needs topping up annually. Sweet fresh juice could be used for vinegar production too in a similar way, but I think most cider makers would much rather use their hard-earned precious juice for cider making, or they would be vinegar makers!

CHAPTER 6
USEFUL STUFF

Cider appreciation

There are no rights and wrongs when enjoying your favourite tipple – pleasure is subjective after all – but if you want to get the most out of your cider or develop a greater understanding of flavour, technique, *terroir,* and so on, there are some simple ways to get the best from it.

Keeping anything cold will help preserve it and serving anything cold will add a degree of cool refreshment but too cold and it will mask some of the subtle flavors and aromas that you'll want to appreciate. 'Slightly chilled' or 'cellar temperature' is the best way to describe the temperature to serve cider, somewhere around 10–12°C. Much colder and you won't be getting the most out of it.

A tulip-shaped wine glass to serve a fine sparkling perry will offer you scope to look through it, swirl it and savour its aroma, before sipping it and rolling it around your mouth. Whereas a sturdier flat farmhouse might be more appreciated by the pint in a handmade stoneware mug.

When pouring (or decanting), be it a bottle or a flagon, try to aerate the cider as it pours. Introducing air to it has the effect of driving off any sulphites, livening up the flavours and aromas. Try to wait 30 seconds after pouring before taking a sniff or swig. If your cider is too warm, chill a glass in the freezer rather than adding ice, which will dilute it.

What is flavour?

This is a question we should all ask ourselves once as discerning adults. Flavour is basically the sensory impression of food and drink determined mainly by the chemical senses of taste and aroma – the two working together to bring us what we call flavour.

When analysing a cider or perry, we start with our eyes by examining the colour and opacity of the juice. We note carbonation and look for body, clinging to the glass. Next we smell it, often swirling it around to release its volatile scents and introduce more oxygen to the liquid. If there are any sulphites present, this helps drive them away, so I tend to do this a little longer with a new bottle. Often the aroma is more unexpected than you think. If a cider or perry has been made and allowed to sit on the lees for a significant period of time, the aromas are more likely to be complex. Really wonderful aromas can hold you captivated for several minutes before you've even had a sip. Bouquet and aroma are terms used interchangeably and are made up by both volatile and non-volatile compounds. The variety of aromas you can detect in your cider and perry tasting will be varied.

The first taste is important to note, but be aware, our mouths adjust over the course of a glass, so pay attention to any changes. Our tongues have different areas on them to register different tastes: sweetness, saltiness, sourness and bitterness, so make a mental note about what's happening on your tongue. I always find enough of a glug to cover the tongue wholly gives you a good start. The texture inside our mouth is referred to as mouthfeel. This is predominately looked at in terms of body (how thick or thin the liquid is) and the puckery effect on the cheeks and tongue from the tannins.

Finally, there is the aftertaste. When the drink is swallowed, you can determine the overall 'shape' of the flavour – some drinks will have a long finish while others will disappear rather quickly.

The more varied the cider you can taste from different parts of the world made in different styles, the better you get at naming the aromas and tastes that make up the flavor. Some of the descriptors will come as a surprise to people because they will generally never have considered certain smells or tastes to be seen as positive, and to some people, they won't be.

Cider blogger Dave White from Old Time Cider (www.oldtimecider.com) has compiled a list of descriptors broken down into 11 areas that help describe some of the flavours you may encounter:

FRUITY

Citrus: grapefruit, lemon, orange, tangerine, zesty
Berry: blackberry, raspberry, strawberry, blackcurrant (cassis)
Pome: cherry, rainier cherry, apricot, peach, nectarine, apple
Tropical: pineapple, melon, banana
Dried/preserved fruit: strawberry jam, raisins, prune, fig, winey

HERBACEOUS/VEGETAL

Fresh: stemmy, cut green grass, grassy, sweet grass, herb, bell pepper, eucalyptus, mint
Canned/cooked: green beans, asparagus, green olive, black olive, artichoke
Dried: tea, tobacco, hay, straw

FLORAL

Orange blossom, blossom, rose, violet, geranium

SPICY

Cloves, black pepper, licorice, anise

NUTTY

Walnut, hazelnut, almond

SUGAR

Honey, caramel, butterscotch, toffee, candy, baked, honey, butter, soy sauce, chocolate, molasses

WOODY

Vanilla, cedar, camphor, oaky, smoke, burnt toast, charred, fire, coffee

EARTHY

Mushroom, farm, barnyard, musty (mildew), mouldy cork, mould, dusty

CHEMICAL

Petroleum: tar, plastic, kerosene, diesel
Sulfur: rubbery, garlic, skunk, cabbage, burnt match
Animal: wet wool, wet dog
Papery: wet cardboard
Pungent: acetic acid (vinegar)
Other: soapy, fishy

PUNGENT

Hot: alcohol.   Cool: menthol

MICROBIOLOGICAL

Yeasty, sauerkraut, sweaty, horsey, mousey, banana skin, vinegar, sulfuric, medicinal, band aid, decay

The orchardist and cider maker's year

While each season is different, there is a monthly outline of what apple growers and cider makers can be doing. Any cider maker (or anyone who is lucky enough to own an orchard) will tell you how important it is to spend time among the trees regularly to keep abreast of the season.

Some years, apples will be early, others late. Some years will bring pests, others bumper crops and the only real way to know exactly what's going on is to be there. Therefore the duties mentioned here may extend to adjacent months. Regular visits will tune you in to what to prepare for next.

NB: These dates may be out by up to a month depending on each particular season, and are intended as guidelines and reminders only. Note-taking will help you learn more about your fruit/orchards and cider making than a book can ever teach you!

Month	Apples	Cider
January	In the UK, pruning apple trees is traditionally done in January. Wassail!	Check gravities, prepare/start racking. Wassail!
February	Finish pruning Last chance to plant new trees	A good time for racking and final blending – blend any lower acidity batches with higher acidity ones to help prevent ropiness. Top up any casks that need it to reduce airspace.
March	Start early spraying if you want to prevent scab, etc	Keep an eye on ambient temperatures, watch for start of MLF. Top up any casks that need it to reduce airspace.
April		Final racking and bottling
May	Blossom time – get the sun out and the bees in!	If bottle-conditioning, pasteurise to cease all further activity
June	Check fruit set – earliest suggestion of crop size Watch for pests and disease	Check any unpasteurised, high-gravity ciders and take action
July	Pick out highest lateral buds on young trees to encourage feathering	Check any unpasteurised, high-gravity ciders and take action
August	Need good healthy leaves on your trees for next year's flower buds to be set now	
September	Remove livestock from orchard	Preparation! This is your chance to prepare all equipment, double-check cleanliness, valves/seals, sharpness, *etc*. Clean and re-sterilise all casks/fermenting vessels
October	Start to collect early fruit, sweating fruit.	Pressing season begins
November	Continue collecting fruit	Watch out for warm weather as gravities can drop fast
December	Finish collecting	Finish pressing any fruit, deep clean and sterilise equipment for storage. Initial racking of sweet ciders or excessively vigorous ones may be neccesary

Rules and regulations of selling to the public in the UK

DUTY & HMRC

If you decide you want to sell your cider to the public, you need to learn and follow the rules as set out by HMRC, Trading Standards and Environmental Health. It may seem daunting at first but each body is there to help traders as well as regulate the industry. You need to register as a cider maker, and apply to take advantage of the exemption from duty. This will involve a visit to ensure you don't have big tanks hiding anywhere!

LICENSING

Both your local Planning office and Environmental Health office will need notifying and questioning about trading with the public. If you want to sell or supply alcohol (or authorise the sale or supply of alcohol) you must apply for a *personal licence.* Without a personal licence to sell alcohol, you are limited to selling your cider to premises licence holders only (pubs and festivals *etc*) but not direct to the public. You have a responsibility to check that each licence holder actually has a licence.

If you want to sell or supply alcohol on a permanent basis, you need to apply for a premises licence. A premises licence authorises the use of any premises for licencable activities.

HM Revenue & Customs

HMRC Reference:

Notice 162

Cider production

is this notice about?

notice explains the effects of the law and regulations co
ction, storage and accounting for duty on cider and per

 we say 'cider' in this notice, we include perry and pea
 notice contains various technical terms, you may find
ry helpful - see section 30.

ects of the law and

Temporary events notices

You may apply for a temporary events notice (TEN) in certain cases. If you're organising or attending a temporary event and want to serve or sell alcohol, provide late-night refreshment, or put on regulated entertainment, you'll need to complete a temporary event notice.

A TEN is a form that you provide to the local council, the police and environmental health, letting them know about the planned event.

There are two types of TENs:
 1. A standard TEN, which is given no later than ten working days before the event to which it relates.
2. A late TEN, which is given not before nine and not later than five working days before the event.
See here for more: **https://www.gov.uk/alcohol-licensing**

If you hold a personal licence, you are allowed to sell direct to the public from a registered premises.

TEN guidelines
- You will need a TEN for each event you hold on the same premises.
- You can get up to five TENs a year. If you already have a personal licence to sell alcohol, you can be given up to 50 TENs a year.
- A single premises can have up to 12 notices applied for in one year, as long as the total length of the events is not more than 21 days and one person doesn't make more than five applications for the premises.

Late TENs
You can apply for a late TEN up to five working days before the event. You can apply for up to ten late TENs per calendar year. If you are organising separate but consecutive events, there must be at least a 24-hour gap between them.

If you don't hold a personal licence, you can serve up to five notices (of which up to two may be late). If you hold a personal licence, the limit is 50 notices (of which up to ten may be late).

ENVIRONMENTAL HEALTH

The Food Safety Act requires cider makers selling cider to register as a food production business with their local District Council Environmental Health Department. A basic food hygiene certificate is probably a good idea as it'll bring about a greater understanding of the risks involved with cider making and how to prevent transfer of any problems throughout the process *etc*. Much of it will seem obvious after the care and attention you already give to ensuring your cider is sound and healthy, but it will open your mind to environmental health issues and views on best practice *etc*.

A very good document to have a copy of is *HACCP: Hazard and Critical Control Point Analysis*. It shows that you're thinking about the problems that could occur; how you intend to stop that problem occurring; how you will identify if that problem has occurred and what you will do to fix the problem and so on.

TRADING STANDARDS

Trading Standards are mostly concerned with weights and measures, and ensuring your customers are getting what they think they are getting. Accurate measuring and filling is important to them because it's their job to protect the public from unscrupulous businesses – under-filling casks or pints being a classic example. They too may want to see records regarding starting gravities and final gravities *etc,* so check your cider is as alcoholic as you say it is.

LABELLING

Both Trading Standards and the Food Standards Agency dictate the rules of labelling in the UK and as they change frequently, it's best to look into legal requirements regularly. Basically, it's a case of being clear and honest about what's in your cider. If you've made it well, you should be proud of its ingredients and want to display that fact. See here for more: http://food.gov.uk/business-industry/guidancenotes/labelregsguidance

CUSTOMS AND EXCISE

When selling it, Customs and Excise will require you to list every drop of cider you make (even if you end up discarding it for whatever reason) so accurate record keeping is even more important in that regard.

The good news is that, currently, anyone is allowed to produce and sell up to 70 hectolitres per year without having to pay any duty. Although you do need to register with them, and you do that by reading Notice 162 and applying to register. Notice 162 is a 68-page document produced by HMRC specifically for cider makers who want to sell directly to the public. It describes the legalities and regulations governing small-scale cider production and your obligations as a cider maker.

There are more rules and guidelines that affect your responsibilities and duty payment than I can print here, so it's important to familiarise yourself with those that will affect you. HMRC have helplines and booklets to guide you. Outside the UK, rules and regulations regarding packaging and labelling are very different so anyone hoping to export needs to do their research thoroughly.

Calculating duty

Duty is calculated on cider as soon as it is removed from registered premises.

HMRC duty rates:

Flat cider & perry	1.2%–7.5%abv	£39.66 per hectolitre
	7.5%–8.5%abv	£59.52 per hectolitre
Sparkling cider & perry	1.2%–5.5% abv	£39.66 per hectolitre
	5.5%–8.5% abv	£258.23 per hectolitre.

NB: These are altered annually and could be out of date. Please check with HMRC for current duty figures. HMRC alcohol duty rates can be found at: http://www.hmrc.gov.uk/rates/alcohol-duty.htm

Any cider or perry over 8.5% is considered a wine or made wine and taxed even higher.

The following examples are given by HMRC and taken from section 5.11 notice 162.

Unless HMRC has permitted the use of an alternative methodology that does not disadvantage the revenue, you must work out each constituent stage of the calculation process to a minimum of four decimal places. In order to complete the EX 606 cider duty return declaration, you must round down the quantity of cider to the nearest whole litre.

See the following examples:

(a) 155 cases of still cider, each containing 12 x 500ml x 7% abv

12 x 500ml = 6 litres per case
6 x 155 = 930 litres in total
930 x duty rate of *£0.3966 = £368.838, rounded down to £368.83

*This is the hectolitre duty rate of £39.66 converted to litres for the purposes of completing the duty return.

(b) 237 cases of sparkling cider, each containing 12 x 568ml x 4.5% abv

12 x 568ml = 6.816 litres per case
6.816 x 237 = 1615.392 litres in total
1615 x duty rate of £0.3966 = £640.509, rounded down to £640.50

(c) 419 x 3 litre container of still cider x 7.3% abv

419 x 3 = 1257 litres in total
1257 x duty rate of £0.3966 = £498.5262 rounded down to £498.52

For the adventurous, inventive and frugal cider makers out there, you can always consider making your own kit. It's fun but can take longer than you think so make sure things are ready and working <u>and tested</u> before you need to press!

The following extracts have kindly been donated by fellow cider enthusiasts and serve to show the passion and philanthropy many of us have for helping people get started in cider making. The mill design and instructions are taken from the UK cider website (www.ukcider.co.uk) and was kindly donated by Nigel Cox of Marches Cyder Circle. It's an account of his experience and methodology upon deciding to build his own apple mill.

The press design and instructions are from Mark Evens of North Cumbria Orchard Group. Reading through them shows you just how creative you can be with your ideas, design and approach. It's a great example of the resourcefulness and attitude many cider makers share.

How to make a homemade cider scratter (apple mill)

© NIGEL COX, Marches Cyder Circle

The Codling Grinder was conceived from the outset as a low-budget project, largely using materials that my wife and I had by us, or could obtain at little or no cost. We honed our scrounging skills to perfection along the way, and it became a real challenge to keep expenditure to a minimum. We paid those that contributed in materials or labour with the best of our 2005 liquid gold. We found, time and again, that people, once they knew what crackpot device we were attempting to construct, were more than happy to help out and become involved.

The layout of the Codler is basically a wooden chassis, supporting at one end an electric motor, driving, in the middle, a rotating wooden drum which is surmounted by a plywood hopper. Fruit is chucked into the hopper via an optional sorting tray (more on this later) and is shredded against the front hopper wall by the studded drum. It then emerges beneath as a finely milled pulp ready for the press. Simple. In its basic form, the Codler could be supported on two chairs/trestles above a collecting vessel and fed directly by the bucketful. We decided to refine this by making a stand for the unit and also a fruit-sorting tray, which has proved invaluable, but, if you want to keep yours simple, you can.

THE CHASSIS

Basically, two pieces of timber joined together at the right distance (200mm + in our case) to accept the drum between. We used [7.6 x 5cm] 3 x 2in, as that was what we had; [7.6 x 7.6cm] 3 x 3in would be better. On one end a deck is made to support the motor and on/off switch. A piece of robust plywood forms the front wall (motor side) of the hopper and descends between the main timbers where it is backed by

▲ The scratter ready to press.

a stout cross-member to form the 'crushing face'. Another cross-member runs just behind where the drum will turn, this forms the rear, lower face of the crushing chamber. We used old pallet wood and stainless-steel screws where necessary, we also faced the lower portion of the front hopper panel with stainless plate that we had cut from an old fire extinguisher.

THE MOTOR

We used a 240V single-phase motor of 0.5 horse power, giving 1425rpm. For a (200mm) 8-inch drum this is just right – if you can get a 0.75hp or a 1hp motor, go for it, you could then easily drive a larger drum if you wished. We scrounged our motor, but £25–£50 is normal on ebay, if you simply must use coin of the realm. Car boot sales might be cheaper still. Try to get one with a pulley already on.

▼ The scratter.

▼ The drum.

▼ The motor.

▲ Stainless steel screws ready to insert.

▲ Drive belt and pulleys.

THE DRUM

This is the only bit you're not going to find knocking about – you'll have to get one made. We used sycamore wood for ours, this does not split easily when seasoned and was traditionally used for the rollers on the machines used in the British textile industry. If it was good enough for the mills of the North West, then it's good enough for us. Our drum is 200mm long by 150mm diameter and has a 25mm hole through its centre to accommodate the shaft. Your local tree surgeon will no doubt have a bit of sycamore in his yard; our log cost £2.50. Then it's round to your local woodturner to get it made into something useful (ours cost £10), but make sure the log's seasoned or he'll get drenched turning it! Once you have your lovely smooth drum, you need to 'stud' it. We used [3.2cm] 1¼in No.8 countersunk stainless woodscrews for this. Screw them in so they project no more than about 6mm (make a depth gauge from a lolly stick to help you). The screw pattern you adopt is important. Aim to have a 'cut' every 5mm across the length of your drum, at least twice per 360° rotation. Stagger the screws accordingly in the pattern that pushes buttons for you. Arrowhead pattern, tractor tyre pattern, it doesn't matter. Be artistic. Every 5mm though.

DRIVE BELT AND PULLEYS

Someone you know will have an old car fan belt hanging up in their garage… pulley size affects the RPM of the drum shaft. Here's the formula:

$$\frac{\text{Drive pulley diameter} \times \text{motor RPM}}{\text{load pulley diameter}}$$

In our case it was 2¾in x 1425rpm divided by 4½in, giving 870rpm at the drum. This seems plenty and does the apples a treat. Our load pulley is a three-speed type, we use the large (slower) one, but we can increase speed if needs be by moving the belt over and adjusting tension at the motor end. Make sure your pulley alignment is okay and the belt tight, but not overtight.

BEARINGS

These fasten to the chassis using coach bolts. Use 'plummer block' bearings with an inside diameter (ID) to match your drum shaft (25mm in our case). Ours were not stainless, but as they sit outside the hopper and are well painted, juice contact is really minimal if not non-existent. Cost to us: £20 the pair from a local bearing stockist. On ebay you pay about the same (with postage) and you have to wait for the right size to come up too!

DRUMSHAFT

For this you need a nice piece of stainless rod (we used 25mm solid, 20mm might have done just as well). Unless you're an ace scrounger like us (well, Sharon really!) buying a short piece of this could cost you about £30. Remember that the shaft diameter, bearing ID, and hole in your drum must all be the same. If your loadside pulley won't fit, have it bored out or the shaft end turned down at your local engineering shop (this was more scrumpy expenditure for us). We also had a small stainless flange welded to the shaft (£10), so that when the drum was pushed on, we could screw it to the flange, thereby stopping the drum from rotating on the shaft rather than with it when in use. In practice this may not have been necessary as the sycamore was a very tight fit anyway. Very nerve-wracking knocking the blessed thing on with a wooden mallet and hoping it won't split! It's possible a stainless steel pipe as used by plumbers in bathrooms might be an alternative you could use. Could work out cheaper and should be strong enough.

THE HOPPER

The sides and rear of the hopper were made from plywood and screwed to the chassis inboard of the bearings. Fit a steep rear slope within to guide the fruit decisively onto the all-consuming rotating drum. If you are not going to use the sorting tray and small cover arrangement as we did, you will need to make a full cover. The apple bits fly everywhere.

◀ The hopper.

THE STAND

Made from old pallets, enough said. Make it large enough to accept a large collecting vessel beneath it, as a bucket ain't big enough when the Codler lets rip!

THE SORTING TRAY

This is great. You load your washed fruit into it for further inspection prior to milling. Pick out all the really grotty ones easily. Make a support stand that gives a slight 'fall' to the apples. The business end locates over and into the hopper, secured by battens attached underneath. Don't forget a removable bridge piece at the outlet into the hopper.

THE ELECTRICS

A motor of the sort of size discussed here (0.5–1hp) will run from a UK 13-amp socket. Fit an RCD safety plug top to your flex. This is better than the adaptor type, as it is hardwired to the machine and there can be no temptation to operate without protection because you can't be bothered to get the RCD adaptor from the shed! Fit a splashproof on/off switch to IP54 or 55. Use a double-pole type – with these there's no danger if our budding sparky gets the polarity wrong, they break Live & Neutral. You'll get one of these from an electrical wholesaler (don't worry, they love to sell to the public over the trade counter – about a tenner). Make sure the motor and switch are effectively earthed.

GENERAL

When assembling your Codler, the crucial measurement is between the drum screws and the lower portion of the hopper front wall. Set this at 1–2mm clearance. All other dimensions will relate to belt length, pulley sizes, *etc*. Fit the Drum/Shaft/Bearing/loadpulley assembly first, then work to that.

PERFORMANCE

The Codler gets through 25kg sacks of apples in no time at all (I will time things when next we use it… if memory doesn't fail). The pulp comes out as fine as that out of professionally made machines I have seen and used, and is well suitable for the next stage in its journey… the press!

THE SKIRT

The skirt directs the pulp more directly into your collection bucket and was made with a square flip-top kitchen waste bin with the bottom half cut away and the removable top discarded. We melted some holes in it for cable ties to pass through, enabling it to be fastened to the cup hooks on the Codler.

SAFETY

If in doubt about the electrics, consult a sparky [electrician].
If you have kiddiwinks about, box-in the pulley/belt area. Never put your hands into the hopper while in operation. Bits of you can enter the pulp and taint the cyder… not good that.

▼ The skirt.

▼ The sorting tray.

▼ The crew.

How to make your own press

© **MARK EVENS, North Cumbria Orchard Group**

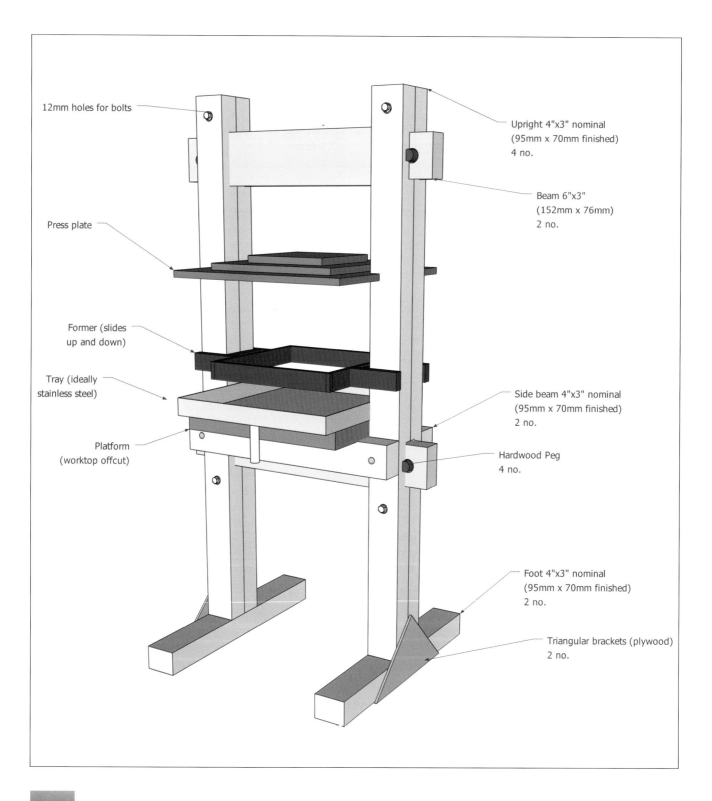

12mm holes for bolts

Press plate

Former (slides
up and down)

Tray (ideally
stainless steel)

Platform
(worktop offcut)

Upright 4"x3" nominal
(95mm x 70mm finished)
4 no.

Beam 6"x3"
(152mm x 76mm)
2 no.

Side beam 4"x3" nominal
(95mm x 70mm finished)
2 no.

Hardwood Peg
4 no.

Foot 4"x3" nominal
(95mm x 70mm finished)
2 no.

Triangular brackets (plywood)
2 no.

WHY BUILD YOUR OWN PRESS?

Cost: A Vigo rack-and-screw cloth press costs approximately £695. This takes 40kg apples in one pressing. My press is a similar capacity and costs about £250–£350 (plus time).

Customisable: You can make your own press to suit your requirements, *eg* add castors, make it 'knock-down' for transportability, *etc*.

Size: You can choose the size. It doesn't make sense to make a small one as a larger one doesn't cost much more. If you want a smaller one (less than about 40kg) then a basket-type press may make more sense than a rack-and-cloth press (Vigo 20L cross-beam press is a good example at approximately £345). A basket press is harder to make than a rack-and-cloth press. The design will scale up fairly well, but you'll need to use appropriate scaling factors (they're not all linear).

Maintenance: If you built it, you know how to fix it if it breaks. Also you can add extra bells and whistles later.

Overall design: See diagram opposite. A key feature is that the sides are used to ensure that the cheeses get built vertically.

SPECIFICATIONS

Tray size

The tray size is what determines the span of the top beam. Bear in mind that you need to leave at least [5cm] 2in all the way round the cheeses, to the inside edge of the tray, so that juice drips into the tray, not on the floor. If you are buying the tray rather than making it, it would be sensible to do this before finalising the size of your press.

Jack size

Jacks come in a variety of sizes, exercising from 2 to 40 tons of force. Larger jacks will give better performance (approx 5 percentage points more extraction for each doubling of force, up to a point) but you need the frame to be more sturdily built. Around 8 tons is a good size for a 16in cheese – beyond that and the additional cost is not justified by the additional yield.

Materials

Main choice is between wood and steel. Both will work. Mine is from wood, because I can work wood. It's also easier for the novice to make. However, stainless steel for the tray is best if you can get it.

Top beam

This is the most critical item as it takes a lot of strain. Main risks are snapping in the middle, bending sideways and tearing at the joints. Stress calculations and joint construction are critical.

Stress calculations

So we need to calculate the size of the top beam (in wood). First, some definitions:

F = the allowable fibre stress (*ie* how strong the wood is)
b = the width of the beam
d = the depth of the beam
l = the span of the beam (between the supports)

Now some sums

Max load at the centre of the beam $= P = \dfrac{Fbd^2}{kl}$

…where k is a constant which depends on the units used. For imperial units, $k = 1.5$.

Observe that the max load goes up with the square of the depth of the beam. So, if you double the length, then you only need to increase the depth by about 50% to sustain the same load. However, you also need to consider the deflection of the beam, which depends on the 'modulus of elasticity' of the wood, rather than its strength. If E = the modulus of elasticity, then:

Deflection of the beam $= y = K\ \dfrac{P}{E}\ \dfrac{l^3}{bd^3}$

(where K is another constant: 0.25 for imperial units)

Now observe that the deflection goes up with the cube of the span and down with the cube of the depth, so if we double the span but only increase the depth by 50%, the deflection will increase by $(^2/_{1.5})^3 = 2.37$ *ie*, more than twice the deflection.

Whether or not this matters depends on the absolute numbers involved, but it is also worth noting that sideways deflection may also be important. If the beam is too narrow, then any off-centre deflection of the jack will apply a sideways load which may bend the beam: the sideways load will then increase and risk of snapping the beam sideways (or permanently bending a metal beam).

So much for the theory, what about some actual numbers?

Wood	Fibre stress propn'l limit (psi)	Modulus of rupture (psi)	Modulus of elasticity (psi *10)
Oak	8000	14000	1.60
Ash	8900	15400	1.77
Pine	6500	9800	1.34

The FSPL is the limit beyond which damage will occur, although it won't actually break until the pressure reaches the modulus of rupture. From this it is clear that ash is the best wood, being both stronger and more elastic. This is why it is used in longbows. Oak is good, but it is important to make sure that the grain is reasonably straight and free of big knots. Pine is a poorer choice, particularly if it has knots, which will reduce the strength. It will therefore need to be larger than an ash or oak beam. We will use the FSPL in our calculations.

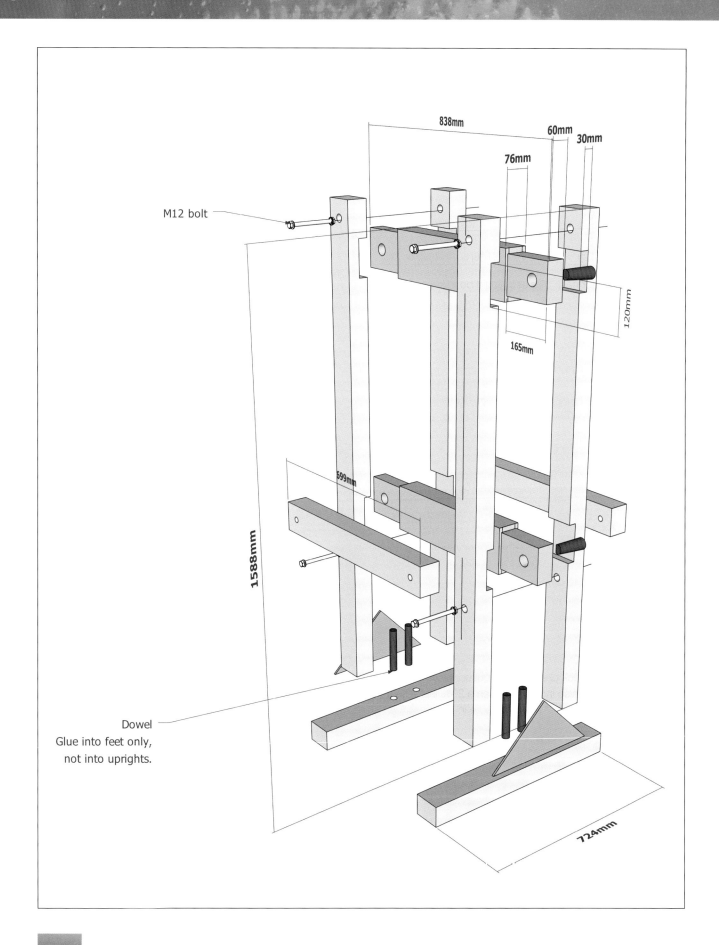

838mm

60mm

30mm

76mm

M12 bolt

120mm

165mm

699mm

1588mm

Dowel
Glue into feet only,
not into uprights.

724mm

A typical [15.2cm] 6in beam (the size of mine in oak) should support almost 13 tons, if it is free of defects and has a straight grain. I use an 8-ton jack, so that sounds more than enough, but my beam is not straight or knot-free. To make the ash and pine beams to the same strength, we would adjust the depths as follows:

Wood	Beam 1 Span [cm] inch	Depth [cm] inch	Width [cm] inch	Max load (ton)
Oak	[50.8] 20	[15.2] 6	[7.6] 3	12.9
Ash	[50.8] 20	[14.5] 5.7	[7.6] 3	12.9
Pine	[50.8] 20	[17] 6.7	[7.6] 3	12.9

The deflection for each of these would be:

Wood	Beam 1 Span [cm] inch	Depth [cm] inch	Width [cm] inch	Deflection [cm] inch
Oak	[50.8] 20	[15.2] 6	[7.6] 3	[0.15] 0.06
Ash	[50.8] 20	[14.5] 5.7	[7.6] 3	[0.15] 0.06
Pine	[50.8] 20	[17] 6.7	[7.6] 3	[0.13] 0.05

As can be seen, the deflection in all cases is fairly low. Some further calculations along these lines show that if using pine 1in thick, you would need a depth of 10.6in. If the load started to go sideways on this beam, then it would soon deflect sideways and exceed the sideways load of 1 ton.

For all of these reasons [15.2 x 7.6cm] 6 x 3in is a reasonable size for a [50.8cm] 20in beam, but is the bare minimum if using (good quality) pine and an 8-ton jack.

Note that if the press is made larger (say, an extra 4in wide), then the rack size will increase by 4in, from 16in to 20in. The area of the cheeses will increase by the square of the increase in width from 256in^2 to 400in^2 – a factor of 1.5625. To maintain the same pressure, a 12.5-ton jack will be needed. To cope with this and the longer beam, at the same safety margin, a depth of 8.5in is needed (assuming still 3in wide). So a 20% increase in beam span requires a 25% increase in depth, assuming the same jack pressure is required. However, if the width of the beam is also increased, then a 20% increase all round works. This is because the pressure in the press (Q) is equal to the force (P) divided by the area (A). ie Q= P/A. Assuming the width of the cheeses is proportional to the span of the beam (say about ¾ of the span), then A= (0.75L)^2 so Q=P/(0.75L)^2. So, double the span requires four times the force. Four times the force requires the beam to be twice as deep and doubling the span can be offset by doubling the thickness, so everything multiplies up by two except for the force which goes up by four times.

All of these calculations are a bit approximate. The intention is to illustrate the complexity of getting the stress calculation right, particularly if departing significantly from the usual size for this type of press. For a significantly larger press, a different design (eg, twin screw) is probably more appropriate, since otherwise the top beam size and jack size get unwieldly.

Choosing a Jack

I have found that an 8-ton jack with a [38cm] 15in cheese width gives a good level of juice yield (about 70%), using a good mill, such as a Vigo. Doubling the pressure might increase yield by about 5%. A 2-ton jack will give about 60%.

Jack (tons)	Cheese [cm] inch	Pressure (psi)	Yield	Approx Cost
2	[40] 16	18	60%	£10
8	[40] 16	70	70%	£22
20	[61] 24	78	71%	£42

MATERIALS

Frame

Wood construction, but ideally ash for the top beam. The rest of the frame can be softwood. The bottom beam can be sized a bit less than the top beam since the load is spread evenly, however, mine is the same size.

Platform

The platform under the tray needs to resist bending – worktop cut-offs are good, or several layers of ply or MDF.

Tray

Mine is stainless steel, fabricated to measure. My first one was just wooden – need to seal the corners well.

Press plate

Built up from three pieces of 12mm ply.

Racks

They don't need to be fancy like the Vigo ones – they can just be of plain plywood, or (better) HDPE. If thick enough, they can be grooved, but I'm not convinced it improves performance.

Former

Plain timber construction.

Cloths

Net curtain material is cheap and works very well.

Sundries

Steel strike plate to protect underside of top beam
Coach bolts – four of M12 x150mm (ideally stainless steel, but galvanised will work)
Coach screws – four of 100mm
Glue
Varnish

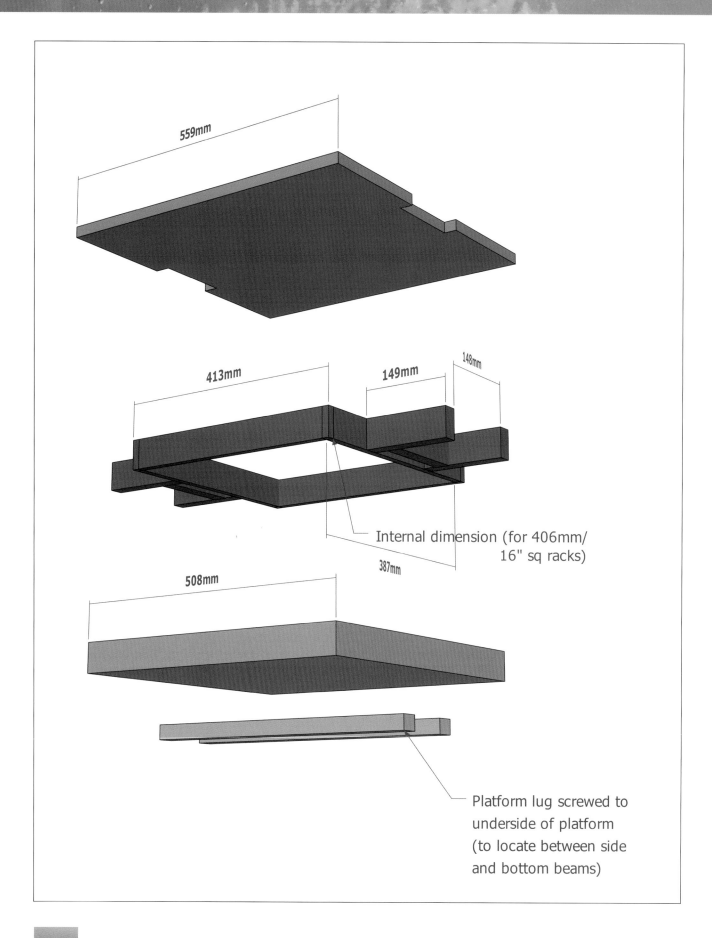

559mm

413mm   149mm   148mm

Internal dimension (for 406mm/
16" sq racks)

387mm

508mm

Platform lug screwed to
underside of platform
(to locate between side
and bottom beams)

CONSTRUCTION

The overall construction is fairly obvious from looking at it. The key features are:

- Other than the top beam, the frame uses [10 x 7.5cm] 4 x 3in softwood (this is the nominal size – the finished planed size is about 9.5 x 7cm). A piece of [15.2 x 7.6cm] 6 x 3in (finished size) oak or ash is assumed for the top beam in these construction notes. Otherwise, glue and cramp together two pieces of [10 x 7.5cm] 4 x 3in (nominal) softwood to make a piece [19 x 7cm] 7½ x 2¾in; the tenons can be the same as for the oak/ash version, so the construction details are otherwise similar.
- It is essential to use a mortice and tenon construction for the top beam. Do not use bolts, as is often seen, as this may cause the wood at the end of the beam to shear under tension. A mortice and tenon joint will place (almost) the whole depth of the beam under compression, which is much stronger.
- The uprights are two pieces of [10 x 7.5cm] 4 x 3in bolted together with four 150mm M12 coach bolts. This gives a stable structure, provides a guide for the cheese former and makes for easy construction of a strong mortice.
- The central bottom beam is also a mortice and tenon construction. The additional bottom beams are principally to keep the tray level and can be bolted or screwed on. The uprights are simply fixed to the base with dowels, then a triangle of ply screwed on. Bed bolts would be another option. Mine has castors, which makes it easy to move, but they only work on a level floor.

The minimum tools required are:
- A good quality handsaw
- A sharp chisel and mallet
- Drill with bits 20mm, 12mm, 10mm, 8mm
- Socket spanners to fit coach bolts & screws
- Try square
- Ruler

If you have a router then the mortices and tenons can be made more quickly and accurately. I will assume you only have the basic tools.

PROCESS

Make or buy the tray > make the frame to fit > add the racks, platform, press plate and former

The tray

Firstly make or buy the tray. It doesn't need to be particularly strong, since it will be supported on a platform. If making it from wood then I would suggest gluing it all with a sealing glue such as Stixall. My tray was made in stainless steel by a local welder for £50. I like to have a tap (as close to the bottom as you can get), but you could just have a hole in the bottom. The taps I use can be dismantled in use if there is a blockage.

The frame

Next make the frame, making the span just fractionally longer than the outside width of your tray. Cut all the frame timber to size and ensure it is square. For my press the sizes are as follows:

- Uprights x four:
  [9.5 x 7cm] 3¾ x 2¾in softwood, [159cm] 62½in long
- Top and bottom beams x two:
  [15.2 x 7.5cm] 6 x 3in oak, [84cm] 33in long
- Additional bottom beams x two:
  [9.5 x 7cm] 3¾ x 2¾in softwood, [70cm] 27½in long
- Base ('feet') x two:
  [9.5 x 7cm] 3¾ x 2¾in softwood, [72cm] 28½in long
- Plywood triangles

Make the mortice and tenon joints

The finished size will be about [6 x 12cm] 2¼ x 4¾in. Cut the mortices first, since it is easier to make the tenons to fit the mortices, rather than the other way round. These will be cut as a 'housing joint' in each piece, then they will be fixed together to form a mortice. Lay the uprights side by side with the 'insides' face up and mark them all together. Mark the depth at 30mm (ie, half the mortice width). Carefully cut on the waste side of each line with a handsaw, then make multiple cuts across the joint, so that chiselling out is easy. Remove the rest of the joint with a chisel (and/or a coping saw if you have one).

Mark out the tenons on the two main beams, to give the required span [50cm] 20in, and cut on the waste side of the marks. Test fit the tenons and chisel any excess so that they are a good tight fit.

Fit it all together, then make a mark along the centre line of each tenon, 8mm away from the upright. Drill a 20mm hole through each tenon and square up with a chisel. Make pegs from the same timber as the beams, from 18mm width at one end up to 24mm at the other. These should fit into the holes and draw everything together. NB: make sure that the tenons are long enough beyond the pegs.

Complete the frame

Mark the positions for the bolt holes and drill 12mm holes. Fix bolts with nuts & washers and tap in pegs to hold it all together. Mark the positions of the additional bottom beams and drill and fix with 100mm coach screws.

Place 'feet' on the bottom of the uprights and drill each with two holes 12mm wide by at least 150mm deep, into the uprights. Glue two 12 x 150mm dowels into each foot. You need an auger bit for this. If you don't have one then use an extra ply triangle and skip this stage. Provide additional strength to the base by screwing on a triangle of 4mm plywood cut from a piece [30cm] 1ft square. (If not using dowels then use two pieces of plywood, on either side). Attach castors if required.

Make the racks

These should be at least [10cm] 4in less than the inside width of the tray, to allow [5cm] 2in all round for drips. Mine are made to measure from HDPE, which is easy to clean, but you could use ply or make fancy hardwood ones. Ten racks should be sufficient. I would also recommend having a thicker (open construction) rack to lift the bottom cheese off the base.

Make and fit the platform

This is best made from a worktop cut-off, but could be built up from three layers of 12mm ply. It should be at least a fraction bigger than the racks, but does not need to be quite as big as the tray (particularly if it has a hole in the bottom). Some strips of wood screwed to the base help to locate it accurately in between the bottom beams.

Make and fit the press plate

This is made from three pieces of 12mm ply, each slightly smaller than the one below, to distribute the force of the jack over the whole cheese. The bottom piece can be shaped so that it slides vertically down on the uprights. Additional timbers may be required above the press plate to extend the reach of the jack.

Make and fit the former

This can be constructed from hardwood or softwood. Mine is made from [1.5cm] ½in thick oak with dovetailed corners, but [2cm] ¾in softwood, glued and screwed would work just as well. The height of the former dictates how high your cheeses will be. On the two sides of the former I have added an H-shaped construction to locate the former on the uprights, so as to keep things vertical when building the cheese. The internal dimension of the former should be just a little less than the racks, so that it sits on them and so that the cheeses don't squash outside the rack too much under pressure.

Finish

All exposed wood should be finished. I used Tung Oil (food safe) but this hasn't worked too well. If I was making it again I would use yacht varnish for the main frame as it is much more easily washed down. You could use polyurethane, but I prefer yacht varnish, even though it takes longer to dry. Any timber that is in direct contact with juice should be coated with a food-safe finish. I like stainless steel and plastic for these pieces as they are easier to clean.

Accessories

Net curtain material works very well for press cloths. Debris netting is very cheap but not as nice in use, or you can fork out on Vigo's fancy stuff. Whatever you use the cloths need to have a minimum width a bit over the area of the former, plus twice its depth. With a little ingenuity, the press can be converted to cope with double pressings, so that one cheese is being pressed while the other is being built. A sliding table on sprung castors runs over the top of the platform.

Costs

Timber: Assuming that the main beams are from hardwood, then the cost will depend on where you source from. Mine were old beams from a barn so they cost nothing. Otherwise green oak or ash should cost in the region of £25–£40; you will need to look for a local supplier. The rest of the frame can be made from four x 8ft lengths of 4 x 3in (95 x 70mm finished size) at a cost of £40–£50. If you are making the beams from softwood then you will need extra softwood at a cost of about £20. In addition, there is ply and timber for the press plate, former *etc*, at about £50. Other than the oak/ash all timber should be available at your local timber merchant. Total cost of timber is approximately £120.

Tray: This is the most expensive single item, if you have a stainless steel one. Mine was made to measure for £50. The taps can be bought online or from your local homebrew shop.

Jack: Clarke CBJ8 8-Tonne Bottle Jack from Machine Mart £22.

Racks: White (natural) HDPE sheet made to measure from www.plasticstockist.com cost £85 incl VAT and delivery for 10 sheets of 385 x 385mm.

Cloths and sundries: Depending on what you use, cloths will be anything from £7.50 upwards. Sundries include coach bolts and screws, dowelling, glue, varnish *etc*. totalling about £30. Should you wish to fit castors, these cost about £15 for two 100mm castoring wheels and two fixed (from Axminster Tools).

Total cost

So excluding your own time and any tools you have to buy, the total cost is about £310 – less than half the price of the Vigo equivalent. If you make a wooden tray and use thin ply for the racks, it would be quite a bit cheaper.

Should you want look at building your own press at a larger or smaller size, a summary of the figures is available in the following table to give you some clear guidelines.

CIDER PRESS – SIZE SPECIFICATIONS

Part	Unit	small press	medium press	large press	Notes
Capacity	kg of fruit	20	40	100	
	yield litres (65% efficiency)	13	26	65	
Tray size	width inches	16	20	28	External width of (square) tray
Rack size	width inches	12	16	24	Size for (square) racks (deduct 2x thickness of tray sides if tray is made of wood)
Internal size of former	width inches	11.25	15.25	23.25	Smaller than racks so that it will sit on them
Max no. of cheeses		7	8	9	2in depth per cheese
Jack size	tons	4	8	20	Bottle jack
Pressure	lbs per square inch	62	70	78	
	lbs per square inch per cheese	8.9	8.8	8.6	
Top Beam	length inches	29	33	41	Made from hardwood such as ash or oak
	height inches	5	6	10.5	(add 15% to height for softwood)
	thickness inches	2	3	3	Thicker timber could be used but thickness of uprights might need to be increased also
	span inches	16	20	28	
Platform	thickness inches	1.5	2	2	
Headroom for jack	distance inches	7.5	8	10	i.e. gap between the top of the cheeses and the bottom of the top beam = min height of jack
Uprights	length inches	59	62.5	71	
	width inches	2.75	3.75	3.75	
	thickness inches	1.75	2.75	3.75	Note that these are doubled up
Bottom beam	length inches	29	33	41	
	height inches	4	5	8	
	thickness inches	2	3	3	
Additional bottom/side beams	length inches	21.5	27.5	35.5	
	height inches	2.75	3.75	3.75	
	thickness inches	1.75	2.75	2.75	
Base feet	length inches	27	28.5	31.5	
	width inches	2.75	3.75	3.75	
	thickness inches	1.75	2.75	2.75	

IMPORTANT NOTES

No guarantees are given that any self-built press will sustain the pressures exerted on it as this will depend on materials used and build quality.

Note on timber sizes when buying from a merchant:

    The main structure (i.e. other than the main beams) can be made out of ready-planed softwood but BEWARE that the nominal size of timber quoted by the merchant is larger than the actual finished size.

An approximate guide is given below:

Nominal Imperial	Metric equivalent	Finished size		
		Metric	Imperial	
4" x 3"	100 x 75 mm	95x70mm	3.75 x 2.75	Used to build a medium or large press
3" x 2"	75 x 50 mm	70x45mm	2.75 x 1.75	Used for a small press
4" x 2"	100 x 50 mm	95x45mm	3.75 x 1.75	
4" x 2.5"	100 x 63 mm	95x57mm	3.75 x 2.25	

CHAPTER 7
CIDER AS AN INGREDIENT

Cider and food

FOOD MATCHING

Cider can accompany a vast range of foods, but it's important to remember that delicate foods will need a delicate match, and more robust foods stand up to more robust cider styles. Its aromatic balance of sweet fruitiness and sharpness mean cider can be put to work with an array of foods. Sharp ciders are great with fatty meats like lamb or chorizo and also seafood, while a dry rustic farmhouse cider goes well with pork and less obvious meals like oily, earthy fish (mackerel) or a simple oven-roasted chicken. The classic combination of farmhouse cider and mature cheddar cheese are difficult to beat and turn a simple snack into an indulgent treat.

For softer, lighter flavour cheeses like mozarella or creamy goats' cheese, an elegant perry or cider will accentuate the flavour.

Soft, but strong flavoured cheeses like Livarot, Camembert and Brie (as well as some of the milder blues like Dolcelatte) suit a sharp, fruity keeved cider. The full spectrum of cheese can be matched with the full spectrum of ciders available today.

Cider brandy suits dark chocolate desserts particularly well, and the more delicate nature of perry compliments light meats like turkey, or fresh salads.

CIDER AS AN INGREDIENT

While I love to play with what ciders go with what foods, it's not until you start cooking with cider that you realise how useful and versatile it is an ingredient. It has become one of my favorites to experiment with. It makes a great (and effective) alternative to white wine and occasionally even water. Its balance of sweetness and sharpness mean it complements many foods, so there are many combinations it goes with. A word of caution, however, by reducing a tannic (bitter) cider too much, you will increase the bitterness as the tannins will condense and intensify too.

The first thing cider does when you include it as an ingredient is to add aroma to your dish. It can be quite perfumed and give a meal a beautiful fragrant appeal before anyone's even tasted it. I nearly always use it in gravy and find it particularly handy for deglazing a pan after browning or cooking some meat. It's a great base for a sauce when cooking something gamey like pheasant or rabbit, and it enhances earthy meats. I once had it served in a dressing over an Egyptian-style salad of cumin and lambs liver and it

Barbecued *andouilles* are a great match.

▲ Many different cheeses suit different ciders and perries.

▶ Field mushrooms baked in cider and garlic.

was fantastic. It accompanies seafood particularly well and will happily twist *Moules Mariniere* into a West Country *Moules-Super-Mare*.

After soaking a gammon for a few hours in some clean water, you can boil it in some sweet cider with some shallots and reduce it into a sticky sweet, salty sauce to serve alongside it.

In Normandy, pommeau is combined with cream to serve over cooked oysters. Cider brandy is used to add panache to a basic sauce or even to flambé Christmas pudding... the ideas go on, and hopefully you get the picture.

Vinegar is a key ingredient in many recipes and cider vinegar is fantastic and best used for salads, dressings, marinades and condiments, although it can be used as any vinegar can.

Desserts

There isn't anything much more satisfying than being able to use your favorite tipple (or one of its derivatives) in a pudding. It's an extravagance worth celebrating.

CIDER BRANDY CUSTARD
(SERVES 6)

This is my luxury version of a classic and a surefire winner for a cider fan on a cold wintery day. Delicious over apple crumble.

Ingredients

- 500ml single cream
- Vanilla pod (scraped out)
- 3 free-range egg yokes
- 85g caster sugar
- 1 teaspoon cornflower
- 35ml cider brandy

Method

In a saucepan, heat the cream and the vanilla seeds to just before simmering and then remove from heat. In a separate bowl, whisk the eggs and sugar until they are smooth then add the cornflower. When mixed in, add a quarter of the warm cream stirring constantly. When mixed, stir back into the cream and return the saucepan to a medium-low heat and stir in the cider brandy. When thick enough to coat the back of a spoon, remove from the heat and serve hot or cold.

CARAMELISED APPLE & CALVADOS ICE-CREAM
(SERVES 6)

It's a labour of love, but is delicious and totally worth it.

Ingredients

- 70ml Calvados
- 4 free-range egg yokes
- 60g sugar
- 1 teaspoon cornflower
- 300ml double cream
- 300ml milk
- 1 sweet eating apple
- Juice of half a lemon
- Knob of butter

Method

Mix four egg yokes and half the sugar together until pale and smooth, then add the cornflower (to help prevent curdling) and the Calvados. Add the cream to the milk and warm the mixture to just below boiling. Remove from the heat and allow to cool for a few minutes.

While whisking the egg mix, slowly pour in the warm cream to the paste (best done in two or three stages to prevent scrambling). Sieve it back to the pan and cook it slowly on the lowest heat for about ten minutes stirring constantly to prevent any egg catching on the pan. It should look like a runny custard. Remove from heat.

When cool, add the lemon juice and then seal into a large plastic container (with a lid) that you can chill overnight in the fridge. When chilled, place into the freezer and take it out after an hour to whisk it thoroughly. This needs to be repeated three or four times, once per hour, to prevent large ice crystals and keep it smooth.

Meanwhile, roughly chop the unpeeled apple into random 1cm or less chunks and fry in the butter and a light sprinkling of sugar, turning them occasionally. Caramelise them to the point of being golden, chewy and tacky, which should take ten minutes. Remove from heat and allow to cool. When the ice-cream is nearly frozen, add in the remaining cooked apple at the final whisk, return it to the freezer for the final freeze until set and ready to serve.

CIDER BRANDY SYLLABUB
(SERVES 6)

Aromatic, creamy, silky, sweet and floaty – it's glorious and extravagant.

Ingredients

- 240ml dry cider
- 60ml cider brandy
- Pinch of cinnamon
- Juice of 1 lemon
- 300ml double cream
- 4 cinnamon sticks

Method

In a bowl, mix cider, cider brandy, ground cinnamon, sugar and the lemon juice until the sugar is dissolved. Stir in all the cream and then whisk until it forms soft peaks (like a meringue.) Over-whipping may curdle it, so somewhere soft and only just holding is perfect. Spoon into martini glasses and place a cinnamon stick in each one like a cocktail.

CIDER GRANITA
(SERVES 4–6)

Granita has to be one of the most simple desserts to make and I think this recipe works best with a naturally sweet cider, particularly an earthy but fruity 3% abv keeved, demi-sec! If you don't have any sweet cider you can use some apple juice, or even sugar to sweeten it. It tastes just like a ripe cider apple and is so refreshing in the summer months.

Ingredients

- 750ml keeved (or sweet) cider
- 1 Gala or Pink Lady apple (or similar)

Method

Pour the cider into a suitable tray or flat-bottomed bowl, sediment included. Using a fine or medium grater, grate a sweet apple and stir into the cider evenly. Put it into the freezer. After 50 minutes it should start to freeze – check it and stir it with a fork to an even consistency. Be sure to move the apple bits around. Every 30 minutes, check it again and keep scraping the edges and turning the mixture, stirring to an even consistency (it should start to look like rock salt) and put it back into the freezer. Repeat until ready. Serve in a steep-sided glass (such as a martini glass). Delicious!

MULLED CIDER (MAKES APPROX. 20 WINE GLASSES)

Mulled cider is actually a very traditional drink that probably originated, or at least was popularised by the Romans as they marched all over Europe. They had access to exotic spices that were becoming more available as trade routes grew.

There are so many recipes for mulled cider, probably because we all have different tastes and cider varies so much all over the world. I suspect people have been mulling it for as long as they have been mulling wine and as new spices and cultures come along, things change and recipes are adapted. It's a winter tradition in cider producing areas and everyone has their own 'special' version. It's pretty easy to prepare and offers guests a warm, comforting drink that hits the spot best when shared with friends outdoors around a massive blazing fire. Wassail!

The spices listed here will compliment a decent cider well if used without excess, but I tend to find I only make mulled cider in times of seasonal excess so I encourage you to use whatever takes your fancy. Personally, I prefer to use a medium cider as it means I have to add less sugar to the final mix.

Ingredients

- 2 star anise
- 3 allspice berries
- 3 cardamom pods
- 4 teaspoons ginger powder
- ½ teaspoon mace
- 1 pinch nutmeg
- 5 teaspoons cinnamon powder
- 2 cloves (whole)
- 5 black peppercorns (whole)
- 2 bay leaves
- 8 dessertspoons muscovado sugar
- 2 large oranges (1 zested & both juiced)
- 1 lemon (juiced)
- 4.5 litres medium traditional/farmhouse cider
- 80ml cider brandy, brandy, or rum if you're desperate!

Method

In a pestle and mortar, coarsely crush the star anise, cardomom and allspice berries and along with the powdered spices (ginger, mace, nutmeg) place into a warm saucepan, on a medium heat. Mix in the whole spices (bay leaves, peppercorns) and sugar. After two minutes of heating through, add a pint of cider to dissolve the sugar.

On a higher heat, infuse the syrupy mix until it starts to simmer. When it does, add the oranges, lemon and the rest of the cider, then turn down the heat to low. Heating the cider will remove some of the alcohol and if you boil it, most of it will go. I estimate 70°C for 20 minutes should retain most of it if you have the lid on.

Serving it is a sticky, messy business so be sure to have a ladle or a jug to hand to minimise the mess. This is a good time to add the brandy into the saucepan or directly onto the glass! Pour directly into the serving vessels through a tea strainer and place the spices back in the saucepan. Thick, handled mugs are often better as they preserve the temperature and protect the drinkers' hands.

Cider cocktails

Whether you are using cider, *eau de vie*, pommeau or cider brandy, there are recipes out there for everyone. A classic punch can be made using a sweet cider as a base to which the other ingredients are added. Here are some of my favourites:

CIDERPOLITAN

A remake of the classic with apple at its core.

Ingredients

- 35ml Triple Sec
- 35ml vodka
- 35ml lemon juice
- 70ml dry farmhouse cider

Add the Triple Sec, vodka, lemon juice and cider into a cocktail shaker over ice. Shake hard and then strain into a Marie Antoinette glass. Serve with a slice of apple.

PICKER'S PERK

A warming reviver for cold autumnal mornings spent apple picking (designed for a 6oz/177ml hip flask).

Ingredients

- 50ml Amaretto
- 50ml Drambuie
- 50ml cider
- 25ml lemon juice

Method

Simply mix all the ingredients together and pop into a hip flask

GOLDEN LION

(élaboré par Marc Bonneton, L'Antiquaire, Lyon)

Ingredients

- 50ml Blanche de Normandie (CD eau de vie)
- 20ml lemon juice
- 10ml liquid sugar
- 1 dash of bitter orange
- 5ml de Pernod Absynth
- Orange peel

Method

Place the ice into a sling glass and add the orange peel.

Pour over the lemon juice, sloe gin and sour cherry liqueur and stir.

Top up the glass with cider.

To serve, hook the apple slice and blackberry or bramble (if using) over the side of the glass. Garnish the cocktail with the cherry (if using).

CHRISTIAN DROUIN TREACLE

(élaboré par Marc Bonneton, L'Antiquaire, Lyon)

Ingredients

- 1 teaspoon of brown sugar
- 3 dashes of bitter angostura
- 20ml apple juice
- 50ml VSOP Christin Drouin (Calvados)
- Orange peel

Method

Mix sugar, bitters, apple juice and Calvados together and shake over ice. Pour into a whisky tumbler over a huge chunk of ice. Shave a large slice of zest from the orange, twist it over the glass and wipe around the drinking edge. Twist again over the glass to form a more thorough twisted peel, as a garnish. Serve.

From Christian Drouin, an award winning third-generation Calvados producer in northern France.

Glossary

adjunct: a substance added to something as a supplement normally to assist in, speed up or intensify an aspect of production.

apfelwein: German equivalent of cider (literally '*apple wine*').

autolysis: the eventual destruction of cells or tissues by their own enzymes. Autolysis has the side effect of increasing complexity and is sometimes used to improve flavour.

bittersharp: a type of 'true' cider apple that tastes both bitter (due to the high levels of tannins) and also sharp (high in acids).

bittersweet: another 'true' cider apple that is high in tannins (bitter tasting) but also has high levels of sugar in.

angels' share: a metaphoric term used by distillers to describe the volume of spirits lost to evaporation through ageing in wooden barrels.

bottle conditioned: a process that allows for a second fermentation inside a sealed bottle to build up carbonation. See *Methode Champagneoise* for more.

chaptalisation: the process of adding sugar to unfermented juice before or during fermentation, in order to increase the alcohol content after fermentation.

cider brandy: Distilled cider as a spirit usually around 40% abv.

cidre: French word for cider.

conditioning: the stage where cider is left to mature and acquire 'condition' – this may be done to improve flavour, clarity, and physical attributes such as carbonation.

dosage: French word describing the addition of sugar and/or yeast to cider at bottling stage as employed in the '*methode champenoise*'.

farmhouse cider: a classic, basic cider style made without fuss or too much interference that has been practised by farmers for hundreds of years.

final gravity (FG): the last measurement of sugar levels in a finished cider using a hydrometer. This is the lowest reading and is normally around 1000 or just below.

gribble: a Somerset word referring to an apple seedling that has grown from an abandoned seed.

grubbed up: a phrase used to describe the removal of orchards and seeing the land put to another use.

ice cider: Canada's greatest gift to the world – a sweet, sharp dessert-style apple wine.

keeving: a traditional technique (referred to as '*defecation*' or '*chapeau brun*' in French) where the juice is split into three parts (either naturally or through the addition of calcium) in order to control the fermentation and help retain natural sweetness.

lees: the detritus of fermentation – what's left behind at the bottom of the fermenter or bottle (normally composed of dead yeast, residual yeast and protein).

maceration: the process of leaving crushed apple pulp to sit (allowing it to oxidise) before pressing it. Often favoured by cidermakers to improve the flavour and clarity of their cider.

malic acid: the acid present in apples that gives a pleasant, sharp and sour taste.

malo-lactic action (MLA or MLF): a secondary action where the sharp, sour malic acid is converted to into smoother, buttery lactic acid by bacteria.

methode champenoise: a French phrase referring to the process of secondary bottle fermentation used in Champagne production.

mulled/mulling: a traditional idea of adding flavour (spices, sugar, fruit *etc*) to cider through heat and infusion.

hydrometer: An invaluable blown glass device used to measure the density of water/amount of sugar dissolved in juice in relation to fermentation.

original gravity (OG): the first and highest measurement of sugar levels in the juice taken after pressing prior to fermentation.

pasteurisation: the procedure of making something free of live bacteria or other harmful organisms (usually by heat).

perry: a close relative of cider, differing in its main ingredient – specialist perry pears.

perry pears: A close relative of cider apples, these rare little pears are mainly inedible and highly tannic and only good for perry making.

PGI: Protect Geographical Indication – a status applied through legal framework designed to protect a regions food or drink heritage.

pippin: name given a seedling grown from a pip.

pomace: the remains of the apple pulp after pressing.

pommeau: French name for an aged blend of apple juice and cider brandy.

racking: the process of moving cider from its current fermenter into another in order to clear it up and leave the sediment behind. This is often done several times.

scratter: the traditional name for a cider mill used to crush apples.

scrumpy: a term applied loosely to various types of cider today, but often used to describe a style akin to a basic farmhouse cider that may be perceived as rougher or more dubious in quality than preferred!

sharps: another classification of cider apple type that relates to highly acidic apples giving rise to a sharp flavour and increased acidity.

sidra: Spanish word for cider.

specific gravity (SG): a measurement of sugar levels in the juice at a specified stage of a fermentation, often done several times to track the progress of sugar conversion.

sweet: another type of cider-apple classification that relates to apples that are predominantly sugar and contain relatively low levels of acidity and tannin.

tannin: an astringent compound found naturally in cider-apple skins that causes a dry puckery feel in the mouth which offers both texture and a pleasant bitterness to cider.

tumping: the traditional practice of piling apples on the orchard floor in sunlight to increase ripeness and boost sugar levels.

Top Tips Team

Andrew Lea
Author, professor and legend!
http://www.cider.org.uk

Andy Hallett
Cidermaker
http://www.halletsrealcider.co.uk
http://blaengawneycider.co.uk

Neil & Helen Worley
Cidermakers
http://www.worleyscider.co.uk

Eduardo Coto
Cider blogger, Spain & Germany
http://sidraglocal.blogspot.com

Louisa Spencer
Farnhum Hill Cider, US
http://www.povertylaneorchards.com

Henry Chevallier Guild
One half of Aspall Cider – Britain's oldest family cider business
http://www.aspall.co.uk

Matt Veasey
Cidermaker & Craft cider advocate
http://www.nooksyard.com

Tom Oliver
Cidermaker
http://www.oliversciderandperry.co.uk

Ben Watson
Author, US
"Cider: Hard & Sweet"

Ed Landen
Commercial Cider Apple Grower

SUPPLIERS

Vigo Ltd
Dunkeswell
Honiton
Devon EX14 4LF
UK
www.vigoltd.com
01404 892100

Overt Locke
West Street,
Somerton,
Somerset TA11 7PS
UK
www.overtlocke.co.uk
01458 272626

Societies and associations

Experience is the biggest help when it comes to the murky waters of red tape and administration involved with selling to the public and there are various associations, local, regional and national that you can join to learn more and seek out further advice from.
These include:

SWECA (South West England Cider makers Association)
http://www.sweca.org.uk

Three Counties Cider & Perry Association
http://www.thethreecountiesciderandperryassociation.co.uk

Welsh Perry & Cider Society
http://welshcider.co.uk

NACM (National Association of Cider makers)
http://www.cideruk.com

Cider Workshop
Probably the most useful resource for any scale cider maker wishing to make good cider, as well as advice on related aspects such as insurance, planning, duty *etc.*
http://www.ciderworkshop.com

FSA (Food Standards Agency
http://food.gov.uk

HMRC (Her Majesty's Revenue and Customs)
http://www.hmrc.gov.uk

Further reading:

BLOGS:
iamcider.blogspot.com

HISTORY & CULTURE:
'*Worlds Best Cider*' by Pete Brown & Bill Bradshaw. (2013, Jacqui Small)
'*The History and Virtues of Cider*' by Roger French. (1982, Robert Hale)
'*Golden Fire*' by Ted Bruning. (2012, self pub)
'*Ciderland*' by James Crowden. (2008, Birlinn)
'*Cider –The Forgotten Miracle*' by James Crowden. (1999, self published)
'*Ripest Apples*' compiled by Roy Palmer. (1996, Big Apple Association)
'*Treatise on Cyder-Making*' High Stafford. (2009, Fineleaf Editions)
'*Cider Hard and Sweet -History Traditions and Making your Own*' by Ben Watson. (2013, Countryman Press)

CIDERMAKING - TECHNIQUES & SCIENCE:
'*Cider Making*' by A. Pollard & F.W. Beech (1957, Hart Davis)
'*Craft Cider Making*' by Andrew Lea (2012, Goodlife Press)
'*Perry Pears*' edited by L. Luckwill and A. Pollard (1963, Univ. of Bristol)
'*New Cidermakers Handbook*' Claude Joliecouer. (2013, Chelsea Green.)

APPLES:
"Growing Cider Apples" R. Umpelby & L.Copas, (2002, NACM)
'*Cider Apples: The New Pamona*' by Liz Copas (2013, self-published)
'*Bulmers Pomona*' (1987, HP Bulmer Ltd)
'*The Story of the Apple*' Barrie E. Juniper & David J. Mabberley (2006, Timber Press)

▷ **Opposite is a two-page template that you can use to record and make notes about each batch of cider you make. It's available to reproduce at your leisure. Good luck!**

CIDER BATCH RECORD

Batch/Fermenter no: . . . . Press date: . . . .   by: . . . .

Intended style/plans: . . . .

Apple variety	Weight	Fruit Source & Notes:
. . . .	. . . .	. . . .
. . . .	. . . .	. . . .
. . . .	. . . .	. . . .
. . . .	. . . .	. . . .
. . . .	. . . .	. . . .
. . . .	. . . .	. . . .
. . . .	. . . .	. . . .
. . . .	. . . .	. . . .
. . . .	. . . .	. . . .
. . . .	. . . .	. . . .

Macerated: Y / N   (length: . . . .)

Pressing notes: . . . .
. . . .

Juice Analysis:

volume collected: . . . .   original gravity: . . . .   pH: . . . .

Additives:

SO_2	type:	amount:	date: . . . .
SUGAR	type:	amount:	date: . . . .
YEAST	type:	amount:	date: . . . .
NUTRIENT	type:	amount:	date: . . . .
ACID	type:	amount:	date: . . . .
OTHER	type:	amount:	date: . . . .
OTHER	type:	amount:	date: . . . .

Juice Notes: . . . .
. . . .

CIDER BATCH RECORD

Notes: . . . .

. . . .

Fermentation:

      Date started: . . . . Date air-locked: . . . .

progress:

date. . . . . .gravity. . . . . activity/notes . . . .

. . . .

. . . .

. . . .

Racking:

                                                    sense notes (visual, smell, taste, other):

Number: . . . .   date: . . . .

Number: . . . .   date: . . . .

Number: . . . .   date: . . . .

Number: . . . .   date: . . . .

Storage/bottling

date & notes . . . .

. . . .

. . . .

. . . .

Tasting notes: . . . .

. . . .

. . . .

. . . .

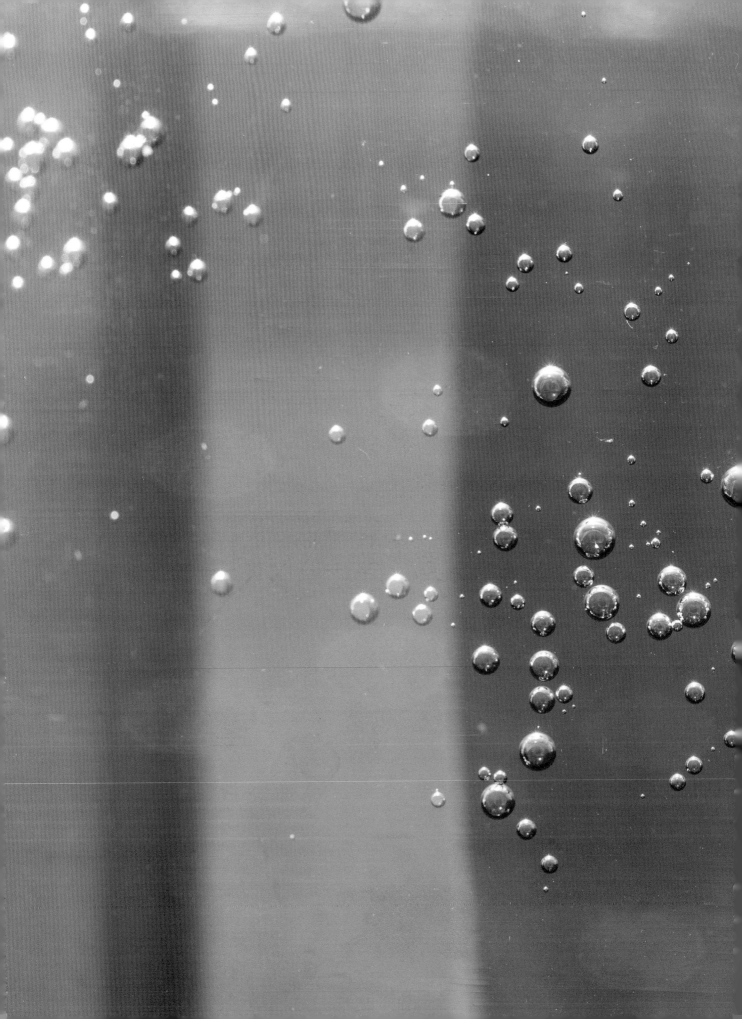